MASTERING THE NATIONAL ADMISSIONS TEST FOR LAW

MASTERING THE NATIONAL ADMISSIONS TEST FOR LAW

by
Mark Shepherd

Cavendish
Publishing
Limited

London • Sydney • Portland, Oregon

First published in Great Britain 2005 by
Cavendish Publishing Limited, The Glass House,
Wharton Street, London WC1X 9PX, United Kingdom
Telephone: + 44 (0)20 7278 8000   Facsimile: + 44 (0)20 7278 8080
Email: info@cavendishpublishing.com
Website: www.cavendishpublishing.com

Published in the United States by Cavendish Publishing
c/o International Specialized Book Services,
5824 NE Hassalo Street, Portland,
Oregon 97213-3644, USA

Published in Australia by Cavendish Publishing (Australia) Pty Ltd
45 Beach Street, Coogee, NSW 2034, Australia
Telephone: + 61 (2)9664 0909   Facsimile: + 61 (2)9664 5420
Email: info@cavendishpublishing.com.au
Website: www.cavendishpublishing.com.au

British Library Cataloguing in Publication Data
Shepherd, Mark
Mastering the National Admissions Test for Law
1 Law schools – Great Britain – entrance examinations – study guides
I Title
340'.076

Library of Congress Cataloguing in Publication Data
Data available

ISBN 13: 978-1-845-68010-7
ISBN 10: 1-84568-010-3

1 3 5 7 9 10 8 6 4 2

Printed and bound in Great Britain

PREFACE

Much debate surrounds the selection processes employed by the top universities to decide which students to admit, with the media frequently carrying stories of able students turned down by universities such as Oxford and Cambridge. Trying to decide how different people will react to a new learning environment and develop over three or four of the most impressionable years of their life is an inexact science and it is unlikely that any truly perfect system will ever be achieved. Nevertheless, the situation becomes more and more difficult each year as increasing numbers of students achieve top grades across the whole range of subjects.

In response to this, a number of the top law faculties in the country have collaborated to devise a new test to provide an additional assessment of candidates' abilities. Known as the National Admissions Test for Law (LNAT), this was sat for the first time in November 2004 by students applying for entry in 2005 or 2006. The test was widely hailed as a success and other universities have already signalled their intention to join the LNAT consortium in future years. Given that students will not be expected to have studied law at an academic level before beginning university, the test is designed to assess general intellectual skills of comprehension, analysis, logic and judgment, rather than focusing on particular factual knowledge. The questions are therefore based on current affairs and an awareness of the world and do not require any specialised knowledge on top of existing A level studies.

Whilst the test is not intended to require specific coaching, the merits of thorough preparation are clear, particularly given the emphasis placed on test success in the application process. This book aims to demystify the test by explaining what candidates will be faced with and the best ways to prepare for, and approach, the test. A number of sample papers, complete with full answers and detailed explanations, are included in order to enable students to familiarise themselves with the format of the test and to facilitate practice of the skills that will be required in order to impress. Throughout, a practical approach is taken and, building on the experience of last year's test, advice is also given on how universities are likely to interpret the test result and what qualities the universities will be looking for. Much of the guidance given is equally applicable to preparing for other tests and interviews and for improving standards of written English generally, and it is hoped that it will build on, and lay the foundations for, study in a number of other areas.

My thanks go to Shelley White, without whose invaluable help and support this book would not have been possible, and to all those who have offered their advice and expertise over the last few months. In particular, I am grateful to the authors (and publishers) who have kindly contributed extracts from their work to be used as the basis of sample examination questions.

Mark Shepherd
London
March 2005

CONTENTS

PART 3

ANSWERS AND EXPLANATIONS

PREPARING
FOR THE TEST

INTRODUCTION

The National Admissions Test for Law (LNAT) was developed to aid admissions tutors in identifying the best students to accept on their undergraduate law programmes, and was intended to counter the criticisms that the existing admissions process discriminated against those from certain backgrounds. The test was devised by a consortium of leading universities, comprised of Birmingham, Bristol, Cambridge, Durham, East Anglia, Nottingham, Oxford and UCL, and was first sat in November 2004. Early indications are that it has proved very successful and King's College London, the University of Glasgow and Manchester Metropolitan University have already signalled their intention to join the consortium for the 2005 test, with many other institutions expected to shortly follow suit. UK students applying to any of the participating institutions are required to sit the test as part of the application process, and this requirement is likely to be extended to overseas students in the near future, thereby developing a more level playing field for all applicants. The requirement to sit the LNAT is in addition to any other requirements of each university concerned, such as interviews or the submission of written work, and, unless exceptional circumstances can be demonstrated, a failure to take the test will result in an automatic rejection by the institution in question.

Application process

The application process has not changed dramatically and candidates will still be required to fill out UCAS forms as usual and, in addition, will be expected to register to sit the LNAT by the published deadline. This is not done automatically by UCAS, and is subject to payment of the test fee, although bursaries are available for those who would suffer serious financial hardship as a result of sitting the test. Registration for the LNAT is carried out online by accessing the consortium's website at www.lnat.ac.uk, which is also a useful source of information about the test. In addition to a candidate's personal details, it is necessary to enter a UCAS reference number to allow the results to be forwarded to the relevant institutions. Amendments or additions can usually be made after registration, but the deadlines imposed by the individual universities must be adhered to, and, in particular, it should be noted that the deadline for Oxford and Cambridge applications is considerably earlier than for other universities.

Administration of the test is carried out by Pearson Assessments and Testing in conjunction with Edexcel. It is overseen by a consortium called LNAT Consortium Ltd, a company jointly owned by the participating universities. The 2004 test was a written paper, sat by candidates at a network of test centres around the UK and abroad. From 2005 onwards, it is envisaged that the test will be sat online in Pearson's network of high street test centres (of which there are 150 in the UK and thousands more worldwide). The passages and questions will appear on the screen and the responses will be keyed in, and the essay will also be typed. There is expected to be a testing window running from early September to mid-January for home candidates and from early September to mid-June for overseas candidates. Those applying to Oxford or Cambridge will need to have completed the test by early November.

Each law school does have an element of discretion with regard to the mandatory nature of the test, and those candidates who can demonstrate exceptional circumstances will not usually be penalised for their failure to take the test. Those candidates with dyslexia or other special needs will be given assistance where necessary, and should specify what support they will require when registering. There is no provision for the test to be re-sat, but there is nothing to stop students from sitting the test again the following year if they are reapplying through UCAS.

Structure of the test

The test is comprised of two sections. The first consists of 30 multiple choice questions, split into 10 groups of between two and four questions each (for the sake of convenience, the sample papers all contain three questions per group). Each group is based on an extract, usually from an article or book, of about 500 to 1,000 words in length. For each question, five alternative answers are given, from which one must be selected. The questions are based purely on the contents of the passage and no specific prior knowledge is required. This section of the test is designed to assess a candidate's ability to read, understand, analyse and make logical deductions based on passages of text. The time limit for the multiple choice questions is 80 minutes. The second section requires candidates to write an essay on a subject chosen from a given list. Normally, there will be about five titles to choose from, covering a range of general knowledge, current affairs and conceptually based questions. This is designed to assess originality, ability to structure thoughts and use of written English. Although, again, no specific area of knowledge is being tested, it will be necessary in any essay to bring in a range of facts to back up the argument. The time limit for the essay is 40 minutes.

How the test is used by universities

The multiple choice component is marked out of 30, with the scores being sent automatically to all of the participating law schools to which the candidate has applied. The essay component is not centrally marked, but is passed to the relevant law schools for them to assess in accordance with their own criteria. There is no specific pass mark and it will be up to each institution to decide how they mark the essay component and interpret the multiple choice results. Some may, for example, use the essay as the basis for further discussions at interview, whilst others may simply use it as an additional academic result in conjunction with A level grades or predictions. Likewise, the relative weighting given to the LNAT, compared with other indicators of ability, will vary from university to university.

Admissions tutors have been quick to emphasise the positive nature of the test. Those who struggle with the test are unlikely to prejudice their position, whilst those who do well will find their result used to counterbalance poor showings at GCSE or worse than expected A level predictions. The LNAT is intended to be an indicator of potential and therefore good scores on it may offer opportunities to candidates with less strong academic backgrounds. Tutors will, of course, wish to see evidence of previous hard work and commitment in addition to good LNAT results, though, and it is unlikely to be enough simply to show an aptitude for law if there is nothing to back this up.

The general consensus is that the importance of the LNAT will increase over time as it becomes more established and more widely used. Universities like Oxford and Cambridge that traditionally interview a large proportion of applicants are likely to use the test to eliminate weaker candidates earlier on in the applications procedure, thereby reducing the number of interviews conducted. Some universities now rank all applications for law courses on the basis of a combination of their GCSE results, A level predictions and LNAT score. This highlights the importance of the test as, in effect, a similar amount of weight is being given to one two hour exam as to several years of academic work at school or college.

Previous experience of the test

In 2004, 4,325 candidates took the LNAT and there was a considerable variation in success. In the multiple choice section (marked out of 24):

- the highest mark was 21, achieved by four candidates;
- the lowest mark was 3, recorded by three candidates;
- the overall average mark was 13.16;
- the average mark for the 893 candidates from independent schools was 13.63;
- the average mark for the 695 candidates from grammar schools was 13.55;
- the average mark for the 1,050 candidates from comprehensive schools was 13.30;

- the average mark for the 1,406 candidates from further education/sixth form colleges was 12.67;
- the average mark for the 61% of female candidates was 13.02; and
- the average mark for the 39% of male candidates was 13.37.

Despite the considerable overall spread of marks, there were only relatively insignificant differences between those marks achieved by students of different genders and those studying at different institutions, and many of these differences can be attributed to the size of the sample. This is a contrast to A level results where there tends to be a much greater disparity between the results achieved by those attending different types of school or college, and between male and female; this goes a long way to vindicating the claim made by those responsible for establishing the test that it is a fair and unbiased indicator.

The essay section of the paper is not marked in the same way, but the general view from admissions tutors was that many students did not have a sufficient grip of written English and displayed an inability to convincingly articulate their thoughts on paper. In particular, it was felt that many students lacked the skills required to construct a persuasive argument, something which is central to the work of a lawyer. Other comments included suggestions that students did not write enough and did not produce a sufficiently detailed essay.

MULTIPLE CHOICE SECTION

The multiple choice element of the LNAT is dealt with in an entirely objective way. The participating universities that a candidate has applied to will only be given the raw mark achieved and will not have an opportunity to see the actual answers. Accuracy is, therefore, everything: there will only be one correct answer for each question, and getting the correct answer is the only way that you will get any credit. Factual preparation is unnecessary as the questions seek to test understanding and logical reasoning rather than any specific area of knowledge. The main focus of preparation should be to familiarise oneself with the style of questions used in the test in order to develop an understanding of what the markers will be looking for. Although most students will at some point have experienced multiple choice questioning in examinations, the questions in the LNAT are of a style that may not previously have been encountered. This makes it all the more important to attempt sample questions and, where possible, discuss them with either a fellow student or ideally someone more experienced in the field who will be able to explain to you any unforeseen nuances or complications.

Tied in with this is the issue of timing. Every question carries the same number of marks and there is no suggestion that any marks will be deducted for incorrect answers. You are, therefore, wasting an opportunity if you do not answer every question. Although the number of passages and questions has been increased for the 2005 test (and future tests), it appears that the time limit may remain the same, which is likely to introduce an element of time pressure on the paper. Indications are that the time allowed for this section of the test will be 80 minutes, which equates to just over two and a half minutes a question. You should, therefore, work through each passage quickly and efficiently, without rushing. There is no point wasting time on questions that you do not understand, but given the relatively short time limit, you may not have time to return to ones that you have left out so it is always best to select one answer and then mark down the question as one to consider again if possible. Time permitting, it is always beneficial to check over your answers at the end, but do not fall into the trap of hastily changing something unless you have identified a clear flaw in your earlier reasoning.

Wording of the question

With any test it is vital to look carefully at the wording of the questions, but this is especially true of the LNAT as the questions tend to be very specifically worded, and subtle differences of meaning are often overlooked. For example:

'A feature of the illness is ... '

This does not mean the same as:

'A common feature of the illness is ... '

Particular attention should be paid to words such as *common*, *occasional*, *often*, *rare*, *sometimes* and *typical*, as they can alter the meaning of a question without making it appear ostensibly different. Care must also be taken with absolutes: if a word such as *never* or *always* appears in an answer, it is necessary to be sure that no evidence could be found that would prove to be an exception to this. It is also important to identify whether the question has more than one part. For example, with the question, 'What unstated assumption is made by the writer?', you need to identify, first, an assumption that has been made and, secondly, one that has not been stated in the text. Incorrect alternatives to such a question are likely to include ideas not stated by the writer, but not assumed either, and assumptions made that are also stated. In such circumstances, it is easy to be misled into selecting the wrong answer.

Equally as significantly, the answer may have two parts. Consider the following question:

What is stated to be the main aim of the policy?

(a) To reduce waiting times

(b) To improve the quality of care

(c) To reduce the cost of operations

(d) To improve public perception of the NHS

(e) To improve efficiency

Here, it would be easy to skim over the answers and assume that (c) just said reduce cost, or that it was implicit that it was the cost of operations that were being referred to in the original passage. Frequently, this proves not to be the case, and it is vital to read the whole answer, as extra words at the end of the answer can completely change the meaning, making an answer seem appropriate when in fact it is only partly right.

Double negatives commonly feature in questions. For example:

Which of the following is not stated in the passage?

(a) Money will not be a factor in making the decision

(b) Further bids will need to be considered

(c) Insufficient evidence has so far been submitted

(d) Ability to commence quickly is one of the main criteria

(e) The guidelines state the degree of discretion permitted

Here, not only is there a negative in the question, but there is also one in alternative (a). Not only is it important not to miss the second one, but it is also important not to simply think that they cancel each other out. It does not follow from (a) that what is being said is that 'money is stated in the passage to be a factor in making the decision'. Such double negatives are not intended to catch candidates out, but are simply a result of the fact that many questions seek to identify where evidence has, or has not, been provided to support a particular idea, and it is often necessary to phrase this in the negative.

Below are considered the issues raised by some common types of question.

What is implied by [...]?

Writers and speakers *imply* things; readers and listeners do not. In other words, if the writer suggests something without explicitly stating it, that would be said to be implied in the passage. This is subtly different from something contained in the passage that could be interpreted by the reader as having a particular meaning, although in reality the difference is minimal. An implication is usually something that is not stated, but it is unlikely that any questions in the test will seek to exploit this issue alone and you should not allow it to distract you from the real meaning of a question.

What can be inferred from [...]?

Conversely, readers and listeners *infer* things; writers and speakers do not. To infer something is to form an opinion on the basis of the information with which you have been provided, in this case in the relevant passage or a part thereof. In other words, what a question like this is asking is what interpretation it is possible to put on what the writer has said. Generally, an inference is made from something that is not explicitly stated, but again this is a subtle difference and one that is unlikely to form the sole basis of a question.

What can be gathered from [...]?

This is virtually the same as asking 'what can be inferred from' some evidence, although it is more likely to encompass ideas that have been explicitly stated, in addition to those that can be deduced from the text.

What is stated to be [...]?

Stated means something that is explicitly said, rather than just implied. If any given statement is true, it will be possible to find evidence of where that sentiment is expressed in the relevant passage. This is, however, not to say that the material must be expressed in precisely the same form, provided that it means the same thing.

What conclusion is reached by the writer [...]?

This type of question seeks to test whether you have followed and understood the point the writer is making. The question may be phrased in a general sense, encompassing the entire passage, or may refer to one specific part of the text. Either way, what is important is to follow the writer's line of argument right through, in order to see where it is heading and thus what final conclusion is reached. Sometimes the conclusion may be spelt out for you and the writer may summarise what he or she is arguing at the end of the passage or section, and it is therefore simply a case of identifying to which part of the text the question is referring. Where this is not the case, it is necessary to look at what weight is given to particular pieces of evidence and what tone is adopted in relation to different ideas, in order to determine the direction that the writer is taking.

What (unstated) assumption is being made [...]?

This is a relatively frequently used question and seeks to test logical reasoning. Generally, you will be asked to identify an assumption underlying a particular idea or argument in the text. The majority of the time, this will be something that is not specifically stated in the text; where the word 'unstated' is used in the question, it is particularly important to check whether the assumption features in the text. The simplest way of dealing with this type of question is to ask yourself what would be the effect of not making the assumption contained in the answer, or of making the opposite assumption. If this fundamentally undermines the idea or argument in question, then it must be a necessary assumption.

Which of the following is merely an assertion?

This is testing the candidate's ability to distinguish between fact and assertion. The main difference is that an assertion is a view put forward without sufficient facts to show that it is correct. You therefore need to look for the existence of evidence to show that it is correct. In doing so, you should confine yourself just to the text and not consider any external evidence that would back up the statement in question. You may also be asked to identify a particular assertion that features in the text. This is a slightly different question and may not require consideration of whether or not the alternatives are assertions, but merely whether they feature in the text.

What point is made by [...]?

This will generally refer to a specific example or analogy made by the writer of the relevant passage, and seeks to test whether you have understood why it is being used. The most important thing here is context. The writer is not going to have put the example or analogy randomly into the text, as this would completely defeat their purpose. Instead, they are likely to be using it to illustrate a point that has just been made, or as an introduction to a point that is about to be made. Start by looking at how the example is introduced and then consider its possible meanings and which of the arguments and ideas put forward in the text are most closely related to that meaning.

Which of the following is an argument in favour of [...]?

Such a question looks to test your ability to understand how an argument is constructed. When answering the question, there are two aspects to consider. First, how is the factor or idea used in the passage? Does it precede a particular conclusion? Secondly, in isolation from the text, what does the factor or idea actually mean? What necessarily follows from it? Ideally, these two aspects should coincide where you have selected the correct answer, but it may be the case that the writer has not considered the idea or has considered it in a different sense, and this does not necessarily preclude it from being the correct answer.

What is meant by [...]?

This may be seeking an explanation of a word or phrase, or of an idea. The nature of the test is that it is not generally necessary to rely on too much outside knowledge, and the question is not therefore testing for the normal definition of whatever is mentioned, but rather is testing how it is used in the text. Again, context is the most importance guide, and you should look at the surrounding text to see if any definition is implied or stated.

What is the main idea in the passage?

This is a common style of question on the LNAT, but can be difficult to answer due to the inevitable degree of subjectivity it involves. Although it is often possible to eliminate a couple of answers on the basis that the arguments that they contain are not advanced at all in the passage, you are likely to be left trying to decide which of several arguments is the main one. This will be judged on a number of factors, including the introduction and conclusion of the passage, the number of references to the argument, the use of particular evidence and the implications contained in the text. This is one of the main reasons why it is advisable to carefully read the entire passage before you start answering the questions as your first impression when reading it through is often the best indication as to the main theme or themes.

Verifying your answer

A number of different approaches can be taken when deciding which answer to select or when verifying an answer that you have selected. One way is to 'positively' validate the statement selected. Consider the following question:

Based on the evidence in the passage, which of the following can be inferred to be the principle determinant of intelligence?

(a) Social class

(b) Wealth

(c) Access to education

(d) Gender

(e) Race

If you selected (d), then you would, in effect, be making the following statement:

From evidence found in the passage, gender can be inferred to be the principle determinant of intelligence.

This can be tested as a proposition and if it determined to be true, then (d) must be the answer. If, on the other hand, evidence can be found in the passage to disprove the theory, then you will need to consider an alternative answer.

More care needs to be taken where there is a greater degree of subjectivity in the question. For example:

What is the writer's main argument in the article?

(a) Cannabis should be legalised

(b) All drugs should be legalised

(c) The negative effects of drugs are exaggerated

(d) Some drugs can have benefits

(e) Public opinion on drugs is overly influenced by the media

Here it is still possible to form a statement in the same way. If you chose (b), you could say:

The writer's main argument in the article is that all drugs should be legalised.

It is not difficult to prove or disprove the idea that the writer makes the argument in the article that all drugs should be legalised. It may, however, not be possible to establish in isolation whether that was the main argument being advanced. In such a situation, it may be more useful to 'negatively' verify the answer by forming statements from all the alternatives and eliminating those that cannot be said to be true.

As a rule, it is unwise to rely on tricks to determine the answers to multiple choice questions as it is hard to develop any that are foolproof and it is easy to be misled into selecting an answer that you would not otherwise have considered. One useful technique, however, is to identify any answers which mean exactly the same thing as each other. Given that there can only be one correct answer, multiple answers must by definition be incorrect. Likewise, it is worth checking for consistency between your own answers to questions on the same passage to ensure that there are no inherent contradictions in what you have selected. On the whole, techniques that involve identifying common distractors and patterns of correct answers tend to offer little accuracy and it would be extremely unwise to rely on such methods.

ESSAY SECTION

The only part of your paper that will actually be seen by admissions tutors is the essay, and it goes without saying that it is essential to produce the kind of answer that will leave tutors with a favourable first impression of you as a candidate. An ability to produce high quality written English is essential both to academic success and, subsequently, to success in many professions, and is a skill that is highly prized amongst lawyers. It is, however, something that is commonly taken for granted, with many people incorrectly assuming that the skills needed to write well are somehow inbuilt and not capable of being developed. Most students, when asked what their greatest failing is in respect of essay writing, tend to answer that they should have done more revision of the required factual knowledge. Whilst this is often true, it is far more common to come across students who have sufficient knowledge to answer a question, but are let down by the way in which they approach the writing itself.

This is particularly true of the essay question on the LNAT paper. One of the most important aims of the test is to look for an ability to develop reasoned arguments and clearly articulate them on paper. To ignore the importance of written English is, therefore, to do yourself a disservice and will inevitably lessen your chances of creating a good impression on those reading your answer. With this in mind, this chapter aims to cover some of the fundamentals of constructing an essay, from choosing a question to planning your answer and constructing sound arguments. It is not intended to be a definitive guide to English grammar, as it would be counterproductive to cover an excessive amount of material, but is aimed at providing you with the information that is relevant to the test that you will be sitting. Above all, it is intended to be a practical guide that all students can relate to, and not one that is littered with technical terms and arcane rules, which are often what discouraged people from learning these kinds of skills in the first place.

The guidance given is applicable to any kind of written work, not just the LNAT, but throughout you should keep in mind the specific constraints and characteristics of this particular test. First, the time limit is very short: you only have 40 minutes to choose a question, plan your approach, write your answer and check over your work. This means that you need to work quickly and efficiently and be decisive about what you intend to say, as there is little spare time to spend reconsidering things. Secondly, guidance may be given in the rubric as to the recommended length of the essay, or a word limit imposed. As a result of the difficulties experienced by many previous candidates in writing sufficient material in the available time, it has been suggested that an increased focus in subsequent tests will be placed on economical writing. This must be balanced with the need to write a sufficiently full answer to convincingly develop and back up your arguments. Thirdly, the essay will not be on a specific subject that you have prepared for beforehand. You must, therefore, be ready to adapt what knowledge you already have to the given subject, and should appreciate the importance of answering the question posed rather than trying to display excessive knowledge of the broad area.

Preparation

Preparation is the cornerstone of success and can broadly be split into two areas: literary and factual. For many students, the former will come relatively naturally as essay writing will be an everyday part of A level studies. For those who are studying science- and mathematics-based subjects, though, this may be an area that requires considerably more work. Either way, there are very few people who cannot benefit from improving the standard of their writing. The first step toward doing this should be to study the basic principles contained in this chapter, in order to give yourself the tools necessary to progress. You should then read essays written by you or others to get a feeling for the kinds of skills involved, as well as familiarising yourself with ideas on how to structure pieces of writing and the kind of material to include. Once you are confident about what you are aiming to achieve, you should attempt as many practice questions as possible in order to refine your technique and highlight any areas that require further work.

With regard to the latter, the best preparation is simply to keep in touch with current affairs over a lengthy period prior to sitting the test. Ideally, this will involve reading a quality newspaper on a regular basis and, where possible, also reading more detailed periodicals, books and websites. This should facilitate an understanding of the issues involved in each of the questions and allow you to make a choice from a larger number of alternatives. A deeper factual knowledge will be required to write an excellent, rather than just a good, essay and it is therefore advisable to focus in depth on a number of different topical and theoretical issues. Some element of choice is involved; as you are only required to answer one question, you may decide to gamble and narrow your preparation to some degree or rely more on knowledge that you have already acquired. Not all the questions will require as much factual knowledge as each other and there are likely to be titles that lean more towards the abstract and the theoretical than towards current affairs. It should also be noted that it is perfectly acceptable to base your arguments on assumptions rather than specific factual knowledge, providing that you state what assumptions you are making, although this is difficult to do without some understanding of the background. The fact that it is impossible to predict the likely essay titles does, however, mean that it is always something of a risk not to be prepared to write on a range of subjects. In any case, many people will be called for interview as part of the application process and much of the preparation done for the LNAT will be highly relevant to the interview stage.

Choosing a question

In many ways, choosing the right question is as much of a skill as answering it. For strong candidates, it is all about choosing the question that they feel gives the best opportunity to show off their knowledge, ideas and writing skills. For weak candidates, on the other hand, it can often come down to scrambling around to find the one question that they know enough about to even be able to attempt an answer. In one word, the difference between these two types of candidates is preparation. Those who have prepared well will give themselves much greater choice and will not be forced into answering a difficult question simply because it is the only one which they know anything about.

The first task is to identify which of the questions you are capable of answering. Clearly, you should immediately cross off those that you do not have the factual knowledge to write about, even if the question seems superficially appealing. More than that, though, you should also eliminate those that you do not fully understand, those that you cannot think of enough arguments on, and those that you do not feel you can provide any useful insight into, as not to eliminate such questions would lead to a bland and generic essay. Next, you need to think about which question gives you the best opportunity to demonstrate your writing skills. Providing that you have the necessary knowledge, this may not be on the topic that you have researched in most detail, but should be the one that you feel most confident in writing a top class answer about. You should consider whether you are better at essays that demand greater factual knowledge and analysis or more subjective ones calling for greater creativity and evaluation. You should also consider how much of a risk you are prepared to take as some topics will be more difficult than others to answer competently, but will give you the opportunity to really shine, whilst others will tend to attract middle of the road answers.

Below are detailed some of the main forms of question you are likely to encounter and a consideration of what each will entail.

[Assertion]. Do you agree?

Invariably this will be a fairly controversial assertion, which probably only reflects one side of the story. This is useful as it gives you something to argue against and makes it easier to include some of your own opinions. To answer the question successfully, it is important to understand exactly what is meant by the assertion and this must be conveyed to the reader in order for there to be any purpose in putting forward arguments for and against it. It is useful to set the assertion into context by explaining whose view it is likely to represent, as this makes for more realistic analysis and allows other perspectives to be brought in. As well as simply putting forward both sides of the argument and forming a conclusion, the more sophisticated answer will look laterally at the assertion and see what other meanings could be placed on it, and also consider alternative assertions or qualifications that are more tenable than the existing one. The answer should express some personal opinion and this should be supported both by factual information and opinions expressed by others.

How would you assess [idea]?

At first glance, this may seem to be identical to the question above. The difference is that it is asking for a critical assessment of a particular idea, rather than an opinion as to whether or not it is desirable. This is a fairly precisely defined question and it requires you to identify the issues involved in a particular idea and then to analyse and evaluate them. To do this, it is necessary to first identify what it is that the idea is trying to achieve, and where this concept has arisen from. This naturally leads on to a consideration of what the alternatives are and whether they would have been more or less successful. A top-class answer is never going to arise if you consider the question in a vacuum and you should look to bring in details of those individuals or groups that oppose or support the idea, and whether there is any difference between the theoretical justification for the idea and what is experienced in practice.

What are the alternatives to [present position]?

How you decide to approach this question is very much a matter of personal choice. An average answer would be to consider what the present position is, and then run through a number of alternatives to it, perhaps coming to a conclusion as to which of the alternatives would be best. A more sophisticated answer will look to challenge the question, looking at the question of why as well as what: Why is the position as it is? Why are alternatives being considered? Why would some be more successful than others? Do not simply assume that the present position is some kind of absolute that does not need to be analysed. Looking at the political, social, economic or other factors that have led to the current situation will help to explain what change may be possible and why it may be that there has been no change so far. Above all, you should look at what aim or role the policy or situation is looking to fulfil, considering whether it does, could do in the future and should do in the future.

What are the arguments for and against [idea]?

Although, and largely because, this is a straightforward sounding question, it can be a difficult one to write a high calibre answer to. The key thing is not simply to fall into the trap of just describing various alternatives, but instead to provide an evaluation of the merits of each and form a definite conclusion as to which would be the better position. Structure is particularly important with an essay of this type, and it is necessary to plan your answer in even more detail than you normally would in order to avoid it becoming a list of disparate points. You should go beyond a simple consideration of the arguments by showing an appreciation of which individuals and groups support each side, how their respective positions have evolved and how they are likely to evolve in the future. There is also the potential to question the idea itself and the validity of the overall argument, where possible bringing in alternatives and putting forward your personal view.

[Statement]. Is this a good idea?

You may encounter this question in a number of slightly different guises, but all require evaluation of a particular position. Depending on the statement, this can be a potentially far-reaching question and, before attempting it, it is important to be completely clear in your mind what the statement actually means and what all the potential implications of it are, even if some are more obscure than would be expected. It is unlikely that the idea will be exclusively a good or a bad one and balanced argument is called for before coming to a conclusion. There may be various nuances in the wording of the question, such as whether something is still a good idea, or whether further change is a good thing. These should not be dismissed as being peripheral to the question, as they can sometimes completely change the situation. A more sophisticated distinction can be drawn between what is a good idea in theory and what is a good idea in practice, and you should consider why particular ideas and policies have or have not been adopted and what the different motivations may be for the different parties involved. Where possible, consider whether past experience or the experience of other people or countries is useful to justify your conclusion.

[Two opposing viewpoints]. Is either of these views correct?

This type of question will tend to see two polar extremes placed against each other and, for that reason, it can be an interesting opportunity to examine some unusual perspectives. A good starting point is to consider where the viewpoints have come from, whose opinions they represent and what they arose in relation to. From here, you can distil the main issue in question and set the debate in some kind of context, which will allow you to consider more meaningfully what view should be taken. Although it is preferable to lean towards one viewpoint or the other, it is vital to examine the merits of both. To provide a first class answer, you may then want to go on to consider whether a third viewpoint might be sustainable and what advantages it would have over the two originally suggested. An interesting question to consider is whose view ultimately matters. For example, it is often the case that the majority view is the most important one, but it could also be the case that one person or group has such power that their view will prevail. In such circumstances, it would then be necessary to consider how valid the overall debate is, and how relevant the views espoused are.

What do you think should be done about [topic]?

Generally, this will be asking for your ideas as to how to solve a particular problem. This is therefore a good question for someone who enjoys creative thinking and can develop unusual ideas of their own beyond those conventionally cited. This is best achieved by first setting the topic in context and explaining why there is any need for action to be taken. It is then advisable to put forward the more mainstream arguments before bringing in a personal dimension. You should not feel constrained from introducing unusual ideas, providing that you justify the rationale behind your thinking and put forward appropriate evidence to back up what you are saying. The most compelling evidence is likely to derive from past experiences of a similar issue or from the experiences of other countries, and it is always desirable to use practical examples to back up what you are saying. A distinction can then be made between the practical realities of the situation and what appears, theoretically, to be most desirable.

Has [policy] been successful with respect to its aims?

This question is a lot broader than it may initially seem as there is the potential to question and discuss not only the success of the policy, but also the validity of the original aims. The importance of the latter should not be underestimated, and it is important to clearly define at the outset of the answer exactly what the aims were; any subsequent analysis will otherwise be meaningless. A good answer will go further than just forming a conclusion as to the success or otherwise of the policy and will look at what alternatives there are to the policy and in what context it was adopted in the first place. It is likely that different parties may be pursuing different aims, and also that there may be a difference between those aims made public and those that are actually being pursued. A particular policy may also succeed in relation to aims that it was not originally pursuing, and it can be important to look at the question in reverse.

Which is more important, [idea] or [idea]?

This may involve a comparison either of two conflicting concepts or two different ways of dealing with a situation. At the outset it is, therefore, important to be clear who or what is the judge of importance, and what the aim of the idea is. There is then the option of considering one idea followed by the other, or mixing them together, and building your analysis on an issue by issue basis. The first of these is probably to be preferred in so far as it avoids confusion and repetition. A likely conclusion that you will reach is that both ideas are valid to some extent and this must be related back to the ultimate aim that is being pursued in order to decide which of them is the more important. Equally, it may be the case that a third idea is more viable and it is always desirable to include personal opinion of this nature, providing that it is backed up appropriately. A top-class answer will also consider the extent to which the two ideas can co-exist and whether there is any potential to combine the two, or at least retain the advantages of both.

[Idea]. Discuss.

This is a typical kind of open-ended question, which is used to allow the candidate some flexibility as to how to approach their answer. Sometimes the idea will be a very general concept, in which case the scope of the answer can be extremely broad, and other times it may be a statement which narrows the scope somewhat. Either way, the same basic principles apply. Before doing anything else, you should define what is meant by the idea. This should include both what you mean by it and what the writer or other people may mean by it. Where there is a discrepancy between these two, you should explain how this has arisen and what the consequences are. Sometimes it may not be obvious how best to structure your answer, and you should ensure that you have a plan in mind before you begin writing, otherwise it is all too easy to write an answer that lacks focus and is not moving toward any definite conclusion. The model of putting forward the arguments for and against the idea is likely to be a good starting point for most essays that respond to this type of question. This should then be backed up by appropriate factual knowledge and opinion and, where possible, some ideas of your own that either are complementary to what is being suggested or illustrate a different perspective. Above all, you should not waste the opportunity presented by the style of question by simply repeating, in isolation, the same basic facts that everyone will be aware of. Instead, look to lay solid foundations and then develop your own style as the essay progresses.

Structure

The effort that goes into an essay should not be underestimated. Each sentence is the result of a never-ending stream of decisions as to the most suitable words, spelling, grammar, punctuation, structure and style. Each paragraph then requires care and attention to mould it into something coherent and informative before it can take its place in the overall essay in such a way that the total created is greater than the sum of its parts. To do this even moderately successfully is something of a feat, and to do it flawlessly is an almost unrealistic aim. Nevertheless, although there may be plenty of potential to make a mistake, there is even more potential to do well, and essay writing should always be viewed as an opportunity and not something to worry about. An analogy can be made with a building. You are the architect and your building blocks are all the skills and knowledge that you have accumulated over many years. Your task is to arrange them together into a logical and coherent design that will inform and entertain the reader.

Proper planning is as crucial to essay writing as to building, and the first thing to consider when writing an essay is how to structure it. This is very much a top-down process, where you start by considering things at the highest level and then move down stage by stage into the detail. Many people like to conduct this planning by sketching out an outline of the essay before they begin writing. This is an excellent idea, but even if you prefer not to actually put it down on paper, what is crucial is that you are clear in your own mind how you are going to tackle the question. Leaping straight in to the first paragraph can often seem appealing when you have a limited amount of time available, but inevitably results in a less well-directed answer, regardless of the quality of the writing. This is especially true of the kind of question that you will encounter on the LNAT paper. Unlike some essays that you may have written in the past, these essay questions do not seek to test factual knowledge so much as understanding and the ability to develop persuasive arguments. Almost without fail, there will be subtleties to the question that are not immediately obvious and that will set apart those candidates with a genuine understanding of the subject from those with a superficial knowledge. It is therefore worth spending a few moments considering what the question is actually asking before you even begin considering how to answer it.

Everyone is familiar with the idea of dividing an essay into an introduction, a middle and a conclusion, and it is easy to gloss over this as being too straightforward. Ultimately though, this so-called 'rule of three' is the basis of most essay writing and is more important than may initially appear to be the case. To illustrate how this can be so, even with non-academic subjects, let's take the example of a report about a football match. One option would be to provide a chronology of the match, minute by minute, describing everything that happened. However, this would not tell the reader that much about the game and would be very boring to read. The alternative would be to split the report up into, say, eight paragraphs. The first would be an introduction, the next two would be about the players involved and their preparations for the game, the next two would be about the key incidents during the match, the next two would be about the reasons for the result and the tactics employed and the last one would be a conclusion. In this way, the essay itself has been split into three sections and the middle section has also been split into three. The advantage of the 'rule of three' is that the essay mirrors the logical thought processes that the reader will be going through and is much more persuasive than would be the case with an unstructured narrative. This kind of structure is very flexible as there is no requirement for all the sections to be the same length and it can be applied to almost any subject on which you are asked to write. Crucially, it acts as something of a safety net in that it prevents you from writing the kind of shapeless answer that would lead the reader to question your ability to argue points effectively, the very skill that you are trying to demonstrate. The fact that propositions are introduced first in the introduction and then backed up in the middle section also encourages the use of relevant factual information in the correct place and avoids material being lost in the wrong section of the essay.

There is no hard and fast rule about how many paragraphs you should include, although between seven and ten is usually about right for an essay of this length, particularly given the requirement to limit yourself to no more than four sides of A4 and the time allotted. Each paragraph should roughly be between a third and two-thirds of a side, depending on the size of your handwriting. Longer paragraphs can distract from what you are saying, whilst shorter paragraphs can be indicative of disjointed ideas that are not properly integrated into the essay. It is a matter of personal choice as to how far you choose to deviate from these basic guidelines, but it must be appreciated that all the best essays have simple structures and needlessly complicating things does not indicate good quality writing. Likewise, structure should be viewed as being just as important, if not more so, than content and the temptation to cram in excess facts at the expense of good organisation should be avoided. The secret to success is being able to see the broader picture, rather than becoming obsessed with including everything you know about a subject.

It is also worth making the point that writing is very different from speaking. When you are having a conversation with someone, whether consciously or subconsciously, you gauge their reaction to what you are saying and adjust your future speech accordingly. Any mistakes that you make can be instantly corrected and it is unlikely that people will even notice that there was anything wrong in the first place. This is not a luxury that you have when you are writing: you only have one chance to communicate your ideas to the reader and by the time they come to see your essay, it is too late to make any changes. In addition, when speaking, it is not necessary to know how a word is spelled, or how a sentence should be punctuated, but once something is committed to paper these issues become important. Likewise, any emotions and expressions, which would have been conveyed by way of tone, delivery and body language, are lost on the page unless they are correctly conveyed through your style of writing. To counter these difficulties, you should develop the habit of, as you are writing, taking a step back from what you have written and making an objective judgment of whether it is correct, something which you would not consciously do when speaking.

The introduction

The old adage that you can only make a first impression once is as applicable to essay writing as it is to meeting people. Whether deliberately or subconsciously, people tend to be influenced by what they read at the beginning of essays and the introduction can often set the tone for the rest of the piece. Two common faults exist in relation to introductions: first, failing to properly introduce the essay and, secondly, writing too much. The former results from lack of planning and is more common when under time pressure. It is an unnecessary mistake to make and can prove costly as it undermines any subsequent attempt to impose a structure on the essay and can lead to confusion from the outset. The latter, whilst perhaps being more understandable, can be more difficult to remedy. The important factor when deciding what to include in the introduction is relevance rather than length; generalised material that adds nothing to what is being said should be avoided. It is often desirable to set the question in context by providing some background information, but this must be limited to that which adds something to the interpretation of the question.

Different writers advocate different styles of introduction, with some preferring to specifically explain how the question is to be approached and others preferring to leave it somewhat more up in the air. On the whole, the former style tends to be the safer option and is also useful to clarify your thinking on a subject. The latter can be extremely effective if done properly, but can also lead to disjointed introductions, which are not readily understood by the reader and which do not lead smoothly into the main body of writing. Either way, it is important to leave something for the rest of the essay and it is pointless to state all your conclusions at the outset. The better option is to summarise the main strand of your thinking on the subject whilst also leaving some questions up in the air to be resolved in the conclusion.

The conclusion

We have all read essays that start brilliantly, but then tail off toward the end. Sometimes this is due to time constraints, meaning that the end is rushed and there is no proper conclusion. Other times, plenty is written, but the essay simply fails to arrive anywhere. Both of these faults can be attributed to poor planning and are entirely avoidable. When you initially plan your answer, you should plan to set an issue up, develop it and then draw it to a conclusion, and one of the things that you should bear in mind is how much time it will take to do each of these. In reality, it almost always takes longer to write things than you expect it to and you should always build some time into your calculation for unexpected delays and to read the essay through at the end. Also, you should prioritise the order in which you introduce material. For each essay there will be a number of arguments and facts that are vital to the answer and a number more that it would be desirable to mention. These facts and arguments that are vital should be dealt with first as this eliminates the danger of not having time or space to include them and also tends to make the reader more forgiving if, by the time they reach the end of the essay, you have already mentioned most of what they expected you to. This should not discourage you from constantly challenging the question with new and interesting material throughout the essay, but is intended to highlight the danger of leaving the main points until late in the essay.

All good essays have good conclusions, and there is more to this than simply writing a good last paragraph. Throughout the essay your aim should be to advance arguments to a logical and well-reasoned conclusion and by the time you reach the end of the main section it should be apparent to the reader what conclusions you have drawn. The last paragraph is a chance to draw all of this together in such a way as to focus the reader's attention on the main points that you have made. It is complementary to the introduction and where you have opened up particular questions at the beginning of the essay you should ensure that they are properly closed at the end. As a general rule, you should not introduce any new material in the conclusion. This is not to say that you have to repeat verbatim things that you have said elsewhere, but the conclusion is really a chance to recap what you have told the reader throughout and, if a point was worth making, it was worth making in the main part of the essay.

Constructing paragraphs

The foundation of any well-structured essay is a collection of well-structured paragraphs, and a degree of conscious organisation is required to achieve this. The rule of three, discussed above in relation to the essay as a whole, is equally as applicable when writing each paragraph. It is sometimes said that in the introduction you should tell the reader what you are going to tell them, in the middle section you should tell them and in the conclusion you should tell them what you have told them. This is a useful guide as it provides a simple, but effective, format that can be applied to almost any essay or writing situation.

Let's imagine you have been asked to write under the title *'What are the arguments for and against reforming UK licensing laws?'*. One of the arguments you might want to consider is that reform would reduce binge drinking. In the introductory sentence you would set up the issue:

> The UK has the highest rate of binge drinking amongst 18–21 years old in the whole of Europe and this is often attributed to the requirement for pubs to close at 11pm.

The next sentences contain the argument following on from the proposition in the introductory sentence:

It is a familiar sight in pubs around the country to see people rushing to the bar as closing time approaches to stock up with large quantities of drink. Such behaviour is often thought to stem from a perceived pressure to enjoy oneself in the limited time before pubs close, and it is suggested that people would feel more able to relax and drink slowly if they know that they had more time. This reasoning is largely based on the experience of other European countries where the rate of binge drinking is considerably lower and where it is commonplace for pubs and bars to stay open until 4 or 5 in the morning. Experts, however, question whether the more realistic explanation is that there is simply a different attitude towards drinking in the UK, something which is unlikely to be changed by any of the reforms so far considered. Such a view is borne out by the reality of all day opening for pubs; despite the increased drinking time available, the rate of binge drinking has carried on increasing.

Finally, a concluding sentence is used to draw the paragraph to a close:

Ultimately, it is highly questionable whether there is a causal link between binge drinking and pub opening hours, and there is little compelling evidence to suggest that changing the opening hours will be sufficient to change the overall drinking culture.

In the above paragraph, the issue has quickly been located, discussed and then advanced to somewhere new. This kind of structured procession is the hallmark of a good paragraph and of a good essay as a whole. By setting out at the beginning of the paragraph the main thread of what you are saying, the reader's attention is immediately focused toward the idea you are addressing, and they are then more receptive to the argument and the evidence that follows. Similarly, by using the last sentence to draw together what has been said, the idea is reinforced in their mind, adding more weight to your writing.

Constructing sentences

Whilst high level organisation of an essay is absolutely crucial to its success, a good structure is to no avail if the quality of writing is inadequate. Having such a structure in place from the beginning does, however, afford you the freedom to concentrate on the minutiae of constructing each sentence. This need not be a laboured process and it is unlikely that you will have the time or patience to dwell for too long on each sentence, but it is important to have an overall idea of what you want to achieve in each sentence. Many advocate applying the 'rule of three' to sentences as well, and this provides a useful starting point. In the same way as with paragraphs, and indeed the essay as a whole, you should look to introduce an idea, develop it and then bring it to a conclusion. Whether or not you choose to follow this rule rigidly is a matter of preference, but what is important is that every sentence you write adds something to the essay rather than just filling space. If you cannot yourself explain what point you are seeking to make in the sentence, then it unlikely that the reader is going to be able to either.

It can be counterproductive to lay down too many rules about how a sentence should be constructed as everyone has their own style, and it is important not to feel unduly constrained when writing an essay. Broadly speaking, though, you should be looking at five elements in each sentence:

1 *Style*: does the sentence read coherently and engage the reader's attention?

2 *Content*: have you gone into a level of detail appropriate for the question being answered?

3 *Length*: is the sentence long enough to stand on its own, without being confusingly long?

4 *Language*: are the punctuation, spelling and grammar correct?

5 *Purpose*: does the sentence achieve a specific intended purpose?

Consider the following examples where one of these elements is missing in each:

Style

> Henry VIII is famous for having six wives; the first was Catherine of Aragon; he divorced her in 1533.

Stylistically, this sentence is poor. Although it serves the purpose of conveying some potentially relevant information and, on the whole, adheres to the appropriate rules of punctuation, it is very disjointed and is unlikely to hold the reader's attention. A better way of expressing the same idea would be:

> Henry VIII is famous for having six wives; the first of these was Catherine of Aragon, who he divorced in 1533.

Content

> The European Union, a diverse body encompassing a number of different countries, was formed many years ago by way of a treaty signed by its founding members.

This bears all the telltale signs of a sentence written by someone with insufficient factual knowledge of the subject. Although its construction is adequate, more content is required in order for it to be a meaningful addition to a piece of writing. An improvement would be to say:

> The European Union, a diverse body now encompassing some 25 different countries, is the modern incarnation of the original European Coal and Steel Community, which was formed following the 1951 Treaty of Paris between West Germany, France, The Netherlands, Belgium, Luxembourg and Italy.

Length

> William Hague, elected as leader of the Conservative Party in 1997 following John Major's resignation, endured a turbulent four years at the helm of the party that had been in power for so much of the 20th century, ultimately being replaced by Iain Duncan-Smith following the Tories' dramatic failure at the 2001 election, and has since faded somewhat into obscurity having declined offers to become more involved in front-bench politics again.

This sentence contains a lot of factual information and serves a clear purpose. The fact that it is so long, however, substantially detracts from this. It would be much better split into more than one sentence:

> William Hague was elected leader of the Conservative Party in 1997 following John Major's resignation. He endured a turbulent four years in office, facing the difficult task of leading the party that had been in power for so much of the 20th century. Ultimately, the Tories' dramatic failure at the 2001 election was to prove costly for him, and straight after the election he was replaced by Iain Duncan-Smith. Since leaving office, he has faded somewhat into obscurity, having declined offers to become more involved in front-bench politics again.

Language

> A number of music teacher's cited there top priority for the coming year as being to encourage students to practice more.

It is perfectly obvious what is meant by this sentence, but the spelling and punctuation errors in it immediately catch the reader's attention and diminish their opinion of the writer and distract from the content of the sentence. Where a number of common errors like this are made, it is much harder to have confidence in the rest of what the writer has said. The correct version would be:

> A number of music teachers cited their top priority for the coming year as being to encourage students to practise more.

Purpose

> The driving force behind the treaty was France, and the other signatories were Spain, England, Ireland, Italy, Germany, Luxembourg, Belgium, Norway, Sweden, Finland and Greece.

Unless it is necessary in order to answer the question, it is inadvisable to simply list factual information without any explanation. This sentence could be better developed to say:

> Of the 12 European countries that were signatories to the treaty, France was clearly the driving force, a fact which goes a long way to explaining why Article 3 was drafted so broadly.

When looking at the structure of sentences, a basic point to remember is that a sentence must be capable of standing on its own. In other words, fragments of text do not automatically constitute a sentence. Consider the following example:

England finally prevailed 2–1 at the end of an epic encounter. Which was a great relief to all the supporters.

Here, the second sentence is not capable of standing on its own and does not fulfil the basic grammatical criteria for a sentence. Instead, this should be written:

England finally prevailed 2–1 at the end of an epic encounter, which was a great relief to all the supporters.

Alternatively, it could be said:

England finally prevailed 2–1 at the end of an epic encounter. This was a great relief to all the supporters.

At its simplest, a sentence must consist of a subject, and object and a verb. For example:

John loved Sally.

Here, *John* is the subject, *liked* is the verb and *Sally* is the object. It is not important to be able to attribute grammatical labels to each word of a sentence, but what is important is to appreciate what goes into forming a sentence. More complicated structures can then be used:

John loved Sally deeply, regularly commenting on her beauty and charm.

Here, an extra clause is added after the comma. In this case, such an addition improves the sentence, but it is important not to misuse the comma by writing sentences consisting of a number of fragments which do not fit properly together. Consider the following example:

The result was never in doubt, Ian had clearly won, the crowd were delighted.

Here, although each part of the sentence makes sense on its own, the overall sentence does not fit together properly and is difficult to read. Instead, it would be preferable to say:

The result was never in doubt, with Ian having clearly won, much to the crowd's delight.

When looking at the grammar of a sentence, agreement is very important. First, there should be agreement between words in the sentence. For example, there must always be agreement between the subject and the verb: we say 'I like' not 'I likes', whereas it is 'he likes' not 'he like'. Secondly, there must be agreement between different sentences. For example, it is illogical and inconsistent to use the past tense in one sentence and the present tense in another, unless there is a good reason for doing so. Likewise, you should try to ensure a consistency in the way that people and places are referred to, and in the tone adopted towards different situations. Such consistency is one of the hallmarks of good writing and is vital in ensuring that the essay reads fluently. Ultimately, writing a good sentence is a case of finding a balance between a sentence that is too straightforward, which suggests conceptual simplicity, and one that is too complicated, which suggests an inability to structure thoughts clearly. Consistency must be complemented by high quality spelling, punctuation and grammar in order to create the best possible impression.

Spelling and word usage

Unlike the essays that you may have written as part of your GCSE or A Level studies, which were largely concerned with testing specific knowledge, the essay component of the LNAT is intended to test how well you think and how well you express yourself. As such, there is no fixed mark scheme and it is not a case of having to include a particular list of facts in order to do well. The reader will start with an open mind and as they read through your essay they will form an opinion on the basis of a number of different factors. On the whole, this will be a 'positive' process, whereby every good point you include will improve their overall impression, rather than a 'negative' one, whereby marks are deducted for every mistake that is made. Spelling, however, is one area that can cross over into this second category. Students applying to top universities will be expected to have an excellent grip of the English language and be able to write high quality material. This is not to say that you are expected to produce a flawless piece of writing, particularly given the time constraints, but misspelling a word is a mistake that is always avoidable and, as such, care should be taken not to do anything that will detract from the overall quality of your essay. There are three stages to achieving this. First, you should prepare properly by doing practice essays and reading through previous work to identify any mistakes that arise. Secondly, during the test you should ensure that you do not rush and that you think carefully before using words that you are not entirely familiar with. Thirdly, you should leave yourself sufficient time at the end of the test to be able to go back over what you have written to check for any errors.

Commonly misspelled words

The following list contains 100 of the most commonly misspelled words in the English language. At first sight, you will probably look at these and think that you would never make a mistake with any of them. In reality, almost nobody gets every one correct, and it is therefore a good idea to familiarise yourself with them to avoid elementary errors in your writing. Many people tend to find that there are a small number of words that they consistently spell incorrectly. By identifying yours it is possible to dramatically increase the quality of your writing.

accidentally	eliminate	neither	rhythm
accommodate	embarrass	ninety	ridiculous
acknowledge	especially	nuclear	sacrifice
allotted	exaggerate	occasionally	schedule
all right	excellent	opinion	secretary
amateur	experience	opportunity	separate
analyse	familiar	pamphlet	severely
appearance	foreign	parallel	similar
appreciate	government	persuade	sincerely
beginning	grammar	physically	straight
belief	guarantee	pleasant	substitute
business	guard	possession	succeed
commitment	height	preferred	success
counsel	humorous	prejudice	supersede
criticism	immediately	privilege	surprise
definitely	independent	probably	thoroughly
dependent	initiative	proceed	though
difference	intelligence	psychology	tragedy
disastrous	irrelevant	receipt	twelfth
discipline	knowledge	receive	unfortunately
disease	leisure	recommend	unnecessary
dissatisfied	lying	reference	until
dysfunctional	meant	relieve	unusual
eighth	miniature	religious	usually
eligible	misspelled	repetition	yield

Using the right word

The English language is not unique in having a large number of words that look or sound very similar, but in fact mean different things. The following are some of the most common examples of words frequently used in the wrong sense, with explanations and examples of how they should be used. These words between them account for a substantial proportion of the mistakes people make when writing essays, partly because people do not appreciate the difference between them and partly because people use them carelessly. Sometimes it can be useful to think of mnemonics or other tricks for remembering which word means what. In each case, it should be appreciated that the formal or most common usage is shown and there may be exceptions where more than one spelling or meaning is used, particularly where informal uses of the words have become accepted over time as part of the language. Many of the words also have other meanings of no relevance to the comparison being made.

a: precedes a word beginning with a consonant sound (*A horoscope*)

an: precedes a word beginning with a vowel sound (*An employee*)

a/an: used where per is not appropriate (*I visit the cinema twice a week*)

per: used where it is appropriate to say 'by the' (*The speed limit was 30 miles per hour*)

accept: to take or receive (*I accept the gift*)

except: excluding (*Everyone except Clare was at the party*)

ad: abbreviated form of advertisement (*He saw an ad in the paper*)

add: to put together (*You need to add the two numbers*)

affect: to influence (*The whole island was affected by the hurricane*)

effect: to bring about (*The new committee effected an immediate change*) or the result (*The effect of the rise in taxation was grave*)

all together: gathered in one place (*The family was all together for the first time in years*)

altogether: in total or completely (*That amounts to £100 altogether*)

all ways: all methods (*I will look at all ways of approaching the problem*)

always: forever (*I will always be a Spurs fan*)

among: preposition where there are three or more people or things (*We are among fellow supporters*)

between: preposition usually used in relation to two people or things (*There is a strong bond between the girls*)

amount: an unquantifiable collection (*An enormous amount of wine was consumed*)

number: a quantifiable collection (*There were a large number of people on the beach*)

anxious: nervous (*He was anxious before the interview*)

eager: looking forward to (*They are eager to complete the deal*)

are: part of the verb 'to be' (*We are very grateful for your help*)

our: used to indicate possession (*We asked for our ball back*)

assure: to give confidence to (*He assured me that the result was never in doubt*)

ensure: to make certain (*He called the airline to ensure that the flight was leaving on time*)

insure: to guarantee against loss (*It is compulsory to insure every vehicle*)

brake: noun meaning a device to make a vehicle go slower or stop (*He hastily applied the brake as another car pulled out in front of him*) or verb meaning to slow down or stop (*He braked suddenly as the traffic light changed to red*)

break: noun meaning where something has separated (*He had a bad break to his left leg*) or verb meaning to cause something to separate or be damaged (*David is always breaking things*)

bring: to carry in the direction of the speaker (*Please bring me a drink from the bar*)

take: to remove away from the speaker (*Please take this to the post office when you leave*)

can: ability to do something (*I can run faster than Ian*)

may: used to ask for permission (*May I borrow your car?*) or give permission (*You may borrow my car*)

choose: present tense of to select (*Please choose from the following options*)

chose: past tense of to select (*In hindsight, I chose the wrong option*)

complement: to balance or enhance (*Those shoes complement your trousers*)

compliment: praise (*Several people complimented me on my promotion*)

continual: happening repeatedly (*We are continually recruiting new staff*)

continuous: never ending (*Our radio station has been broadcasting continuously for the last ten years*)

disinterested: having no involvement (*It is vital for judges to be disinterested in the cases they hear*)

uninterested: not interested (*He was uninterested in the contents of the book*)

each other: between two people or things (*The twins always enjoyed talking to each other*)

one another: between three or more people or things (*The staff always enjoyed socialising with one another*)

eminent: well known (*Nelson Mandela is one of the most eminent people in the world*)

imminent: about to happen (*The eruption of the volcano is imminent*)

farther: to a greater, and usually measurable, distance (*The airport is farther away than the station*)

further: to a greater, and usually immeasurable, distance (*It's still a lot further away*) or additional (*Further consideration of the plan is necessary*)

fewer: used where the subject is quantifiable (*There were fewer people than usual at the party*)

less: used where the subject is not quantifiable (*There is less chance of winning a prize this year*)

formally: officially or properly (*The Mayor formally opened the fete*)

formerly: in the past (*He was formerly a director of the company*)

good: describes nouns (*She is a good teacher*)

well: describes verbs (*She teaches well*)

hanged: the past tense of 'to hang' in relation to executions (*The prisoner was hanged yesterday*)

hung: the past tense of 'to hang' in all other contexts (*I hung up the sign yesterday*)

hear: to receive or become aware of a sound (*I hear what you are saying*)

here: in, at or to this place (*They'll be coming back here later on*)

imply: suggested by the writer (*He implied in my appraisal that I had nothing to worry about*)

infer: deduced by the reader (*From what was said in my appraisal, I inferred that I had nothing to worry about*)

its: possessive pronoun (*Its main aim was to improve productivity*)

it's: shortened form of 'it is' (*It's unlikely that we'll have to pay anything*)

know: to have knowledge (*I know the answer to that question*)

no: not any (*I have no money left*) or to answer in the negative (*No, I don't want any help*)

later: further on in time (*Justin will be coming to visit later*)

latter: the second of two items already named (*I prefer the latter of those suggestions*)

lead: present tense of 'to show the way' (*I am currently leading the expedition*)

led: past tense of 'to show the way' (*Yesterday, I led the expedition*)

loose: not closely fitting (*She was wearing very loose clothing*)

lose: not win (*I think we're going to lose this match*)

maybe: perhaps (*Maybe the weather will improve this afternoon*)

may be: might to be the case (*It may be that we will have to cancel the event*)

nor: used with neither (*Neither Matt nor Tony will be there tonight*)

or: used with either (*Hopefully either Ian or Chris will be able to help*)

onto: preposition used where there is physical movement (*I climbed onto the roof*)

on to: preposition used in other circumstances (*I really think we should move on to the next item on the agenda*)

practice: noun meaning regular activity (*In some restaurants it is common practice to leave a tip*) or place of carrying out an activity (*The doctors have just opened a new practice*)

practise: verb meaning 'to train' (*She practised the piano for three hours a day*) or 'to work' (*He practised as a dentist*)

principal: main (*The principal language spoken is English*) or person in charge (*The school has just appointed a new principal*)

principle: rule (*The answer can be derived from the basic principle*)

quiet: the opposite of loud (*It was very quiet in the church*)

quite: not completely (*I am quite confident that I'm right, but I may be mistaken*) or completely (*I'm quite certain that's the answer*)

shall: used after 'I' or 'we' (*I shall be back tomorrow*) but reversed in the imperative (*I will be in trouble!*)

will: used after 'he', 'she', 'it' or 'they' (*He will be back tomorrow*) but reversed in the imperative (*They shall be in trouble!*)

should: used to express a duty (*I should go to the gym today*) or in place of would with the pronouns 'I' or 'we' (*I should be grateful if you would call me as soon as possible*)

would: used to express a wish (*He would love to win that prize*) or possibility (*We would consider that offer*)

stationary: not moving or changing (*The car remained stationary at the traffic lights*)

stationery: writing materials (*The office used a large amount of stationery every day*)

that: used with restrictive clauses (*Here is the woman that I hope to marry*)

which: used with non-restrictive clauses (*Those programmes, which are hugely expensive to make, tend to prove very popular with younger viewers*)

their: belonging to them (*That's their best result of the season*)

there: adverb introducing a sentence (*There is no time to do that*) or indicating a place (*He's over there*)

they're: contraction of they are (*They're in a hurry*)

to: used to form infinitive of verb (*I'm looking forward to playing football later*)

too: also (*I'll be joining you too*)

two: the number (*That car is available in two different colours*)

weather: climatic conditions (*We've enjoyed some lovely weather this summer*)

whether: if (*I'm not sure whether that idea will work*)

were: past tense of the verb 'to be' (*We were on our way home from the shops*)

where: an adverb or conjunction used to refer to a place or situation (*Rebecca lived in London, where she worked as a shop assistant*)

who: used where 'he' or 'she' would be appropriate (*It was James who won the competition in the end*)

whom: used where 'his' or 'her' would be appropriate (*It was Alice whom I originally knew*)

who's: contraction of 'who has' or 'who is' (*Who's coming to the cinema with me?*)

whose: used to signify possession (*The man whose car I borrowed*)

your: belonging to you (*I think that's your coat*)

you're: contraction of 'you are' (*You're a lucky man*)

A note of caution should also be sounded with regard to words that do not formally exist, despite being used in everyday conversation. For example, *irregardless*, in so far as it has a meaning, means the same as *regardless* and should never be used; *snuck* is an Americanism which is now incorrectly used by some instead of *sneaked*; and *alright* is sometimes used instead of the correct *all right*.

Rules of spelling

People often joke that the main rule of spelling in the English language is that there are no rules. Although a slight exaggeration, this is not so far from the truth, and as a general principle there is no substitute for learning how to spell words by way of experience rather than looking for a quick-fix solution, which can often cause more problems than it solves. There are, however, a number of rules that are of use, provided that you appreciate the potential for exceptions to each rule.

'i' before 'e' except after 'c'

If there is only one rule that people remember being taught, it tends to be this one. We are well used to the idea that words like *grief, piece, mischief* and *shield* should be spelt like this rather than with the 'e' before the 'i'. We are also happy with the fact that this situation is reversed with words like *conceit, deceive, receipt* and *receive*. There is, however, a further component which must be added to the rule for it to be more effective: '*i*' before '*e*' only applies where the sound is '*ee*'. This is to say that with words like *deign, eight, rein* and *weight*, where the sound is different, the '*e*' should go before the '*i*'. This latter part of the rule is much less well known than the rest of the rule, but goes a long way to explain many of the anomalies that arise.

adding 'dis-', 'mis-' and 'un-' to words

There are times when you will want to reverse the meaning of a word by adding one of the prefixes '*dis-*', '*mis-*' or '*un-*'. There is no universal rule for deciding which of these prefixes will be appropriate and, indeed, there are times – for example with *disinterested* and *uninterested* – where different prefixes can give the word a different meaning. The rule for spelling words like this, though, is that you should always add the prefix to the entire original word, even where the result is that a letter is duplicated. For example, it is common when '*mis-*' is added to *spelled* to see it written as *mispelled* when, in fact, it should be *misspelled*. Likewise, it is *unnecessary* rather than *unecessary* and *dissatisfaction* not *disatisfaction*.

single or double consonants

There is no universal rule for determining where there should be a double consonant in the middle of a word, for example *exaggerate*, and when there should be a single consonant, for example *skilful*. There is, however, a rule for the endings of words, albeit a fairly complicated one: you double the final consonant if you are adding the suffix '*-ed*' or '*-ing*' when the word ends in a single consonant that is preceded by a single vowel and the accent is on the last syllable. For example, *shop* becomes *shopped* and *travel* becomes *travelled* because all of these conditions are satisfied, whereas *unparallel* becomes *unparalleled* because the emphasis is not on the last syllable of the word *unparallel*. Similarly, *sleep* becomes *sleeping* because the final consonant was not preceded by a single vowel.

other suffixes

It can often be confusing to try to work out why the addition of a suffix can require the removal of the last letter of the original word, for example with *manage* and *managing*, and why at other times it would be incorrect to remove the last letter, for example with *manage* and *management*. The general rule is that if the word ends in an '*e*', you retain the '*e*' if the suffix begins with a consonant, but not if it begins with a vowel. There are, though, a number of exceptions to this, such as *argue* and *argument*, and there is unfortunately no alternative but to learn such words individually.

There is no firm rule for deciding when a word should end '*-able*' and when it should end '*-ible*'. On the whole, it tends to be that if the word has a Latin root, '*-ible*' is used, but this is not a realistically useful reference point. The more common ending is '*-able*' and it is therefore useful to consider the following list of exceptions to this: *edible, eligible, fallible, feasible, flexible, forcible, intelligible, negligible, perceptible, permissible, plausible, possible, tangible* and *visible*.

Further confusion with regard to suffixes arises over the endings *'-ise'* and *'-ize'*. The commonly held view is that *'-ize'* is the American spelling, which is incorrect in everyday English spelling. This is actually something of a misconception in that *'-ize'* was the original English spelling, which has now been largely abandoned except by the Americans. As a general rule it is therefore usually best to use *'-ise'* for most words, apart from those like *capsize* which do not have this alternative spelling.

forming the past tense

Regular verbs form the past tense by adding *'ed'*, for example *warn* becomes *warned*. There are, however, a number of irregular verbs, such as *sleep*, which form the past tense in a different way, here by adding a *'t'* to give, for example, *slept*. A third category allows the past tense to be formed in either way: for example *burn* can change to either *burnt* or *burned*. There is no hard and fast rule on what is correct, although the use of *'ed'* is now increasingly prevalent.

Capital letters

The incorrect use of capital letters should be regarded as a spelling mistake and again is something that is easily rectified. The default position should be that you do not used capitals apart from at the beginning of a sentence and otherwise you should ask yourself whether a capital is required in a given situation. The only other occasion when you should use capital letters is for proper names. This includes the names of people, for example *Isaac Newton* and *Ernest Hemingway*, and places, for example *London* and *Madrid*. They should not, however, be used for words subsidiary to either of these: it is *Isaac Newton's father* and the *east of London* not *Isaac Newton's Father* and the *East of London*, as is sometimes seen. On the whole, there is a trend towards using capital letters less frequently than previously, but this is not to say that you should fail to use them when they are properly required.

Punctuation

The importance of correct punctuation when answering the essay question in the LNAT is twofold. First, it makes the essay read better and will leave the reader with a more positive overall impression of the content. Secondly, it convinces the reader that you have sufficiently good attention to detail to succeed on the degree course that you have applied for. As with various elements of grammar, there is some degree of subjectivity in how you approach punctuation, and you should not think of punctuation in absolute terms, as everyone has their own style. Nevertheless, there are a number of basic principles, not all of which you will necessarily have previously been taught, that you should adhere to.

Full stops

It is a fairly safe assumption to make that everyone reading this book will be familiar with the idea that sentences start with capital letters and end with full stops. Like so much of what normally comes naturally, it is not unheard of for this knowledge to be thrown out of the window under the pressure of exam conditions. What tends to happen more frequently, though, is that students lose the overall sense of how the essay will read and start overusing commas at the expense of full stops. This produces long and poorly structured sentences, which detract from the content of their writing. The subject of how commas should properly be used is dealt with below, but, suffice to say, they are not intended to separate clauses that should form separate sentences.

Consider the following example:

> Tony Blair's Labour Party swept into power at the 1997 general election with one of the biggest majorities in British parliamentary history, in no small way this was due to the wholesale reforms made to the party structure under first John Smith and then Blair himself, which sought, amongst other things, to diminish the power of the trade unions and move the party away from the far left of the political spectrum.

Although it is factually correct, the sentence is too long and contains a number of different clauses, separated by commas, which could be divided up into separate sentences:

> Tony Blair's Labour Party swept into power at the 1997 general election with one of the biggest majorities in British parliamentary history. In no small way this was due to the wholesale reforms made to the party structure under first John Smith and then Blair himself. Such reforms sought, amongst other things, to diminish the power of the trade unions and move the party away from the far left of the political spectrum.

This second example is no more difficult or time consuming to write, but, by using punctuation correctly, comes across much more clearly. Under use, rather than overuse, of full stops tends to be the more common mistake, but it is nevertheless important to be sure that you do not consistently write sentences that are too short. The full stop is the longest pause available and should be used after a unit of information has been put forward, before moving on to the next unit. Short sentences can be useful to emphasise a particular point, but lose their effect if this technique is repeated too frequently.

Exclamation marks

The principal formal use of exclamation marks is to signal the use of the imperative; that is to say a command being given. For example, you might write, *'Dave shouted to his wife, "hurry up!"'*. It is relatively unlikely that you will be using direct speech in an academic essay, unless quoting directly, in which case you should use the existing punctuation. There are other occasions where exclamation marks can be used, such as to inject humour or signal irony. You should not be afraid of using them in this way in your essay, but be aware that it is probably better to err on the side of caution and write in a relatively formal style throughout unless there is a specific reason for not doing so.

Question marks

One of the secrets of good essay writing is to challenge the title you are given, and this may involve posing additional questions. Where the question is straightforward, there is usually little problem with the use of a question mark:

> What can we learn from this example?

The time when people tend to forget to use the question mark is where there is a longer sentence where the question itself becomes hidden amongst other clauses:

> The question one must ask is, in view of the enormous body of support for the plan and the government's reluctance to intervene, could anything really be done to stop it?

Some would argue that a question mark does not add much to a sentence like the one above; ultimately though, it's a good habit to get into to use the correct punctuation and it makes it much easier for the reader if they are clear as to when you are posing questions and when you are answering them. Failing to include a question mark can also change the meaning of a sentence and cause much of the effect of the point to be lost. The general rule is that question marks are required for direct, rather than indirect questions. A direct question is something like 'What was the cause of the war?', whilst an indirect question would be 'People sometimes wander what the cause of the war was'. This distinction is important both in terms of what punctuation to use, and also to determine whether you subsequently answer that specific question or simply continue discussing the topic in a more general context.

Commas

Commas are used to indicate a slight pause or change in direction in a sentence. Despite being one of the most commonly used forms of punctuation, though, they are often seen as being one of the most difficult to use correctly. This is understandable given the variety of occasions in which they are used, but in fact there are a limited number of specific situations where a comma is required and these can easily be learned and understood.

to link clauses

We have seen above that commas should not be used in place of full stops when it would be more appropriate to start a new sentence; this simple rule is one of the most important points to remember when dealing with commas. Conversely, when you are dealing with two clauses that are closely related, it may be more appropriate to separate them with a comma than a full stop. For example:

> John is a keen sportsman. He enjoys playing cricket and tennis. He also occasionally plays football.

This would be better written as:

> John is a very keen sportsman, enjoying cricket, tennis and the occasional game of football.

Sometimes the link between clauses is made by modifying the verb, as is the case with *enjoys* and *enjoying*, and at other times words such as *and*, *but* and *or* are used. The above example joins two main clauses together, but the same principle also applies when joining a subordinate clause to a main clause. For example:

> John decided that the best option was to swim for the shore. There was little chance of being rescued from the shipwreck.

This would be better written as:

> John decided that the best option was to swim for the shore, since there was little chance of being rescued from the shipwreck.

The use of a joining word helps to introduce the subordinate clause. Other examples of such words are *although, before, if, unless, until, while* and *whereas*.

Where the sentence is very short, and the meaning is not influenced by the placement of a comma, it is perfectly acceptable to join sentences together without the use of a comma. For example, '*John is a good footballer and a good golfer*' may stylistically be preferable to '*John is a good footballer, and a good golfer*'.

to distinguish introductory clauses at the beginning of the sentence

Sentences frequently have an introductory element to them, which is separate from the main part of the sentence, and this should be separated by a comma. For example:

> As a result of this, Sarah decided to apply for a new job straight away.

'*Sarah decided to apply for a new job straight away*' is the main part of the sentence and could stand on its own, whilst '*as a result of this*' is an introductory clause. This is an example of an introductory clause that does not add much to the meaning of the sentence, but improves the style of the writing and makes the sentence read more fluently. Words and phrases like *although, however, in the event that, nevertheless, of course, therefore* and *though* fall into this category and should not simply be added to the main part of sentences without appropriate punctuation. The need for commas to separate off the introductory clause of sentences also applies where a preposition is used to relate the main clause to something else. For example:

> Before Christmas, most shops tend to employ additional staff to cope with the increased number of customers.

'*Before Christmas*' is crucial to the meaning of the sentence, but is used to qualify the main clause of the sentence, rather than actually being part of it, and should be separated from the main part by a comma.

to distinguish ancillary elements in the middle of the sentence

Closely related to this is the rule that ancillary elements in a sentence should be separated with commas. This can refer to the same kinds of words discussed above, such as *however* and *though*, where they appear in the middle of the sentence. For example:

> Jane was reluctant to leave her present job, however, and hinted that she might be forced to turn down the offer.

Here, '*however*' does not add anything to the meaning of the sentence, but makes it read more fluently. It should be noted that commas should be used on both sides of the words or expression in question and not just afterwards as is sometimes assumed.

An ancillary element of the sentence can consist of more than just a single word or phrase and can extend to a much longer subordinate clause. For example:

> Lucy was reluctant to enter the competition, despite her convincing win the previous year, due to concerns over her fitness.

Here, '*despite her convincing win the previous year*' is an important clause, but is ancillary to the main part of the sentence and should be separated by commas on either side.

to distinguish additional clauses at the end of the sentence

In the same way as commas are used to separate introductory clauses at the beginning of sentences, they are also used to separate additional clauses at the end of the sentences. For example:

> The letter explained that I had been rejected by the academy, although only after much deliberation.

Here, '*although only after much deliberation*' adds to the meaning of the main part of the sentence, but is not capable of standing on its own. It should, therefore, be placed after a comma in order to allow a brief pause for the reader before reaching it. It can sometimes be difficult to determine where to place the comma in this situation, or even if one is required at all. As a general rule, though, a comma should be used unless the sentence is fairly short and would sound better without one, and a comma should not separate the subject from the verb. In simple terms, this just means separating the main part of the sentence from anything that could be said to be additional.

when redefining meanings

Consider the following sentence:

> Ian Jones, editor of the Daily Post, will be available to answer any questions after the talk.

Here, a noun (*'Ian Jones'*) is introduced, and then modified by a subsequent phrase (*'editor of the Daily Post'*). In other words, from that point on, *Ian Jones* is to be thought of in his capacity as *editor of the Daily Post* rather than in any other capacity. Such a modifying phrase is sometimes known as an appositive and should be separated by commas before and after it.

with series

This is one use of commas that most people are quite comfortable with, although some are unsure of the finer points of the rule. Consider the following example:

> Jen's favourite colours were red, orange, pink and blue.

Here, commas are inserted after all but the penultimate and last items of the list. This is the commonly accepted practice and is applicable in all situations except where the comma changes what is meant by an item in the list. Consider the following example:

> I like bread and butter.

This means that I like bread with butter on it. The following sentence, on the other hand, means that I like bread and I also like butter, but not necessarily together:

> I like bread, and butter.

Where it is not apparent from the context whether the last two items of the list go together in this way, a comma should be used before the *and* to avoid any confusion.

with multiple adjectives

There are various occasions where two or more adjectives are used to refer to the same noun. This can occur where different characteristics are being described. For example:

> Andy ordered a long, cold drink.

Here, *long* and *cold* are discrete adjectives referring to the same drink and it would be possible to rewrite the sentence using *and* instead of the comma. It is a matter of choice whether a comma or *and* are used in these circumstances.

There are other times when the two adjectives are more closely related. For example:

I have several long-term projects on the go.

Here, *several* refers to the *'long-term projects'* and it would not be appropriate to separate the adjectives with a comma.

Apostrophes

The apostrophe is probably the most incorrectly used punctuation mark in the language and every day hundreds of examples of incorrect usage can be seen on signs and in advertisements around the country. Ironically, the most common mistake tends to be using an apostrophe when none is required, and it is common to see *'hundred's of items for sale'*, *'selection of wine's available'* and so on. In fact, apostrophes need not be difficult to use and, broadly speaking, are only required in the two situations detailed below.

to indicate possession

At the simplest level, apostrophes are used to indicate possession. Where the possessor is singular and does not end with an *'s'*, this is very straightforward:

That is Tom's book.

An apostrophe and an *'s'* are added to the end of the original word. The situation is more complicated where the original word already ends with an *'s'*, as sometimes just an apostrophe is added and sometimes a second *'s'* is added as well. There is no hard and fast rule for when an apostrophe is used rather than when both an apostrophe and a second *'s'* are used; the best way of determining this is to think about how the word would be pronounced. For example, if you wanted to talk about a car owned by James you would say *'James's car'* as the second *'s'* is articulated when saying the phrases. On the other hand, if you wanted to talk about a car owned by *Hercules*, you would be more likely to say *'Hercules' car'* as it sounds more natural not to articulate an additional *'s'*. With proper names, the use of the apostrophe is largely dependent on how the person themself chooses to pronounce it.

With plural nouns, the important thing to remember is that the apostrophe has nothing to do with pluralising the word. To signify possession, an apostrophe is added to the end of the already pluralised word. If the plural noun does not end with an *'s'*, an *'s'* is added after the apostrophe. For example a cage in which several tigers live would be a *'tigers' cage'* and a party for more than one child would be a *'children's party'*. A second *'s'* should never be added where the plural noun already ends in an *'s'*. It is sometimes difficult to know how to pluralise proper names. For example, if you wanted to refer to a house belonging to the Jones family, you could say either *'the Jones' house'* or *'the Joneses' house'*. Again, this is a matter of deciding what sounds right, having reference to how the people in question choose to pronounce their name. Either way, the apostrophe should always come last, with nothing after it, when indicating possession. A very important exception to the use of an apostrophe to indicate possession is with pronouns. Consider the following example:

Whose is that car parked outside?

Here, *whose* indicated possession, but is not written *who's*, as this means *'who is'*. The same is true of other pronouns such as *his*, *hers* and *theirs*, and most commonly, *its*.

to indicate contraction

Apostrophes are also used to indicate where words have been contracted, and this is a completely separate usage from where possession is being indicated. The most common such usage, and one that many students get incorrect, is the contraction of *'it is'*:

> It's annoying that the weather is so bad.

Here, the apostrophe is used to indicate that the space and the second *'i'* have been removed. The same principle applies with *doesn't*, *he's*, *she's*, *weren't*, *won't*, *who's* and so on. Two points should be made on this point. First, it is crucial to get the punctuation correct if you are going to shorten words in this way. Secondly, the essay you will be writing will be fairly formal in style and, whilst it may be acceptable to use contracted words, you should avoid shortening too many words and make sure that, where you do, it is appropriate in the context.

In particular, you should avoid contractions where it leads to ambiguity over what is being said. For example, if you wrote *'John's home'*, this could be interpreted as meaning either *'the home belonging to John'* or *'John is home'*.

Colons

Colons are used to introduce a word, clause, list or quotation. Generally, they amplify or expand on what is said before them, usually following on from a clause capable of standing on its own, although they are sometimes used after *'for example'* or similar. Consider the following example:

> Martha excelled at a number of subjects at school: English, French, Science, Maths and Latin.

Here the colon precedes the list of subjects that Martha excels at, this list amplifying what is said in the first part of the sentence. A colon is used to similar effect in this next example, but with a clause instead of a list:

> It's important to think very carefully before you start writing: mistakes in this exercise can prove very costly.

Again, the part of the sentence after the colon amplifies what is said before it. In a similar way, colons are used to introduce quotations:

> Adrian reminded everyone of the company's motto: 'It's nice to be important, but it's more important to be nice.'

An alternative way of introducing quotations is through the use of a comma and this is more appropriate where the quotation is in the middle of the sentence:

> Adrian reminded everyone that, 'It's nice to be important, but it's more important to be nice', explaining that it was the company's motto.

Colons are sometimes used with a dash immediately afterwards, but this is incorrect, as is the use of a space before the colon. A space should, however, always be left after the colon.

Semicolons

The semicolon is often seen as being one of the more sophisticated forms of punctuation, and whilst it can be avoided altogether, its use can often add some extra refinement to your writing. It is primarily used to separate clauses that are linked in theme, but not joined by a conjunction. Unlike where a similar function is performed by commas, the clauses must be capable of standing separately on their own. Consider the following sentences:

> John was the best young pianist in the country, having recently won a number of competitions. As a result he was highly sought after for concerts.

This could be rewritten as:

> John was the best young pianist in the country, having recently won a number of competitions, and a result he was highly sought after for concerts.

This is slightly clumsy and would be better written as:

> John was the best young pianist in the country, having recently won a number of competitions; as a result he was highly sought after for concerts.

The fact that John is highly sought after for concerts is very closely linked to what an accomplished pianist he is and it makes more sense to have both pieces of information in the same sentence, but to join the two clauses by using commas makes the sentence unwieldy. A semicolon offers a further option for linking together ideas, and is indicative of a more confident style of writing.

Semicolons act as a pause and are useful for breaking up your writing without creating as conclusive a break as does a full stop. They do not require the use of a conjunction in the same way that commas sometimes do and in many ways are more analogous to starting a new sentence, apart from the fact that the letter immediately after the semicolon is not capitalised. Ultimately, they are designed to help the reader by providing guidance as to how different ideas interrelate and how the material should be split up.

One of the reasons why semicolons can be an effective writing tool is that they are used relatively infrequently. You should, therefore, use them sparingly and not with the same frequency that you would use full stops or commas. In particular, you should avoid using them where the effect is simply to lengthen sentences with no corresponding improvement in clarity. There are occasions where it may be appropriate to use more than one in the same sentence, but often such use becomes confusing and it is preferable to start a new sentence where possible.

Hyphens

Hyphens have two different uses. First, they are used to join together a single word where it is not possible to fit all of the word onto a line. In such circumstances you should put the first part of the word and the hyphen on the first line, and the second part on the next line. Only one hyphen is ever used and this always goes on the first line. Care should be taken to ensure that the word is split in a logical way. The convention is that the first part should normally end with a consonant and, where possible, syllables should not be split.

Secondly, they are used to join two or more words together. As a rule, hyphens do not go between adjectives and nouns. For example, you would write '*in the 20th century*' rather than '*in the 20th-century*' as *20th* is an adjective and *century* is a noun, and they are, therefore, performing different grammatical functions. Where you are creating a compound adjective, however, a hyphen should be used: it is '*20th-century Britain*' rather than '*20th century Britain*', as *20th* and *century* are both adjectives and they together modify the noun *Britain*.

Probably the best way to think about this is to consider whether adding a hyphen will make clearer the meaning of what you have written. For example, if you said, '*I regularly go for two mile long runs*', it would not be clear whether you were in the habit of going for two runs each of a mile in length, or a single run of two miles in length. It would therefore be better to write: '*I regularly go for two-mile long runs.*' If a hyphen is not required to aid clarity, then its use should be avoided as too many hyphens can make your writing look disjointed and make it more difficult to read.

There are a number of specific situations where hyphens are always used:

1   with fractions (*two-fifths*, *three-quarters*);

2   with compass points (*north-east*, *south-west*);

3   with Latin prefixes such as *anti-*, *ex-* and *non-* (*anti-clockwise*, *non-conformist*);

4   to separate double letters when adding a prefix (*co-operation*, *book-keeper*); and

5   with nouns formed from prepositional verbs (*call-out*, *set-down*).

Double hyphens are also sometime seen in expressions like '*mother-in-law*', although this is more commonly written as '*mother in law*' now. On the whole, the use of hyphens is becoming less common and once words are established in common usage in the language the hyphen is frequently dropped.

Dashes

The dash (–) is often confused with the hyphen (-), but in fact performs a completely different function, separating words where hyphens join them together. Opinion is divided as to how desirable it is to use dashes in written English, and on the whole it is the type of punctuation mark that could be avoided altogether. Nevertheless, there are some occasions where it may be desirable to use dashes.

Dashes should normally be used in pairs, and are used in a similar way to commas when separating off an ancillary element of a sentence. They are used either when an alternative to commas is required in order not to complicate the sentence structure, or when it is desired to have a longer pause than would be achieved with commas. Consider the following example of how dashes can be used:

> Today's horseracing results were a surprise to everyone, with Sunlight Express – fancied by many to win – coming last, and a number of lesser known horses occupying the higher places.

The same result could be achieved with commas, but arguably it is clearer to use dashes as shown. The important thing to remember is that dashes should be used sparingly as they disrupt the flow of the sentence. It should also be remembered that they cannot be nested in the way that commas can, and where possible you should keep the clause between the dashes as short as possible.

Brackets

Also known as parentheses, brackets are in many ways similar to dashes, discussed above. They, too, are always used in pairs and contain information that is ancillary to the main sentence. Brackets are used in preference to commas or dashes where the information to be conveyed is incidental to the rest of the sentence and could be left out without changing the meaning of the sentence. For example:

> Alan (aged 51) recently took over from Elliot as global co-ordinator.

The reader does not need to know that Alan is 51 in order to understand the sentence, and this information is very much peripheral to the main part of the sentence. On the whole, you should minimise, or avoid altogether, punctuation inside brackets.

Quotation marks

It is unlikely that you are going to make extensive use of direct speech in an essay of an academic nature, but you may wish to include the occasional quotation and it is important to be clear how such quotations should be punctuated. Often, people concern themselves about whether single or double inverted commas should be used. In fact, there is no hard and fast rule on this, and it is purely a matter of convention. Traditionally, double inverted commas are used, although there is a move towards using single inverted commas. Either way, the key thing to remember is that material should be quoted exactly as it appears in the source. Where the quotation is short, it is normal to continue on the same line rather than starting a new paragraph as you would with a longer one. Whether you choose to use a colon, a comma or no punctuation before the quotation depends on what is appropriate in the circumstances and, to a great extent, is a matter of personal preference. For example:

> In summing up the case, the judge commented that 'the offence was made far more serious by the dishonesty involved'.

There is no logical break between *that* and *the*, and it is unnecessary to introduce punctuation. There may, however, be times when punctuation is necessary. For example:

> The judgment began: 'In my opinion, this is a most grave case.'

There is a greater degree of separation between the first part of the sentence and the quotation and it is more appropriate to use a colon. In doing so, the normal rules for the usage of a colon apply, and in other circumstances it may be more appropriate to use a comma. With regard to punctuation at the end of the sentence, the determining factor as to whether it falls within the inverted commas is whether the punctuation forms part of the quotation. If it does, it must fall within inverted commas. For example:

> The complete sentence was: 'I would like to thank you for your warmth and generosity from the bottom of my heart.'

The whole sentence is quoted and logic dictates that the final full stop is included as well. Where the punctuation does not form part of the quotation, the punctuation can go after the quotation mark. For example:

> When asked what her favourite colour was, Maria replied 'red'.

When dealing with a quotation within a quotation, the rule is that the other type of inverted comma should be used. In other words, if you started by using a single inverted comma, you should use a double inverted comma for the second quotation, and vice versa. For example:

> The first line of the judgment read: "At the beginning of the trial I asked the defendant whether he was guilty to which question he replied 'certainly not' with some degree of indignation."

Or:

> The first line of the judgment read: 'At the beginning of the trial I asked the defendant whether he was guilty to which question he replied "certainly not" with some degree of indignation.'

Sometimes it may be desirable to remove irrelevant parts of a quotation, and this is done through the use of an ellipsis. The missing words are replaced by three dots. For example:

> Immediately, and fearing that I was already too late, I rushed into the street.

This could be shortened to:

> Immediately ... I rushed into the street.

It is a matter of preference whether a space is left before or after the dots. As with many elements of punctuation, the important thing is that you retain a consistent style throughout the essay.

SAMPLE TEST PAPERS

USING THE SAMPLE PAPERS

One of the key parts of your preparation for the test should be the use of practice tests. As has already been made clear, the LNAT is a test of ability and potential, not knowledge, and good technique is fundamental to maximising both. The sample papers in this section will give you an insight into some of the styles of questions that you are likely to encounter and will help you to understand and develop the skills that you need to answer them. Equally as importantly, familiarity with the format of the paper will help you to feel more at ease when you sit the actual test and will give you more confidence in your preparation.

The subsequent tests are carefully designed to be as similar to the actual paper as possible, although care should be taken not to take this fact for granted, as one of the skills that the LNAT seeks to test is the ability to think on your feet, and the style of the paper is constantly evolving. The LNAT Consortium deliberately limits the availability of sample papers in order not to reveal every intricacy of the forthcoming tests, and there is nothing to be gained by trying to identify specific patterns of questions as this will simply cloud your judgment in future tests. The sample tests should, therefore, be taken as a guide to the way of thinking required, rather than as an example of the particular questions that you will face.

The decision to increase the length of the test from 24 questions to 30 questions from 2005 onward indicates a greater focus on efficient use of time, and is likely to see candidates put under considerable time pressure. Consequently, it is a reasonable assumption to make that some of the extracts may be slightly shorter than those used in the previous test and in the following sample papers in this book, although this is by no means guaranteed. With this in mind, you should work through each of the passages as quickly and efficiently as possible, but it is suggested that it is worth completing each sample test even if you pass the time limit, in order that you are as well prepared as possible. Note how long each test takes you and try to gradually decrease the time taken with each test attempted. Such an approach will ensure the best possible outcome regardless of the length of the extracts in the actual paper that you sit, and you will hopefully then find the actual test a pleasant surprise rather than an unpleasant one.

You may wish to work gradually through one or two of the papers at your own pace to begin with, but it is recommended that you keep at least three to sit under proper examination conditions in order to get some more realistic experience of what you will encounter. In particular, there is a tendency with practice papers not to take them as seriously as you would the actual test, but this is somewhat counterproductive as it makes it difficult to assess your progress and to identify the areas you need to work on. Try also to concentrate on both sections of the test, rather than just the one that you prefer, as the way that the test is marked makes it difficult to compensate for a poor performance in one part with a good performance in the other.

For each test, an answer sheet is provided at the back of the section and that should be completed as you go through the test. A space is also provided for notes and an essay plan, which should be used in order to facilitate revision when working back through the book.

NATIONAL ADMISSIONS TEST FOR LAW

SAMPLE TEST 1

The test has two separate sections, A and B.

Section A: Multiple Choice

This section is divided into 10 subsections; each subsection has three questions.

You should answer **all** 30 questions in Section A, selecting one of the possible answers and indicating your response on the answer sheet at the back of the section.

Time allowed: 80 minutes

Section B: Essay

This section has five essay questions.

You should select and answer **one** question in Section B. Your answer should be no more than four sides of A4. A page is provided at the back of the section for your essay plan and notes.

Time allowed: 40 minutes

SECTION A: MULTIPLE CHOICE

ANSWER **ALL** OF THE FOLLOWING QUESTIONS.

1   Historical Sources

History begins with sources, the material and textual traces of the past. Anything can be an historical source: letters, legal records, financial accounts, literary narratives, paintings, photographs, buildings, discarded rubbish, postcards, tombstones, stained-glass windows, graffiti, royal writs, rebellious pamphlets … anything, in fact, which offers the possibility of catching a small glimpse of the past. The task for someone who wants to do history is first to understand how best to catch that glimpse; and secondly, to explore how the first fragment might be connected to a second, and then a third, and so on.

Through stitching together these small snatches of past knowledge we can build up a composite picture of an historical event or theme or person. The task is therefore something like compiling a jigsaw puzzle. However, it is a strange, rather fluid jigsaw: the pieces uncovered can be made to fit in a number of different ways, and the pictures thus revealed can differ, according to the routes taken. The picture built of the past is therefore affected by two factors. The first is the demands, possibilities and limitations of each piece of historical evidence: what it says, what it suggests, what we think of it in terms of truth, bias and opinion. The second factor is more subjective, and involves what each one of us brings to our pursuit of the past: what kind of picture we want to uncover, what interpretation we place on our evidence, what direction we have chosen to follow.

All good history should make fair use of its sources, treating them with care and attention, and not (for example) bending them out of shape to fit a preconceived idea. The best histories, however, are those that are also aware of the choices they have made. Every history – every picture revealed – involves a degree of choice on the part of the historian. If we are aware of each choice made, we tend to make better decisions, rather than simply following our preconceived ideas and prejudices. This element of choice is inescapable, in part simply because there is so much historical material available to us. This may sound surprising, but – with certain qualifications – it is true. Even for the medieval period, the total number of sources that survive are vast, far more than could be read by any one person in their lifetime. As one approaches more recent times, this vastness becomes one of the major hurdles for historians. Of course, if one decides to restrict one's area of interest to a more specific time and place, the relevant sources available may be smaller in number. Still, we have to choose where and what we wish to explore, and the kinds of sources we want to use. All of these choices will affect the kind of picture we end up producing.

So we need to decide on somewhere to begin. There are a number of ways in which historians might find their starting point. They may have decided that they want to explore a particular theme such as, for example, parliamentary politics in the eighteenth century. In this case, past experience and knowledge would suggest to them that they would look at the centralised records of parliament, the local records of elections, and the campaigning pamphlets of politicians. Alternatively, one might notice a passing reference to some sources in another historian's work, something that the original writer had not found interesting but which looked intriguing to the reader. For example, earlier historians did not think the trials of witches much worth considering, whereas more recent writers (including me) have found the sources relating to witchcraft trials completely fascinating. Yet again, we might be researching one topic and then happen across an unexpected piece of evidence that leads us in a very different direction. The craft of the historian is to focus closely on a chosen topic, whilst remaining alive and alert for those surprising new discoveries that might lie around each corner. It is not always easy; but it is exciting!

(*Source: 'The element of choice: how to work with sources' by Dr John Arnold, May 2001, from BBC News at www.bbcnews.com*)

Select one answer for each of the following questions:

1   Which of the following is an unstated assumption of the writer?

   (a) Different people attach different value to particular sources

   (b) It is impossible to be sure of the validity of a source

   (c) It is ultimately possible to reconcile all the different sources about a subject

   (d) An accurate history needs to be based on sources

   (e) All historians have access to the same sources

2   Which of these can be inferred from the passage?

   (a) Consulting more sources ensures a more accurate history

   (b) All sources are of equal validity

   (c) Not all sources are completely accurate

   (d) Every source can be interpreted in more than one way

   (e) More specialised histories are more accurate

3   What is the writer's main argument?

(a) Anything is capable of being an historical source

(b) Sources should be used with care

(c) History is constantly evolving

(d) Previous historians' work is one of the most useful sources of information

(e) It is not possible to investigate every piece of evidence relating to a given subject

2   Opinion Polls

A brief word on the importance of the low turnout and its effect on the polls. MORI's final poll projection for *The Times* was Conservative 30%, Labour 45%, Liberal Democrat 18%; the 'poll of polls' (average of all the companies' polls conducted during the final week) was Conservative 31%, Labour 45% and Liberal Democrats 18%. Both polls were close to the final result (32.7%:42.0%:18.8%), and within the standard 3% margin of error for all parties – though, naturally, we would like it to be even closer.

But readers of some newspapers will have noticed that it took less than a week before the 'expert commentators' started criticising the polls again, noting that all the final polls overestimated the Labour lead, and rehearsing again their theories about 'shy Tories' and biased samples. As we have pointed out many times, you should watch the shares, and the turnouts, not the gap. Looking simplistically at the lead risks completely missing the point. MORI's final poll found 63% said that they were certain to vote. In fact, only 59% voted. As we said on numerous occasions before the election was likely to happen, 'old Labour' voters in safe seats in particular realised that they didn't need to vote after all – so Labour lost last-minute votes, but not seats, and won the majority that should have gone with a 13-point lead even though in actual votes cast they had only a 9-point lead.

The trouble with percentages is that they depend on the base – if lots of people tell us they will vote Labour and then don't vote at all, that not only reduces Labour's percentage share but it increases the percentage shares of the other parties, because their unchanged numbers of voters are now part of a smaller total. The difference between a 63% turnout and a 59% turnout is big enough to have a significant effect on the party shares, if the extra stay-at-homes are disproportionately from one party. So instead of thinking in percentages, let us think in millions of real voters. On a 63% turnout, a 30% Conservative share translates to 8.2 million votes, 45% for Labour equals 12.2 million and 18% for the Lib Dems is 4.9 million. And the actual votes? The Tories got 8.36 million, Labour 10.7 million and the Lib Dems 4.8 million.

In other words, that final poll almost exactly predicted the numbers of Conservative and Lib Dem voters. But it overestimated the number who would turn out for Labour instead of staying at home, and as a result got the percentages – slightly! – wrong. Interestingly, exactly the same was true of MORI's last poll before the 1999 European elections: the Conservative vote was correctly projected to the nearest tenth of a million, but Labour's turnout was overestimated. So the likeliest explanation of the small error of the polls – which was present in all of them to differing degrees, despite the wide range of sampling methods used – is that, far from there being anything wrong with the samples, the samples were pretty good; the difficulty is identifying all of those who though they would support Labour if they voted at all will decide in the end not to bother in a low turnout election.

The so-called newspaper 'experts' are wrong in their diagnosis! It's not shy Tories at all, it's stay-at-home Labour, and probably old Labour.

(Source: 'What shy Tories?' by Roger Mortimore, MORI, 6 July 2001)

Select one answer for each of the following questions:

4   Which of the following can be inferred from the article?

(a) The number of seats won by a party is not directly proportionate to the number of votes won

(b) The most accurate way to predict an election result is by reference to total vote rather than percentage share

(c) Conservative voters are more reluctant to answer opinion polls

(d) Turnout at elections is declining

(e) Results would be more accurate if opinion polls were conducted nearer to elections

5   What does the writer seek to illustrate through the comparison with the 1999 European election?

(a) The results of previous opinion polls are useful in determining the outcome of future elections

(b) Labour supporters are traditionally less likely to make the effort to vote

(c) Turnout is impossible to accurately estimate

(d) Results from polls carried out by the same organisation tend to follow similar patterns

(e) Newspaper criticisms of the more recent poll are unjustified

6   What assumption must be made in order to accept the writer's principal assertion?

(a) Voters do not always reveal their true preferences to opinion pollsters

(b) It is always the case that some voters will change their allegiance at the last minute

(c) It is impossible to be certain that a representative sample has been taken

(d) People are influenced by others' voting intentions

(e) There is no correlation between voting share and actual votes received

3   Defining Intelligence

The word *intelligence* means so many different things that it is best to use other terms in order to avoid confusion. What I mean by *intelligence* is 'general cognitive ability', or h, which refers to the substantial overlap that exists between different cognitive processes. This overlap is one of the most consistent findings of research into individual differences in human cognitive abilities over the past century. It has been found even in tests of processes that seem to have little in common.

For example, general reasoning is assessed through tests such as Raven's Progressive Matrices, in which subjects need to detect logical progression in a series of matrices consisting of geometric forms. Spatial ability is assessed through solving mazes, identifying simple geometric figures embedded in more complex shapes and deciding whether or not one figure is a rotated version of another. Vocabulary tests assess the product of previous learning, while tests of memory typically involve presenting digits or pictures to see how well they are recalled.

Despite this diversity, individuals who do well in one test tend to do well in others. In a meta-analysis by John Carroll in 1993 of 322 studies that included hundreds of different kinds of cognitive tests, the average correlation was about 0.30, which is highly significant. This overlap emerges not only for traditional measures of reasoning and of spatial, verbal and memory abilities, such as those mentioned above, but also for rates of learning and for information-processing tasks that rely on reaction time.

Psychologist Charles Spearman recognised the overlap in cognitive abilities nearly a century ago. He called it g in order to create a neutral signifier of general cognitive ability that avoided the many connotations of the word intelligence. This g is best assessed by a statistical technique called principal components analysis. This identifies a composite dimension that represents what diverse cognitive measures have in common.

Such analysis indicates that g accounts for about 40 percent of the total variance in people's performance of cognitive tests. The rest of the variance is accounted for by factors such as spatial, verbal and memory abilities, and by variance unique to each test. The more complex the test the higher the importance appears to be of the g factor. For example, g accounts for a high amount of variance in Raven's Progressive Matrices, while it is less important in simple memory, reaction or processing speed tests.

But g is not just a statistical abstraction. A look at a matrix of correlations between cognitive measures will show all overlap strongly while g is also indexed reasonably well by a simple total score on a diverse set of cognitive measures, as is done in IQ tests. In fact, g is one of the most reliable and valid traits in the behavioural domain; its long-term stability after childhood is greater than for any other trait, it is better at predicting important social outcomes such as educational and occupational levels, and it is a key factor in cognitive ageing. There, are of course, many other important, non-cognitive abilities, such as athletic ability, and *g* by no means guarantees success either in school or in the workplace. Achievement also requires personality, motivation and social skills, now referred to as 'emotional intelligence'. But nothing seems to be gained by lumping all such abilities together as the popular notion of 'multiple intelligences' does. For me, *g* is what intelligence is about.

(Source: 'What is intelligence?' by Robert Plomin in 'Big Questions in Science' edited by Harriet Swain, Vintage, 2003; reprinted by permission of The Random House Group Ltd)

Select one answer for each of the following questions:

7   What is the main conclusion reached in the passage?

(a) There is more merit in studying *g* than other forms of so-called intelligence

(b) Intelligence is an innate quality which cannot be altered

(c) There are a number of different types of intelligence

(d) *g* is the most valuable indicator of general intelligence

(e) There is an inevitable variation between different measures of intelligence

8   Which of the following can be inferred to be most closely linked?

(a) *g* and emotional intelligence

(b) *h* and emotional intelligence

(c) *g* and *h*

(d) Non-cognitive ability and emotional intelligence

(e) Spatial ability and non-cognitive ability

9   Which of the following would be expected to increase most as a result of effective education?

(a) Vocabulary

(b) Spatial awareness

(c) Emotional intelligence

(d) *g*

(e) *h*

4   Freedom of Speech

For progressives of many different political persuasions, the idea of the freedom of speech is central to the progress and practices of dialogue and critique that not only bring to light a society's greatest injustices, but can also potentially change them. That speech can be free, and indeed should be free, is a core assumption that forms part of many societies' self-regulating mechanisms, most often codified by a constitution and its political and legal declarations and rights. It is, notionally at least, at the beating heart of politics. Speech and critique are underpinned by the assumed and unqualified good of freedom. The presumption is that democracy and political process and progress are assisted by the protection of free speech. By safeguarding free speech, we are protecting the capacity for a transparent process of critique, instantiated in dialogue and debate, and the possibility for social change.

This is not a view from nowhere. The First Amendment, and similar enshrinements of the freedom of speech in other written and unwritten democratic constitutions, is of course part of the Athenian tradition of free speech. Featured in the earliest writings of Athens (eg Thales ca BC 600), democracy eventually reached its peak in the age of Pericles (BC 450–430), a time during which the creation of the polis (city-state or community) and its decision-making structures for the regulation of public life fully flourished. Under Athenian democracy, political decisions were transferred from the hands of the few in the assembly, to the hands of the many citizens that constituted the polis. Public meeting spaces were created, notably the agora (or the marketplace) in ancient Athens, in which decisions were debated and then agreed to by the public. All decisions needed the support and agreement of the public. It was therefore the job of politicians, through rhetoric and through dialogue, to convince the public of the good of a particular decision. In this context then, speech, or the spoken word, became a key instrument of power in the emergence of the polis. Prevailing upon the minds of others through language, and through dialogue, became the paradigmatic modus operandi of the political system.

Athenian democracy and freedom of speech eventually disappeared, a short time after the death of Socrates and in consonance with the rise to power of Macedonian controlled oligarchies. Despite this, its modus operandi were highly influential in later philosophical and political writings that would shape the purpose and nature of modern political systems, the emergence of the nation-state system, cultures of rationalism and the creation of public spaces for state-civil society relations. Today we continue to live in the West with the paradigmatic spectre of politics as a public space in which decisions come to be made through dialogue and discussion where all are in principle free to speak their mind and where critique is thereby assured.

I would like to challenge a number of assumptions that are often and unquestioningly associated with the projection of a dialogical model of free speech into a public space. Specifically, these are the ideas that: there is such a thing as free speech; that dialogue is an obvious good in which power relations are disavowed in the search for consensus on certain decisions; and that there is in fact a public space that can be used for the purpose of political citizenship and critique.

(Source: 'On speech, critique and protection' by Gavin Jack, in Ephemera (volume 4, number 2, May 2004))

Select one answer for each of the following questions:

10 What is the main purpose of the article?

(a) To suggest that free speech may be an illusion

(b) To suggest that free speech is the best way of regulating government

(c) To suggest that free speech is not a new concept

(d) To suggest that free speech is the basis of democracy

(e) To suggest that the importance of free speech is often underestimated

11 Which of these components can be inferred to be the least important to the achieving of democracy through free speech?

(a) Public spaces

(b) Politicians skilled in the art of oratory

(c) Absence of sanctions for those opposing the government

(d) A requirement for the government to consult

(e) A common language

12 Which of the following is least likely to constitute free speech?

(a) Discussion of government policy in a state owned newspaper

(b) Discussion of government policy in a privately owned newspaper

(c) Discussion of government policy between friends

(d) A speech made by an independent political commentator

(e) Political commentary in an independently published book

5   AIDS Research

The scientific strategic plan of the Global HIV/AIDS Vaccine Enterprise, published in this month's PLoS Medicine, is a clear and cogent document describing how major funders and stakeholders in HIV vaccine development should move forward in a collaborative fashion. There is no doubt that this roadmap will be regarded as a useful instrument to bring greater cohesion and coordination to the field. The individuals who championed this effort should be commended for providing a great service to the scientific community. It is an excellent start to a continuing dialogue of utmost importance.

The Challenge

Why is it that we still do not have a protective vaccine against HIV 22 years after its initial identification? Many possible explanations come to mind.

In the natural course of HIV infection, the virus wins 99% of the time, showing that specific immunity in an infected person is unable to completely clear the virus. We have also known for over a decade that primary HIV isolates are relatively resistant to antibody neutralization, probably because of a 'protective shield' on the viral envelope glycoproteins, consisting of variable loop sequences and extensive N-linked glycosylations. Another explanation is the extreme plasticity of HIV that allows new viral variants to evade immune recognition in the same way that they escape from drugs. Moreover, superinfection by a second viral strain has been documented in a number of individuals who have already mounted immune responses to the initial HIV infection. Yet another problem is that the AIDS research community has yet to uncover the correlates of immune protection *in vivo*. Lastly, proven vaccine approaches from the past have either failed (whole killed virus and subunit vaccines) or faced seemingly insurmountable regulatory hurdles (live attenuated virus vaccine).

Given these daunting obstacles, why have so many continued in the long struggle to develop an HIV vaccine? The answer must lie, in part, in the noble cause at hand. Yet there are also some encouraging clinical and experimental observations. Rare patients do control HIV infection spontaneously. Certain people remain virus-negative despite repeated exposures. That superinfection is not more commonly found supports the notion of immune control. Vaccine-mediated protection against simian immunodeficiency virus is indeed possible using live viruses attenuated by specific mutations or by pharmacological interventions. Finally, and perhaps most importantly, HIV transmission by sex in the natural setting is typically inefficient (and thus easier to block), unlike most experimental challenge systems employed in monkey studies to date. Collectively, these findings provide a ray of hope to push on.

The Enterprise

The scientific strategic plan of the Enterprise is spot-on in identifying the major roadblocks in HIV vaccine development, as well as in establishing the key scientific priorities as we see them today. It rightly recommends the formation of a growing alliance of organizations to foster a better collaborative spirit that could lead to, among other things, stronger political support and increased funding. The proposed greater coordination and management, sharing of information, technologies, and reagents, and harmonization of standards, assays, and approaches could only add to our overall efforts.

One might ask, however, whether there are potential downsides to the plan. In the name of continuing this important dialogue, I would like to offer one general concern. Arguably, the reason for the lack of an effective HIV vaccine today is rooted in the basic problems posed by the virus itself. What we need foremost are new scientific solutions, although a prim and proper 'process and structure' in our approach will be helpful. The needed breakthroughs to develop a vaccine will likely emerge from the creativity of scientists doing fundamental research that is free of preconceived biases. It is my contention that great new ideas are as likely to come from curiosity-driven basic studies as from the mission-oriented approach that is represented by the new proposal. Therefore, the leadership of the Enterprise must safeguard against the kind of 'group think' that is so pervasive in large collaborative endeavors of this nature. The views of a small number of researchers, no matter how smart or accomplished, must not supersede the collective wisdom of the scientific community at large.

No doubt important contributions will be made by scientists working outside of the Enterprise. Measures should be taken to ensure that their views and approaches, even if deemed unconventional, are not stifled by the newly established system. Likewise, their research support should not be compromised because the creation of the Enterprise concentrates the funding into the hands of a relatively small number of designated scientists. To me this is a serious risk given the current 'flat funding' at the National Institutes of Health.

The Future

The authors of the 'The Global HIV/AIDS Vaccine Enterprise: Scientific Strategic Plan' have laid out a timely and insightful plan to address perhaps the greatest public health need of the millennium. This document and its later revisions will serve as useful guideposts for the AIDS vaccine development effort for years to come. To be successful in this mission, our research community will ultimately need a specific 'scientific blueprint' for making an HIV vaccine. That day will come only after we get another shot in the arm, infusing us with new knowledge and know-how. Is there any doubt that we need to redouble our investment in basic research on the challenges posed by HIV?

(Source: Ho DD (2005) A Shot in the Arm for AIDS Vaccine Research. PLoS Med 2(2): e36)

Select one answer for each of the following questions:

13 Which of these is not an argument suggesting that a vaccine is likely to be found?

(a) The ability of some patients to control the virus

(b) The rarity of superinfection

(c) The potential to attenuate live viruses

(d) The ability to provide vaccine-mediated protection against simian immunodeficiency

(e) The inefficiency of sex as a method for transmitting the virus

14 Which aspect of research into the virus does the writer suggest might be limited by the strategic plan put forward?

(a) Depth

(b) Quality

(c) Quantity

(d) Scope

(e) Speed

15 Which of the following most closely reflects the author's purpose in writing the article?

(a) To attack the strategic plan

(b) To support the strategic plan

(c) To build on the strategic plan

(d) To define the nature of the virus

(e) To provide an explanation of the key challenges faced

6   Life's Destiny

In the end then, what is the fate of intelligent consciousness to be? Who will care for it? Amid the gloom, there seem to be two possible, more optimistic answers. One is 'Life itself'; the other is 'God alone'.

Those who give the first answer argue like this. Life has come to be through the evolved complexity permitted by the elaborate and fruitful chemistry of carbon. However, when life reached the stage of human self-consciousness the evolutionary process was radically modified. Natural selection is not given free reign, for human compassion preserves and provides for the weak and the disadvantaged. Above all, culture affords a much more powerful and quickly effective way of transmitting information from one generation to the next than that provided by genetic channels based on DNA. At present, culture (which of course includes science and technology) is simply ancillary to the development of life, giving us means to achieve ends that we could not accomplish unaided. Eventually may not culture go beyond that and create new, artificial, forms of 'life' itself? Those who make strong claims for artificial intelligence, and who believe that truly 'thinking' computers are an inevitable future development, are prophesying that a form of silicon-based life will be humanly created, to take its place alongside the carbon-based life of its creators. Once such a process has begun, it will surely continue. As cosmic circumstances change, either in the freezing of a dying expanding universe or the frazzling of a fiery collapsing universe, so that any form of electrochemical life is no longer possible (whether carbon-based, or silicon-based, or whatever), will not life engineer further (and to us stranger) reimbodiments of itself, taking advantage of whatever purchase it can gain on the increasing hostile cosmic circumstance? In that way life will defy the threat of extinction and preserve itself as long as the universe lasts.

The strongest form of these claims is asserted by what John Barrow and Frank Tipler call the Final Anthropic Principle: 'Intelligent information-processing must come into existence in the Universe, and, once it comes into existence, it will never die out.' Tipler, in particular, has pursued the matter with a peculiar tenacity. He treats the essence of life as being the processing of information. This would imply that there would be an infinite degree of fulfilment in the course of cosmic history if there could be the processing of an infinite number of bits of information. Tipler's conclusion is that, in certain particular and specified circumstances, this would be possible in the hectic period of the final split seconds of a collapsing cosmos. The whole universe would then have been taken over by 'life', in an ever-more-energetic, ever faster racing, computer-like mode, which in its dying gasp would achieve an infinity of information processing operations. The energy for this operation would be derived from the gravitational sheer energy of cosmic collapse. Tipler explicitly compares this ultimate cosmic computerization to the attainment of Teilhard de Chardin's Omega Point. Tipler is a kind of Southern Baptist atheist and he speaks of his ideas as 'physical eschatology', and of the fleeting ultimate state of his universe as the realization of a 'physical god'.

It is a strange, not to say bizarre, vision of the cosmic future. There are considerable difficulties concerning its claims. The first is that it is based on a computer model of the nature of life. Living entities are seen as being finite-state machines and the character of life is the processing of information. Tipler's physical god is the apotheosis of artificial intelligence. I cannot accept so physicalist, reductionist a view of life. The claims of artificial intelligence appear to me to be inflated and implausible. Thought is more than the execution of algorithms; computers can do the latter but not the former.

(Source: 'Beyond Science: The Wider Human Context' by John Polkinghorne, Cambridge University Press, 1996)

Select one answer for each of the following questions:

16 Which of the following can be inferred to be the writer's opinion?

(a) Computers will never be able to perform human functions

(b) Artificial intelligence is undesirable

(c) Silicon-based life can never be identical to carbon-based life

(d) People are well informed about the possibilities afforded by artificial intelligence

(e) Humans are inherently more sophisticated than computers

17 What is the main purpose of the extract?

(a) To provide a synopsis of artificial intelligence

(b) To define what is understood by thought

(c) To refute some misconceptions about the role of computers

(d) To challenge the traditional orthodoxy on the scope of intelligent consciousness

(e) To consider the evolution of life

18 Which of the following is not an assumption made by Tipler?

(a) Intelligent information processing does not yet exist in the universe

(b) Intelligent information processing will be created by a specific being

(c) Intelligent information processing will increase in power

(d) Intelligent information processing will not die out

(e) Intelligent information processing is the essence of life

7   Chess and Gender

Throughout the history of the game, chess has been dominated by males. More men play the game and more spectators are male. Of course, there are many female chess players in the game today, although they are still greatly outnumbered by men in the field. Female only tournaments exist and many women have gone on to become grandmasters. However, the best players in the world are still considered to be male. This leads us, then, to ask why there is such a difference between men and women in chess. Is it purely a social one or are women really less capable of playing chess?

It can certainly be considered a psychological issue and, to a certain extent, an anatomical one too. It is a known fact that men and women's brains differ. Psychologically, men and women also show considerable differences, which play an important part in the game of chess. There have been many theories put forward to explain why women are seen as inferior in the world of chess.

The first is social pressure on women. Women undoubtedly have more demands on their attention throughout life, and thus have less time to devote to a single cause. This could be said to be a gross generalisation, especially in the world today, however the basic principle rings true – women have more responsibility to shoulder. Sex roles for men and women are still vastly different and, until they are equal, the difference between men and women in chess is likely to persist. The rise in women appearing in chess could be attributed to the development of chess programmes in schools. With chess being offered to more young girls at primary and secondary school age, they are starting to become more dominant in the field. This was a similar situation to that of science in schools. Traditionally science was offered mostly to boys, as it was assumed that girls would not be interested in it. However, today, women rival men in the world of science and to restrict female access to a scientific education would be considered preposterous.

Thus, the age of introduction of women to the world of chess may help to explain why women trail in the game. A good example of this is the Polgar sisters. They were taught by their father to play chess from a very young age and now Judit Polgar is the only woman ever to become a US Open Champion and the only woman to ever have made it into the men's top 10 Grandmaster list. She is currently number 19 in the top 100 players in the world and is the only woman present in the list. There are also biological theories for differences. Women typically have less physical strength than men and it is believed that this gives them a lower capacity for maintaining concentration in long matches. The competitive male nature also plays a part in their success at chess. Men as a sex are more competitive than women and it is believed that this drive to succeed is what gives males the upper hand in chess. Although there have been exceptions to the rule (including Judit Polgar and Vera Menchik, two women who have famously challenged and subsequently won against a multitude of male players). Chess is often considered a task that epitomises spatial awareness. Research has shown that women tend to excel in verbal intelligence, whereas men excel in spatial items. This may help to explain why men appear to be better at chess than women. It has even been suggested that these differences also affect whether or not a woman would be attracted to chess in the first place.

However, it is impossible to attribute gender differences in chess to only one factor. It appears to be an interplay of both social, psychological and biological factors. This makes it an extremely difficult area to investigate and therefore until women equal men in the game of chess, it will be impossible to attribute the differences to any one factor.

(Source: 'Chess and gender' by Amit Bhaduri, Celine Vousden, Weng Tak Poon, Chris Staines, Ashraf Khan and Christine White, University of Edinburgh Medical School website)

Select one answer for each of the following questions:

19 Which of the following does the writer imply would be the most successful way of narrowing the gap between men and women in chess?

   (a) Having more all female tournaments

   (b) Encouraging children into the game at an earlier age

   (c) Having a shorter time limit on games

   (d) Changing the general perception of chess

   (e) Offering more women the chance to play in high level competitions

20 Which of the following cannot be gathered by reading the article?

   (a) The differences between men and women's brains means that they have differing capacities to succeed at chess

   (b) Women may never be as successful at chess as men

   (c) The standard at all female tournaments is lower than that at comparable male events

   (d) Physical characteristics can affect mental capacity

   (e) Chess is easier to succeed at if learned from a young age

21 What point does the writer seek to make through the analogy with science?

(a) Similar skills are required to succeed in chess as in science

(b) Gender differences exist in all areas of life

(c) Differences can only be properly analysed when both genders have equal opportunities

(d) The principal reason for the difference in both fields is the traditional perception of women

(e) It may not be long before women overtake men at chess

8   Quasi-states

The totalitarian state is easy to define, easy to identify, and thus offers a recognisable target at which the archers of human freedom can direct their darts. Not so obliging is what I have referred to as the quasi-state, that elusive entity that may cover the full gamut of ideologies and religions, contends for power but is not defined by physical boundaries that identify the sovereign state. Especially frustrating is the fact that the quasi-state often commences with a position whose basic aim – a challenge to an unjust status quo – makes it difficult to separate from progressive movements of dissent, with which, too, it sometimes forms alliances of common purpose. At the same time, however, there lurks within its social intent an equally deep contempt for those virtues that constitute the goals of other lovers of freedom. Thus, to grasp fully the essence of power, we must look beyond the open 'show of force', the demonstration of overt power whose purpose is to instruct a people just who is master. We are obliged to include – indeed, to regard as an equal partner in the project of power – the elusive entity that is conveniently described here as the quasi-state. We shall return to that mimic but potent entity in a few moments.

The formal state, in its dictatorial or belligerent mutation, represents power at its crudest – African nations, caught in an unending spiral of dictatorships and civil wars, are only too familiar with this exegesis of power. Equally familiar, to many, are the daylight or night-time shock troops of state, storming the homes and offices of dissidents of a political order, carting away their victims in total contempt of open or hidden resentment. The saturation of society by near-invisible secret agents, the co-option of friends and family members – as has been notoriously documented in Ethiopia of the Dergue, former East Germany, Idi Amin's Uganda, among others, all compelled to report on the tiniest nuances of discontent with, or indifference towards, the state – these constitute part of the overt, structured forces of subjugations. To apprehend fully the neutrality of the power of fear in recent times, indifferent to either religious or ideological base, one need only compare the testimonies of Ethiopian victims under the atheistic order of Mariam Mengistu with those that emerged from the theocratic bastion of Iran under the purification orgy of her religious leaders. The Taliban remains a lacerating memory of anti-humanism, as does the Stalinist terror in the former Soviet Union.

Gruesome as we may find the histories of formal dictatorships both of the left and of the right, however, it is to be doubted that the fear engendered by such regimes ever succeeded in percolating through to a visceral level as the totally unpredictable state-in-waiting, one that repudiates even the minimal codes of accountability that are, admittedly, often breached by the formal states. It is these that constitute the quasi-states, often meticulously structured by shadowy corporations of power that mimic the formal state in all respects except three: the already noted lack of boundaries, the lack of government secretariats with identifiable ministries and, by extension, the responsibility of governance. The quasi-state, complete with a hierarchy of elites and its own monitoring – ie policing and enforcement – agencies, may indeed look to a future world order but, in the process, humanity is blatantly declared expendable, and the actualisation of that new order is limited to a close cabal, proliferating through warrens and cities, and contemptuous of boundaries.

(Source: 'Climate of Fear' by Wole Soyinka, Profile Books, 2004)

Select one answer for each of the following questions:

22 Which of the following can be gathered from the article?

(a) Formal states tend to be better defined than quasi-states

(b) Quasi-states tend to be better defined than formal states

(c) Formal states tend to have wider aims than quasi-states

(d) Quasi-states tend to have wider aims than formal states

(e) None of the above

23 Which of the following cannot be inferred to be a defining characteristic of a quasi-state?

(a) It has limited accountability

(b) It does not have fixed boundaries

(c) It seeks to mimic a formal state

(d) It has less responsibility than formal states

(e) It is a state about to assume formal power

24 What point does the writer seek to make with regard to religion?

(a) It is the cause of most discontent towards the state

(b) It is the basis of the ideologies adopted by quasi-states

(c) It is not a primary determinant of the degree of subjugation experienced by citizens

(d) It is central to the development of formal states

(e) Its importance is diminished by the rise of quasi-states

9   Changing Public Attitudes

The last five years have seen a seismic shift in public attitudes which one can see every time one opens a tabloid. For decades concern about race, immigration and asylum was seen as a national issue by only around 5% of people. Since the late 1990s, however, it has soared up the public's agenda. Today immigration and asylum is consistently seen as one of the top three issues facing Britain – only terrorism/Iraq and the NHS and education are seen as more pressing.

This is a remarkable change which cannot be ignored by anyone, even if it is uncomfortable. It also cannot be dismissed as solely the result of media hype – if you plot public concern against the rising volume of asylum seekers you will find they are broadly correlated. The problem for the government is that while concern rose alongside an increase in asylum applicants (and after 9/11), it has plateaued at a high level, even as numbers have fallen. The public does not believe the government on this one and many do not think David Blunkett is doing anything like enough. In 2003, some 90% of the public disagreed that the government had the issue under control, and there are no signs that this has improved much. Some 80% of the public favour ID cards, and 83% are happy to carry one at all times – the reason? It will help tackle illegal immigration.

Much of the concern bears no relation to reality. As a nation we think that around 23% of the population of our islands were born elsewhere – the correct figure is 6%. And when one looks at regional differences the picture is stark. The two regions with fewest asylum seekers or BME residents are most opposed to multiculturalism – the North East and South West: in contrast white Londoners – a minority in some Boroughs – are among those least concerned. What this highlights is the two key issues which most affect attitudes: education and experience. People with degrees are much more realistic about the scale of the issue, and people who have regular contact with people from other ethnic backgrounds are more accepting. The very most racist people in Britain tend to be older, working class people with no qualifications, who have had very little personal contact with Black or Asian people; there tend to be more of these in the regions which are more concerned about Britain being multi-racial.

Given the absence of any direct link between levels of concern – which is definitely there – and actual numbers of new immigrants in each region – it does prompt the question of whether local government should be doing more to address these issues at a local level. If one feels that the public is irrational, pointing out that there are only 35 asylum seekers in your town, out of population of 100,000 plus, might help. In the North East, according to the Home Office, there are only circa 300 asylum seekers, compared to over 100 times that many in London, but attitudes of white residents in each region could not be more different.

All is not lost; more of us agree (59%) than disagree (20%) that Britain is a place where different ethnicities get on well – but we still think there are too many immigrants. The experience of the last few years suggests that local government must address these issues more directly than it has done in the past. We need to be able to acknowledge the genuine tensions that new arrivals and separated communities can bring, while being realistic about the scale of the problem. For local politicians, of course, one problem is the massive skew in the age profile of those who bother voting in elections: older people are most concerned of all about asylum and immigration. If you are a Labour politician in the North of England, your natural constituency in a local election – older, working class people – are least likely to be sympathetic to messages to consider the actual facts, as opposed to what they hear elsewhere. Nevertheless, unless more is done to state the facts, by mainstream parties, as opposed to airing the hype, those who revel in talking about it – the BNP – will continue to do better than in the past.

And things will change, whether public services own the agenda or not. With rising public concern, we are starting to see a shift in a fairly uniform liberal consensus about multi-culturalism, which praised and respected all manifestations of diversity as positive, to a more considered view. This is extremely sensitive ground, but we need to be able to confront more directly the challenges that increasing diversity brings, as well as simply acknowledging its benefits. We need to look at what increasing fragmentation might do to society and think harder about the real challenges it poses for those delivering public services.

(Source: 'The second death of Liberal England?' by Ben Page, MORI, 1 September 2004)

Select one answer for each of the following questions:

25 Which of the following cannot be inferred from the passage about the rising volume of asylum seekers?

(a) The majority of the public are concerned about the issue

(b) Concern about the issue is not directly related to the number of applicants

(c) An increase in applications may lead to an increase in concern

(d) The upward trend in applicant numbers has now been reversed

(e) Media coverage of the issues can have the effect of increasing public concern

26 What is the main point being made by the writer in the article?

(a) Those who are better educated have a clearer impression of the issues

(b) Those with personal experience of other races tend to be less prejudiced

(c) We should consider the issue of immigration from a more objective standpoint

(d) There is considerable regional variation in attitudes towards immigration

(e) Different generations have different attitudes towards race

27 Which of the following does the writer suggest to be a key factor in the BNP's popularity?

(a) The lack of involvement of local government

(b) The reluctance of other politicians to state the true facts

(c) The inability of the main parties to agree a joint strategy

(d) The fact that the BNP is a single-issue party

(e) The fact that Britain has tended to have a liberal consensus

10   American Values

What are the beliefs and values most commonly found in American politics? It is important to know these beliefs and values if one is to understand the political psyche that exists in America and which has percolated into the executive, legislative and judicial systems that make up America's political structure. This political culture does change and modify as a result of several complex processes such as socialisation and feedback from the political system. Individuals may develop political beliefs from their parents, friends etc (socialisation) or they may develop in response to certain political issues and/or political responses (feedback).

In 1996, a much higher percentage of Black Americans voted for Bill Clinton than Bob Dole presumably as they felt that one through his experience of being president was better able to deliver than the other who had no experience of executive power. Likewise, far more women voted for Clinton than Dole. In 2000, this trend continued with a significantly higher number of women voting for Gore and 90% of Black Americans also voting for Gore. A much larger number of men voted for Bush and what are classed as small towns and small cities voted in much higher numbers for the eventual winner – Bush.

Why have these patterns occurred? The political culture in America effectively supports the political structure and as a result there is very little likelihood of the structure changing. There are radical social scientists like Katznelson and Kesselman who believe that America's political culture is imposed from the top in an attempt to legitimise the political structure. This belief is known as the 'dominant ideology' and those who support this theory believe that its logic is to instil in the people that the political system in America is the only one possible and that any change could do enormous damage. Samuel Huntington in his book 'American Politics' summarised America's political culture as 'liberty, equality, individualism, democracy and the rule of law under a constitution'.

Research has indicated that Americans are very keen to support free speech when associated with general statements eg 'People who hate America's way of life should still have a chance to express their views and be heard'. However, there would appear to be a much lower level of support for specific statements eg 'This book which contains unacceptable political views cannot be a good book and does not deserve to be published'. Research indicates that about 80% of Americans would agree with the first statement but only 50% would support the second one.

In 1954, only 37% of those surveyed in America believed that people had the right to make atheist comments. By 1972, this had increased to 65% and by 1991, to 72%. In 1954, 27% of those surveyed in America believed that people had the right to state their support for communism. By 1972, this had increased to 52% and by 1991, to 67%. In 1954, 17% of those surveyed in America believed that people had the right to express racist views. By 1976, this had increased to 61%, and by 1991, to 62%. Research from the above study also indicated that support for specific freedom of beliefs was much higher among the educated 'elite' as opposed to the mass public.

The belief in freedom of speech and thought is not uniquely American and there have been times in America's history where they have not been upheld – such as during the 'Red Scare' of the 1950's and the attitude of some white southerners during the civil rights campaigns in the 1960's. The expression of 'un-American' views during the protests during the Vietnam War brought a similar response. However, in general, America has moved towards greater social tolerance and the above statistics would seem to bear this out. But these same statistics could provide other interpretations.

If in 1991, 67% of those surveyed believed that people had the right to express their support for communism, then 33% either were neutral on this issue or believed the opposite. With an adult population of 200 million, this would represent a sizeable figure if such a sentiment is true for the whole of America and if the sample group for this survey was truly reflective of American ideals.

Regardless of this, Americans do enjoy considerable legal rights that protect the rights of freedom of speech and thought etc. Likewise, within the confines of the law, the media and the newspapers enjoy a great deal of freedom to investigate and publish or produce. It was a newspaper investigation by the 'Washington Post' that started the proceedings that lead to the resignation of Richard Nixon.

If problems occur with regards to freedom of speech it is frequently a problem on a local arena as opposed to a national one, though with the growth of communications throughout America, any violation of individual freedoms at a local level can be quickly dealt with by higher authorities … at least in theory.

(Source: 'Beliefs and values in America' by Christopher Trueman, www.historylearningsite.co.uk)

Select one answer for each of the following questions:

28 What is the writer intending to show through the use of the example of Richard Nixon?

(a) The media provides the most effective check on government

(b) The government does not exert an overriding control over the media

(c) Freedom of speech is an absolute right

(d) Freedom of the media is always a good thing

(e) The media always acts in the best interests of the country as a whole

29 Which of the following is not merely an assertion?

(a) Bill Clinton's experience was seen as a positive quality

(b) Clinton's policies proved favourable to ethnic minorities

(c) Bush's policies were aimed at promoting the interests of men

(d) Education leads to more tolerant beliefs

(e) A majority of people would be prepared to forego freedom of speech in the event of a national emergency

30 What can be inferred about the number of people supporting communism in the US?

(a) It has increased

(b) It has decreased

(c) It is a majority of the population

(d) It is a minority of the population

(e) There is insufficient evidence to say

MCQ ANSWER SHEET

Historical Sources	AIDS Research
1	13
2	14
3	15

Opinion Polls	Life's Destiny
4	16
5	17
6	18

Defining Intelligence	Chess and Gender
7	19
8	20
9	21

Freedom of Speech	Quasi-states
10	22
11	23
12	24

Changing Public Attitudes	American Values
25	28
26	29
27	30

SECTION B: ESSAY

ANSWER **ONE** OF THE FOLLOWING QUESTIONS.

1 What are the arguments for and against reforming the voting system currently used for parliamentary elections in Britain?

2 Is religion a good thing?

3 'Prison is no more than a school for criminals.' Discuss.

4 Which do you believe is more important in explaining human development: nature or nurture?

5 'Scottish and Welsh devolution was a weak compromise that has satisfied no one.' Do you agree?

ESSAY PLAN AND NOTES

NATIONAL ADMISSIONS TEST FOR LAW

SAMPLE TEST 2

The test has two separate sections, A and B.

Section A: Multiple Choice

This section is divided into 10 subsections; each subsection has three questions.

You should answer **all** 30 questions in Section A, selecting one of the possible answers and indicating your response on the answer sheet at the back of the section.

Time allowed: 80 minutes

Section B: Essay

This section has five essay questions.

You should select and answer **one** question in Section B. Your answer should be no more than four sides of A4. A page is provided at the back of the section for your essay plan and notes.

Time allowed: 40 minutes

SECTION A: MULTIPLE CHOICE

ANSWER **ALL** OF THE FOLLOWING QUESTIONS.

1   Cultural Relativism

Cultural relativism is the view that all ethical truth is relative to a specified culture. According to cultural relativism, it is never true to say simply that a certain kind of behaviour is right or wrong; rather, it can only ever be true that a certain kind of behaviour is right or wrong relative to a specified society.

The cultural relativist might thus be happy to endorse the statement that it is morally wrong to deny women equality in the work place in modern America, but would not endorse the statement that it is morally wrong to deny women equality in the work place. The latter statement implies the existence of an objective ethical standard of the kind that cultural relativism rejects. There are societies, the cultural relativist would say, where for historical and cultural reasons it is acceptable that women are limited in their freedom.

The strength of cultural relativism is that it allows us to hold fast to our moral intuitions without having to be judgmental about other societies that don't share those intuitions. If we reject cultural relativism then we face a difficulty: if we are to be consistent about our moral beliefs then it seems that we ought to condemn those past societies that have not conformed to our moral code and perhaps even seek to impose our moral code on those present societies that do not already accept it. This, though, smacks of imperialism.

Cultural relativism allows us to evade this difficulty. On cultural relativism, our moral code applies only to our own society, so there is no pressure on us to hold others to our moral standards at all. On cultural relativism, we can say quite consistently that equality in the work place is a moral necessity in our society but is inappropriate elsewhere around the globe. In an age where tolerance is increasingly being seen as the most important virtue of all, this can seem to be an attractive position.

This strength of cultural relativism, however, is also its weakness. Cultural relativism excuses us from judging the moral status of other cultures in cases where that seems inappropriate, but it also renders us powerless to judge the moral status of other cultures in cases where that seems necessary. Faced with a culture that deems slavery morally acceptable, it seems appropriate to judge that society to be morally inferior to our own. Faced with a culture that deems ethnic cleansing morally acceptable, it seems appropriate to condemn that society as morally abhorrent.

In order to make such judgments as these, however, we need to be able to invoke an ethical standard that is not culturally relative. In order to make a cross-cultural moral comparison, we need a cross-cultural moral standard, which is precisely the kind of moral standard that cultural relativism claims does not exist.

(Source: 'Cultural relativism' by Tim Holt, www.philosophyofreligion.info)

Select one answer for each of the following questions:

1 Which of the following can be inferred to be inconsistent with cultural relativism?

(a) A country which lays down laws for its own citizens

(b) A country which lays down laws for foreign visitors

(c) A group of countries which impose rules on themselves

(d) A group of countries which impose rules on other countries

(e) A religion which lays down rules to be adhered to by its followers

2 Which of the following is stated to be the case with cultural relativism?

(a) Exceptions are provided where an underlying moral principle is breached

(b) Objective standards are fundamentally invalid

(c) What has happened in the past is irrelevant

(d) It is wrong to describe actions as morally inferior to others

(e) It allows for the holding of consistent moral beliefs

3 Which of the following could be said to be most strongly promoted by cultural relativism?

(a) Morality

(b) Equality

(c) Acceptance

(d) Empathy

(e) Prosperity

2   Trade and Health

Trade is the lifeblood of all commerce. The exchange of goods and services has played a defining role in human history, creating vast empires, encouraging mass migration, and sometimes tipping the balance between peace and conflict. It is thus unsurprising that protecting and encouraging international trade has remained a top priority for governments, businesses and international organisations.

Historically, the protection of health has been a permitted reason for restricting trade. Trade brought plague to Athens in 430 BC, killing as much as one-third of the population, as well as to fourteenth century Europe after which quarantine practices were introduced. During the nineteenth century, flourishing trade also facilitated the spread of diseases such as cholera. This prompted a series of International Sanitary Conferences among leading trading nations, and the adoption of International Sanitary Conventions (forerunners of the present day International Health Regulations). While protecting health was a clear aim, in reality the primary task was to minimise interference by health matters on trade.

Today, there are greater tensions than ever before between promoting trade and protecting health because of globalisation. Successive rounds of trade negotiations held since the Second World War, under the General Agreement on Trade and Tariffs and, since 1995, the World Trade Organization (WTO), have substantially reduced tariff levels and standardised trading practices across countries. This process of trade liberalisation has significantly increased trade volumes, bringing more and more countries into the world trading system. For the public health community, trade has raced ahead of corresponding measures to protect health. Efforts to ensure that there is an appropriate balance between the two policy areas has become a difficult challenge.

Tensions between Trade and Health

The right to restrict trade to protect the health of humans, animals, and plants is recognised by the General Agreement on Trade and Tariffs (Article XX) under two conditions: (1) the restriction is applied in a non-discriminatory way; and (2) the restriction is based on recognised scientific evidence. Countries are allowed to restrict trade, for example, of certain goods such as radioactive waste or infected food products.

Disputes can arise if the restriction is believed to be discriminatory or there is disagreement about the scientific evidence supporting it. The ban introduced by the European Community in 1989 on hormone-treated beef imported from the US led to two rulings by the Dispute Settlement Body of the WTO in favour of the American government. The assessment of the evidence primarily by trade experts, rather than public health experts, is a clear problem of the existing dispute settlement process. The process also makes it difficult to regulate inappropriate production methods which do not lead to problems in the end product but may be of public health concern. For example, the practice of using hormones to boost meat production may prove problematic in future research, even if residues in the meat are not judged high enough at present to warrant sufficient proof of health concerns.

Moreover, tight regulations on trade that are intended to protect health can come under fire from the trade lobby. Two World Bank studies argue, for instance, that European Union (EU) regulations on pesticides in bananas, as well as aflatoxins, could be interpreted as barriers to trade and market access. The short shrift given to precautionary measures to protect health, where existing scientific evidence is deemed insufficient, reflects a further inbuilt priority given to trade. Growing concerns over the development and use of genetically modified organisms (GMOs), for example, have been dismissed by major companies such as Monsanto and Cargill on the basis of a lack of existing scientific evidence of harm to health. Consumer groups and public health advocates, however, argue that the subject is still in its scientific infancy. Where new causal pathways or systemic impacts of environmental exposures are of concern, such as with GMOs, at best one can say that the jury is still 'out'. Hence, allowing GMOs to be spread widely, rather than taking precautionary measures, could prove to have irreversible consequences.

The classification of certain goods as a risk to health, and thus subject to trade restrictions, is also a source of dispute. The best example is tobacco products, which manufacturers argue should be treated like other traded goods. Public health advocates, however, argue that because tobacco is harmful to health, it should be subject to special restrictions. A battle over tobacco is currently being played out in regional trade negotiations and will be raised at forthcoming multilateral negotiations over agricultural trade. Whether the public health community will be able to argue successfully to protect health, when pitted against the vast resources of a multi-billion dollar industry, remains to be seen.

(Source: Lee, K and Koivusalo, M (2005) Trade and Health: Is the Health Community Ready for Action? PLoS Med 2(1): e8)

Select one answer for each of the following questions:

4 What, from a health perspective, is identified as being the main concern with the current trade regime?

  (a) Decisions are always made by trade experts not health experts

  (b) The trade lobby has greater financial resources than the health lobby

  (c) Little attention is paid to future health risks

  (d) GMOs are not adequately regulated

  (e) Tobacco products are not adequately regulated

5 What is the main idea in the extract?

(a) Efforts should be made to ensure a realistic balance between health and trade

(b) Health concerns should override trade concerns

(c) Health risks posed by trade are greater than in the past

(d) Trade is an area in which there are a number of vested interests

(e) Historically, trade has been regarded as more important than health

6 Which of the following is not stated by the writers?

(a) Globalisation has created new threats to the protection of public health

(b) Tobacco products should be subject to a stricter trade regime

(c) Health consequences of GMOs are not currently known

(d) It is difficult to circumvent measures designed to protect trade, even on health grounds

(e) Health consequences are judged largely on the basis of final outcome rather than on method of production

3   Hieroglyphs

With Walter Benjamin's postulation that '[e]very expression of human mental life can be understood as a kind of language', divisions between verbal and non-verbal language have been eclipsed by major questions waged by the indeterminacy of the visible and invisible. The translation of the hieroglyph or the portrait follows this approach. The hieroglyph, the Egyptian script, as visual/verbal representation cannot be expressed in any fixed sequence of words, and the message it bears may only be reproduced via a process of enactment. Although the portraits are considered a rupture in Egyptian iconography, they bear several characteristics suturing the abstract and the mimetic.

However, at the time the portraits were executed, the hieroglyph, the script adapted for the requirements of a harmonious culture, was in decline with the conquest of the last pharaohs who harmoniously combined political and religious power. Henceforth, the hieroglyph became the secret language of the priests, the custodians of a cultic tradition practised by an oppressed populace. The sacerdotal monopoly of the hieroglyph is held responsible for its decline. By making the script more intricate, the priests were practising a politics of exclusion safeguarding the hieroglyph against foreign invasions, whilst sustaining the myth of their professionalism, reinforcing their power among the practitioners of the old beliefs, the majority of the oppressed population. The transformation made in the hieroglyph bred false conceptions of its symbolic significance, attributing it to an obsolete tradition, stultifying its dynamic cultural role. Consequently, its reception in the Greek philosophic circles induced recurrent debated. Through Plotinus (204–270 CE) hieroglyphic studies were enmeshed with Neo-Platonism until the eighteenth century. Hieroglyphs were used by the Neo-Platonists to explain the allegorical nature of things, as they illustrated the relation between sign and meaning. This generated the notion of a symbolic system of writing expressing the abstract by means of concrete images or material objects. Eventually, the predominance of alphabetical writing set demarcations between word and image for several centuries. Mitchell propounds that the word/image divide only reflects the Western divide between spirit and body.

Lately, with the deconstruction of the logos prevailing in Western thought since post-Platonic times, the hieroglyph has been re-evaluated by several thinkers, Jacques Derrida, Roger Cardinal, Martin Bernal, and Mario Perniola, among others. In his writings, Derrida praises the Egyptian hieroglyph on account that it is a form of writing, a muteness that replaces speech, in order to recapture presence, when speech threatens life. Derrida adds that as a design, the hieroglyph is closer to writing, not only because it traces a movement, but also because, 'the signifier first signifies a signifier, and not the thing itself or a directly present signified'. In my view, the pictorial turn from the hieroglyph to the portrait should be visualised as a sort of 'picto-hieroglyph' to expand on Derrida's term in a different context, or a suturing of the image/word divide.

Perhaps the Fayoum portraits, in some sense, mark a renaissance of the hieroglyph, at a time when sacerdotal fanaticism reduced the hieroglyph to the condition of the 'logos'. The portraits have filled a gap the newly acquired alphabetical language has created, by its linearity, by its effacement of the visual incorporated in the hieroglyph. In the former times, the hieroglyphs transmitted the solemn proclamations of royalty to gods and men. As pictorial representations representing sacred, royal or mundane inscriptions they have acted as artistic representations following the Egyptian artistic canon with its tendency to abstraction, a style suited to represent the in/visible divine. Hieroglyphs were called the 'writing of the divine word' and the Greeks called them 'sacred letters'. The visual language of the Fayoum portraits supplements the hieroglyph by representing the visible and invisible.

(Source: 'Reading the hieroglyph/traversing death' by Marie Thérèse Abdel-Messih, in Ephemera (volume 3, number 1, February 2003))

Select one answer for each of the following questions:

7 Which of the following is implied by the writer?

(a) The general populace did not understand the role of hieroglyphs

(b) Priests were not well respected in the times described

(c) The more advanced hieroglyphs were too complicated even for many of the priests to understand

(d) The priests were not as professional as they sometimes claimed

(e) The hieroglyphic script used by priests was not as complicated as they claimed

8 What does the writer mean by a 'suturing of the image/word divide'?

(a) There was an increasing difference between the function of images and words

(b) Portraits should not be regarded as so different from hieroglyphs

(c) Words and pictures had become totally interchangeable

(d) There was no relevance in studying how words were distinct from pictures

(e) All languages rely on the use of images to some extent

9 The writer suggests that the main reason for the widespread use of portraits was the fact that:

(a) They were easier to create than hieroglyphs

(b) They did not have the same religious overtones as hieroglyphs

(c) They could convey sentiments not capable of being conveyed by alphabetical language

(d) They were less time consuming to create

(e) They could be understood by everyone

4   Speeding

The government's favourite cash cow, taxation of petrol, has recently found a friend in the shape of proceeds from speed cameras. All around the country, unsuspecting motorists are being flashed by these anonymous boxes by the sides of the road, which annually generate millions of pounds for the treasury.

Or so we are led to believe. For in fact, despite the government's supposedly hard line attitude to road safety, the new Road Safety Bill contains a measure designed to reduce speeding which could ultimately have the effect of actually increasing road deaths.

Why? Well it's certainly not for want of a focus on meeting targets. Amongst the many benchmarks laid down by the government, the Department of Transport has resolved to reduce the number of people killed or seriously injured in road accidents by 40 percent by 2010, compared with the average during the mid-1990s. Not only that, but this is one target which we are actually on course to meet, unlike so many others in fields like health and education.

Surely then, it's not that the government doesn't understand the implications of what it's doing. Well maybe. Above all, the new policy on speeding is guided by the misconception that the current system of fixed penalties discriminates against those who are only speeding a little bit. Those who claim that they face punishment for driving 1mph above the limit are wrong. At present the police policy is to allow a certain amount of discretion – usually 10 percent of the speed limit plus 2mph. This means you'd need to be exceeding 79mph to be penalised on a motorway. Such is the public opposition to the current regime that the government has decided to implement a scheme of variable penalties based on how far above the speed limit the driver is.

What is being proposed is that those doing between 31 and 39mph in a 30mph zone will be fined £40 and given two penalty points, those doing between 40 and 44mph will be fined £60 and given three penalty points and those doing more than 45mph will be given a £100 fine and six penalty points.

On the face of it this kind of approach makes good sense and would be perfectly reasonable if applied to motorways, which are the safest roads in the country. The problem arises when it comes to residential roads. Given the near certainty that there will no change to the current enforcement threshold, the practical effect of the policy will simply be to reduce by a third the penalty for driving at between 35 and 39mph in a 30mph zone, and with it the deterrent against such speeding. This is the very kind of speeding that dramatically reduces road safety, given the now well accepted view that as a pedestrian your chance of being killed if you are hit by a car travelling at 40mph is twice that if the car was travelling at 35mph.

This shift in policy towards appeasing the drivers' lobby is reflected in the policy on speed cameras. Previously the guidelines for the placement of such cameras required at least eight crashes per kilometre of the road in question in a three-year period, including at least four resulting in death or serious injury. Now 'only' four such crashes are required. What is the logic in the road having to be piled high with casualties before the speed limit can even be enforced?

True, a degree of flexibility is called for in order to reflect the reduced safety risks posed by slight speeding in the small hours of the morning in areas where there are no pedestrians around, but to reduce the penalties for speeding in built-up areas is madness and can only lead to more road deaths. Such a policy does little but pander to the drivers' lobby and discredits what is otherwise a soundly thought through Bill.

(Source: 'Speeding towards danger' by Ian Edwards, Daily News, January 2005)

Select one answer for each of the following questions:

10 What is the writer's main purpose in putting 'only' in inverted commas?

(a) To show the change from the previous policy

(b) To highlight what a small number of crashes are required before a speed camera is installed

(c) To highlight what a large number of crashes are required before a speed camera is installed

(d) To suggest that crashes should not be one of the criteria for deciding where to place speed cameras

(e) To show that he disagrees with the use of speed cameras

11 What is the writer's main argument in the article?

(a) Speed limits on motorways could safely be increased

(b) Government policy on transport should not be influenced by public opinion

(c) Penalties for those caught speeding should be increased

(d) Speed limits in built-up areas need to be reduced

(e) Increasing the number of speed cameras would improve road safety

12 **What does the writer imply would be the most likely practical consequence under the new legislation for those driving at 33mph in a 30mph zone?**

(a) They would be fined less

(b) They would be fined more

(c) They would be more likely to have an accident

(d) They would be less likely to have an accident

(e) There would be no change

5   Community Cohesion

Community cohesion has become increasingly important on the national, regional and local government agenda following the disturbances in the north of England in summer 2001. Draft guidance issued by the Local Government Association, along with the Home Office, Office of the Deputy Prime Minister and the Commission for Racial Equality to all local authorities provides a toolkit for maintaining and enhancing community cohesion.

A 2001 survey and series of focus groups conducted by the MORI Social Research Institute for the CRE exploring issues of community shows that a lack of community cohesion is not simply seen as a 'race' issue, but rather, problems relating to access to employment, education and housing. Race is often used as a shorthand for these problems and they tend to be exacerbated in areas of high deprivation.

The lack of daily interaction and communication with people from a different background is also a key driver of intolerance and lack of cohesion – physical, social and economic polarisation of different ethnic groups is highlighted in the Cantle report.

While problems of cohesion are acknowledged, there is evidence to suggest there is much that unites people from different ethnic groups. Regardless of ethnicity, people strongly identify with their local area; 44% of white people say they identify most with their local area compared with 57% for ethnic minority groups, which suggests that where one lives is often a more powerful determinant of perceptions than race.

The survey also shows that while race and immigration is increasing in importance nationally, all groups place a greater importance on the NHS, crime and education. The picture is similar at the local level, where issues around race are not rated as important as 'big' local priorities such as a lack of things for young people, health and community safety – which again are shared concerns for all ethnic groups.

The survey does show that while we have come a long way in terms of race relations, there is still a lot of work to do. Nearly half (49%) think that race relations are better than ten years ago but a similar proportion think they have got worse (47%). This is not surprising since the research was conducted at a time when race relations were a prominent issue in Europe (with Jean Marie-Le Pen securing a victory in the first round of the French presidential elections).

What is interesting about the survey is that people of all ethnic backgrounds massively overestimate the proportion of the British population that is made up of ethnic minorities – most think it is one in five, compared to only one in twelve in reality. Those who are dissatisfied with their area are most likely to overestimate the proportion – which again underlines that the local area is important in determining people's perceptions.

Clearly, building community cohesion will mean looking at what brings people together, and highlighting common goals as well as tackling genuine feelings of inequality. This will be key in overcoming racial tension which is often a result of a lack of cohesion rather than a cause. There will be a need for a grassroots approach, given the importance the local area plays in people's lives.

(*Source: 'Community cohesion' by Kully Kaur-Ballagan, MORI, 29 April 2004*)

Select one answer for each of the following questions:

13 Which of the following does the article imply is the most commonly cited cause of a lack of community cohesion?

(a) Race

(b) Employment

(c) Education

(d) Housing

(e) There is insufficient evidence to say

14 What conclusion could be reached about race relations during the last 10 years from the evidence in the survey?

(a) Relations have remained unchanged

(b) Relations have consistently worsened

(c) Relations have consistently improved

(d) The issue has decreased in importance

(e) There is insufficient evidence to say

15 Which of the following cannot be gathered from the survey evidence presented in the penultimate paragraph?

(a) Many people have a negative view of the effect of ethnic minorities on a locality

(b) Perception of race is not always based on reality

(c) The state of race relations affects how people view their community

(d) Ethnic minorities themselves have a distorted view of the racial make-up of the country

(e) None of those surveyed correctly estimated the percentage of ethnic minorities present in the country

6   Democracy

Democracy is a word frequently used in British politics. We are constantly told that we live in a democracy in Britain and that our political system is 'democratic' and that nations that do not match these standards are classed as 'undemocratic'. D Robertson, writing in 1986, stated that: 'Democracy is the most valued and also the vaguest of political terms in the modern world.' Robertson continued by stating that the word only starts to mean something tangible in the modern world when it is prefixed with other political words, such as direct, representative, liberal and parliamentary.

Direct Democracy

This belief is based on the right of every citizen over a certain age to attend political meetings, vote on the issue being discussed at that meeting and accepting the majority decision should such a vote lead to a law being passed which you as an individual did not support.

Part of this belief is the right of everyone to hold political office if they choose to do so. Direct democracy also believes that all people, who have the right to, should actively participate in the system so that it is representative of the people and that any law passed does have the support of the majority.

Direct democracy gives all people the right to participate regardless of religious beliefs, gender, sexual orientation, physical well being etc. Only those who have specifically gone against society are excluded from direct democracy. In Britain, those in prison have offended society in some way and, therefore, their democratic rights are suspended for the duration of their time in prison. Once released, and having 'learnt a lesson', their democratic rights are once again restored.

Direct democracy is fine in theory but it does not always match the theory when put into practice. Direct democracy requires full participation from those allowed to. But how many people have the time to commit themselves to attending meetings especially when they are held mid-week during an afternoon? How many wish to attend such meetings after a day's work etc?

If Britain has 40 million people who can involve themselves in politics if they wish, how could such a number be accommodated at meetings etc? Who would be committed to being part of this system day-in and day-out when such commitment would be all but impossible to fulfil? How many people have the time to find out about the issues being discussed whether at a local or a national level? How many people understand these issues and the complexities that surround them? How many people understood the complexities of the problems surrounding the building of the Newbury by-pass, the installation of Tomahawk cruise missiles at Greenham Common etc?

If people are to be informed on such issues, who does this informing? How can you guarantee that such information is not biased? Who would have time to read all the information supporting the building of the Newbury by-pass and then read the material against it, before coming to a balanced personal decision?

Because of the realities of direct democracy, few nations use it. Some states, ie New England, USA, do use it at a local level but the number of people involved is manageable and the culture of the towns involved actively encourages participation. The issues discussed are relevant purely to the town and, therefore, there is a good reason for involving yourself if you want your point of view heard. Meetings are held in town halls across New England – which, apart from cities such as Boston, is not highly populated. But how could the system work in heavily populated areas?

...

Technological developments in the future may change this. The expansion of the Internet and the speed with which communication can now be achieved may favour direct democracy. The present government set up a system in 1997, whereby 5,000 randomly selected members of the public (the so-called 'People's Panel') are asked about their reactions to government policy. However, there is no system in place which allows the public to help formulate government policy, and critics of the 'People's Panel' have called it a gimmick with no purpose.

(Source: 'Democracy and British politics' by Christopher Trueman, www.historylearningsite.co.uk)

Select one answer for each of the following questions:

16 What can be inferred to be the main reason why the formation of the 'People's Panel' could not be said to have led to direct democracy in the UK?

(a) Only a small number of people are involved

(b) The participants were chosen randomly

(c) The participants do not form a cross-section of society

(d) The panel is not consulted on all issues

(e) The panel has limited influence

17 What is the main implication of the reference to countries being labelled undemocratic?

(a) Democracy has certain widely accepted requirements

(b) The definition of democracy is somewhat arbitrary

(c) Democracy is seen as a superior form of government

(d) Britain is seen as the birthplace of democracy

(e) Britain is the arbiter of democracy

18 Which of the following is not a practical difficulty with direct democracy?

(a) Size of the population

(b) Ignorance amongst citizens

(c) Insufficiently advanced technology

(d) Lack of time

(e) Lack of suitable meeting places

7   Unemployment and Health

It has been established for many years that people registered as unemployed generally have poorer health and higher mortality than those in work. Two main reasons have been postulated to explain this: people who are sick are more likely to lose their jobs and swell the ranks of the unemployed (health selection) or the experience of unemployment itself is damaging to health. These explanations are not mutually exclusive. It is important to understand more about this relationship, not only to match health services more closely to need, but also for the development of broader public health and social policy to address the social determinants of health. A key policy-relevant question is whether the relationship between unemployment and health varies with the local economic environment. Are the unemployed who live in high unemployment areas better or worse off in health terms than their counterparts living where unemployment has traditionally been low? By using the new questions on health and class in the 2001 UK Census, we recently showed that the relationship between social class and self-rated health varied not only across, but also within, regions of Great Britain. Each of the seven main occupational classes had higher rates of poor health in Wales, the North East and North West of England than elsewhere. The widest health gaps between classes within regions, however, were to be found in London and Scotland. Does unemployment exhibit the same or a contrasting pattern?

Data for men and women of working age (25–64) were analysed. We obtained data for England, Wales and Scotland from reports on the 2001 UK Census produced by the Office for National Statistics (ONS) and the General Register Office for Scotland. Unemployment data for the regions for 1984–2001 were obtained from NOMIS.

There are two main hypotheses to explain the differences we found in the self-rated health of the long-term unemployed in relation to the economic history of the regions. First, the composition of the long-term unemployed group may be different in different regions. In areas where jobs are easier to come by, it may be largely the more sick people who are left out of the labour market. Conversely, in the high unemployment areas, there may be a higher proportion of long-term unemployed people who are healthy but have difficulty in finding work. This is a health selection effect. Added to this, there was the administrative practice in the 1980s and 1990s of re-classifying the unemployed as incapacitated, thereby reducing the unemployment claimant count. This practice was followed particularly rigorously in some of the areas with the highest unemployment rates. Even before this period, there is evidence that the unemployed were more likely to report themselves as retired or permanently sick when unemployment rates were high, as both an economic and psychological coping strategy. These factors may have resulted in a healthier profile for the 'officially' unemployed in such areas.

Second is the idea that the experience of long-term unemployment may be less stigmatising, and hence less stressful and health damaging, in areas where unemployment rates have been traditionally high. Where the chances of unemployment are perceived as higher and jobs, once lost, more difficult to re-gain, being unemployed may be seen as more of the norm, rather than a deficiency of the individual. Conversely, in more prosperous areas, with lower unemployment, being unemployed for a long time may be perceived as an aberrant and personally stigmatising situation. In epidemiological terms, our findings may provide a specific example of 'ecological effect modification', in which the local context has an independent effect on health, which modifies the impact that individual characteristics have on health outcome. This phenomenon has been noted in the psychiatric literature. For example, the suicide rate for members of ethnic minority groups is lower in areas where they represent a larger proportion of the population. A similar relationship between ethnicity and schizophrenia has been noted. In relation to health inequalities, Mitchell and colleagues have demonstrated a significant relationship between a person's attitude to their community (ie whether they feel part of it) and their health, which is independent of individual and area characteristics. We cannot differentiate between these hypotheses in a cross-sectional analysis and with the available census data. This would require several different types of investigation. What this study does do, however, is identify a paradox, which challenges common assumptions about the relationship between unemployment and health. It points to the need to take more account of the geographic and socio-economic context in which long-term unemployment is experienced when considering policy implications.

(Source: 'Is the health of the long-term unemployed better or worse in high unemployment areas?' by Margaret Whitehead, Frances Drever and Tim Doran, Health Statistics Quarterly, Spring 2005, www.statistics.gov.uk; Crown copyright material is reproduced with permission of the Controller of HMSO)

Select one answer for each of the following questions:

19 Which of the following is suggested in the article?

   (a) Not everyone who is unemployed reports themselves as such

   (b) Not everyone who is sick reports themselves as such

   (c) More people report themselves as unemployed than actually are

   (d) More people report themselves as sick than actually are

   (e) None of the above

20 Where in the UK can be inferred to have the worst overall health?

(a) North West, North East and Wales

(b) Scotland

(c) London

(d) None of the above

(e) There is insufficient evidence to say

21 Which of the following is identified as having the most negative effect on health?

(a) Poverty

(b) Location

(c) Ethnic origin

(d) Unemployment

(e) Variation from the norm

8   Dreams

Dreams fascinate us. Whether they are recurring nightmares or benign, surreal images, we are desperate to know what they mean. If only we could interpret them, we believe, we could unlock the hidden depths of our personalities and show the world what interesting people we truly are.

They have also fascinated different ages and cultures, playing a huge role in literature, philosophy and religion. The earliest recorded dreams date back to the Sumerians of Mesopotamia in 3100 BC. Aristotle thought dreams, being absent from external stimuli, could heighten awareness of internal sensations. Artemidorus, author of the first 'Interpretation of Dreams' in the second century, classified dreams into two types: prophetical and realist, that is dreams which deal with current concerns and are affected by the dreamer's state of mind and body. From the Sumerians and ancient Greeks, through to modern psychotherapy, people have seen dreams as a heightened form of communication – as divine messages, creative inspiration, prophecies, or the keys to hidden desires. Yet many have also dismissed them as nonsense. Francis Bacon wrote in his Essays in 1625: 'Dreams and predictions of astrology ... ought to serve but for winter talk by the fireside.'

It is only relatively recently that dreams have moved from the realms of the mystical and literary into the world of science, and a glance at the numerous dream exchange sites on the Internet shows that the mystical still holds sway. Sigmund Freud was tackling the science of dreams around 1900. In his 'Interpretation of Dreams', he described dreams as 'the royal road to the unconscious', an unconscious made up of (mainly sexual) desires that had been blocked out or repressed by waking thought. By getting patients to talk about their dreams, Freud uncovered the tension between conscious and unconscious thought, and linked the resulting repression to mental illness. His book was the first systematically scientific work on how the mind works.

At first, Freud used hypnotic suggestion to get at the unconscious, trying to induce a dreamlike state in his patients. He then moved on to what later became known as 'free association', simply asking patients to say the first thing that came into their head and to connect ideas loosely from there. This provided insights into their unconscious mind, although he came up against resistance from the patient's conscious will. From this, Freud developed his theory of the three-dimensional mind, divided between the id, which applied to instinctive thought; the ego, which applied to organised, realistic thought; and the superego, which covered moralising and critical functions.

Freud's work had a huge impact on ideas about identity, creativity and mental health, although some of his theories may now appear dated or subjective. In literature, for example, his work was crucial to the surrealist movement, whose followers used his ideas about the unconscious in their own experimentations on writing. Many writers practised what became known as automatic writing, which was supposed to come directly from the unconscious and represent unblocked desire.

However, Freud was not the only scientist to show an interest in dreams at the turn of the twentieth century. The Dutch psychiatrist and novelist Frederik van Eeden also developed a theory of the dream that still has an impact today, although many of his conclusions have been contradicted. He is credited with coining the term 'lucid dreaming', meaning dreaming while you know you are dreaming. Van Eeden began studying his dreams from 1896 and wrote down the most interesting in a diary. In 1898, he began to record a particular type of dream, later dubbed the lucid dream. In 1913, he published 'A Study of Dreams', in which he distinguishes nine different types of dream, from initial and pathological dreams to lucid and symbolic dreams. He believed that dreams were not purely arbitrary, and that there must be some kind of scientific order behind them. 'To deny may be just as dangerous and misleading to accept,' he stated.

(Source: 'What is a dream?' by Mandy Garner in 'Big Questions in Science' edited by Harriet Swain, Vintage, 2003; reprinted by permission of The Random House Group Ltd)

Select one answer for each of the following questions:

22 Which of the following cannot be inferred to be a view held by Freud?

(a) Repression is a fundamentally bad thing

(b) There is a link between conscious and unconscious thought

(c) There is a benefit to discussing dreams

(d) It is possible to control what one dreams

(e) There are a number of different aspects of the human mind

23 Which of the following assumptions must be made in order for there to be merit in the theories discussed in the passage?

(a) Everyone dreams

(b) Everyone is capable of remembering their dreams

(c) There is a scientific basis to dreaming

(d) Everyone is honest in describing their dreams

(e) The same dreams mean the same things to different people

24 Which of the following cannot be inferred from the passage?

(a) People believe that they can learn about themselves from their dreams

(b) We are now more able to accurately understand dreams than in the past

(c) Not everyone attaches the same significance to dreams

(d) The term 'dream' means different things to different people

(e) There is the potential for the content of dreams to be deliberately influenced by conscious acts

9　Einstein

Sorry to spoil the party … but Einstein got it wrong. The whole theory of relativity is invalid. The speed of light is not an absolute limit: it is not even constant. Einstein was a genius and a truly original thinker but that doesn't make him right. Does this sound like complete heresy? Read on: allow me to convert you. Not only will we be able to travel faster than light-speed, light itself can be accelerated or decelerated. This is not science fiction: let me say it again – Einstein was wrong.

It is not entirely his fault. He believed that the speed of light had been shown to be constant; that it had been shown to breach fundamental Newtonian principles – but actually no such proof had been found. In Einstein's day, the idea that the speed of light could be a constant was brand-new. For that idea, we have to thank two American scientists, Albert Michelson and Edward Morley. They ran a series of experiments in the 1880s designed to demonstrate the existence of something called 'ether'. This was a beautifully engineered experiment: beams of light were shone at angles to the surface of the Earth, along the plane of Earth's orbit with and against that motion.

In accordance with 'classical' Newtonian principles for the summation of velocities, they expected to see the speed of light vary; boosted or degraded both by Earth's own motion through space and by the presumed 'drag' created by the presence of the ether. To their astonishment, almost to their horror, they couldn't find any change in the speed of their light-beams, no matter what they did. How staggering a result this was may be hard for us to imagine now. Up until that moment no one had ever suggested that light's speed could be a constant. The very idea that anything at all could breach Newtonian principles was incredible, but this was exactly what the scientific community had come to accept. The only other possible explanation would have to be that the Earth was actually standing still. But this idea was dismissed as absurd.

Which left as the only alternative the idea that light's speed must indeed be a constant. Newton's laws, so reliable everywhere else, had been broken. Many scientists struggled to come to terms with this radical new concept: the most famous – and lasting – of all these attempts is Einstein's work on Relativity. But was Newton truly beaten? Were the Michelson-Morley results valid?

No. Their beautiful experiment was in fact useless: light, far from breaching Newtonian principles, had behaved in the experiments exactly as those principles predict. Indeed, had they obtained any other result, then (and only then) would Newton's Laws have been broken. The error they made was to presume that light was a 'thing' that could be carried or projected. Take the standard example of a 'summation of velocities' problem – one that Einstein himself uses: the example of a man walking along in a moving train. His velocity will be the sum of his own walking pace and the velocity of the train. If he carries a gun in his hand and fires it, the initial velocity of the bullet will be the projective velocity added to the above. This is the effect they expected to measure for light but they overlooked one key point: light is an emission. A very high-speed emission. That makes all the difference.

The man might be carrying a torch but he cannot carry the light it emits. Nor does he 'fire' the light from his torch as if it were an ordinary projectile. An emission is a very special 'case' of projection. The emission-particle is not 'pre-loaded': it is both created and given motion by the emission process.

(Source: 'Did Einstein get it all wrong?' by Pat Dean, Mensa Magazine, March 2005)

Select one answer for each of the following questions:

25 Which of the following is not challenged by the writer?

(a) The Michelson-Morley results

(b) Einstein's Theory of Relativity

(c) The idea that Newton's Laws were wrong

(d) The existence of 'ether'

(e) None of the above

26 Based on the definitions which can be inferred from the article, which of the following is an emission?

(a) Heat

(b) Steam

(c) Fire

(d) A jet of water

(e) A column of smoke

27 Which of the following can be gathered from the evidence in the article?

(a) Emissions travel faster than standard projectiles

(b) Standard projectiles travel faster than emissions

(c) Emissions are easier to measure than standard projectiles

(d) Standard projectiles are easier to measure than emissions

(e) None of the above

10   Nature of Intelligence

Intelligence and Racism

Intelligence tests have been involved in the promotion of eugenics, the idea that you could control the human race by selective breeding. Francis Galton – one of the pioneers of intelligence tests – was also a founding member of the Eugenics Society in the UK. The belief that intelligence is biologically determined in the make-up of the brain, and therefore to some extent genetically determined, is widely accepted. But a number of researchers over the years have used this idea to advocate social change. Using intelligence as one of their factors, Hernstein and Murray's controversial book, The Bell Curve (1994), argued that differences in IQ scores between racial groups reflect innate biological differences.

The Bell Curve

The Bell Curve is a graph that plots the range of IQ scores of an average population. However, it can be interpreted in many ways, and when the intelligence of the whole human race is in question, the stakes are high. Critics argue that the way intelligence is measured contains a high level of random variation and therefore it's impossible to generalise it all into one graph. However, belief in the Bell Curve and in the genetic, rather than social, basis for intelligence has unfortunately led to the propagation of many racist ideas.

Evidence to suggest social factors are important in 'intelligence' is strong. The US military tested recruits to assign rank and found that black applicants scored lower than whites. However, discrepancies were found to be due to educational differences; black recruits scored very low until the 1950s, when an increase in score corresponded to improved educational standards for all.

Is Intelligence Genetic?

In spring 1998, Robert Plomin claimed to have discovered a gene linked with intelligence. More recently, the Human Genome Project was cautious when approaching areas implying racial differences since research actually shows greater genetic differences within races than between races. However, not all individuals are endowed with the same intelligence and many believe this must have something to do with our genes and the way they interact with the environment. Identical twins are more likely to obtain the same score in an IQ test than twins from two separate eggs that have a different genetic make up.

It is important to remember that genes work by interacting with the environment, so social factors will also influence intelligence. Intelligence tests may be more of an assessment of social factors, such as your educational background. Black children adopted into white middle class families score significantly higher on average than those in working class families – implying a cultural slant to tests. It is impossible to devise questions without some cultural or gender bias; boys tend to do better in spatial tests whereas girls score higher on linguistic tests.

Recipe for Intelligence

Better schooling, parenting and increased leisure time for activities are believed to have influenced improved IQ scores across the board. Good nutrition means an individual is able to function well both physically and mentally. Although many believe this plays a role in intelligence, it is very difficult to assess. A balanced diet will provide all the foods required to maintain the correct balance of neurotransmitters.

Emotional Intelligence

Emotional intelligence, or EI, is the ability to understand your own emotions and those of people around you. The concept of emotional intelligence, developed by Daniel Goleman, means you have a self-awareness that enables you to recognise feelings and helps you manage your emotions. On a personal level, it involves motivation and being able to focus on a goal rather than demanding instant gratification. A person with a high emotional intelligence is also capable of understanding the feelings of others. Culturally, they are better at handling relationships of every kind.

Just because someone is deemed 'intellectually' intelligent, it does not necessarily follow they are emotionally intelligent. Having a good memory, or good problem solving abilities, does not mean you are capable of dealing with emotions or motivating yourself. Highly intelligent people may lack the social skills that are associated with high emotional intelligence. Savants, who show incredible intellectual abilities in narrow fields, are an extreme example of this: a mathematical genius may be unable to relate to people socially. However, high intellectual intelligence, combined with low emotional intelligence, is relatively rare and a person can be both intellectually and emotionally intelligent.

Does Socialising Make You Clever?

Both emotional and intellectual problems are more easily resolved when in a good mood, which to some extent depends on emotional intelligence. Self-motivated students tend to do better in school exams. The ability to interact well with others and having a good group of friends means students are more likely to remain in education, whereas those with emotional difficulties tend to drop out.

On the negative side, low emotional intelligence can affect intellectual capabilities. Depression interferes with memory and concentration. Psychological tests show feelings of rejection can dramatically reduce IQ by about 25%. Rejection increased feelings of aggressiveness and reduced self-control. It is this quality of self-control, rather than being impulsive, which is regarded as necessary to perform well in IQ tests. So a low emotional intelligence may limit intellectual performance.

(Source: 'Are you born brainy?', 17 November 2004, from BBC News at www.bbcnews.com)

Select one answer for each of the following questions:

28 What can be inferred to be the link between emotional and intellectual intelligence?

(a) Those with low intellectual intelligence have a lower emotional intelligence

(b) Those with low intellectual intelligence have a higher emotional intelligence

(c) Those with high intellectual intelligence have a lower emotional intelligence

(d) Those with high intellectual intelligence have a higher emotional intelligence

(e) There is insufficient evidence to say

29 What purpose does the writer seek to achieve through the example of black children being adopted into white middle class families?

(a) To show that intelligence is not genetic

(b) To show that social environment is the main influence on intelligence

(c) To show that children from non-white families tend to achieve lower IQ scores

(d) To show that IQ tests are not a perfect test for raw intelligence

(e) To show that children raised in middle class families always do better at IQ tests

30 Which of the following is not suggested in the article as being a determinant of intelligence?

(a) Social background

(b) Genetic factors

(c) Mental stability

(d) Gender

(e) Race

MCQ ANSWER SHEET

Cultural Relativism	Community Cohesion
1	13
2	14
3	15

Trade and Health	Democracy
4	16
5	17
6	18

Hieroglyphs	Unemployment and Health
7	19
8	20
9	21

Speeding	Dreams
10	22
11	23
12	24

Einstein	Nature of Intelligence
25	28
26	29
27	30

SECTION B: ESSAY

ANSWER **ONE** OF THE FOLLOWING QUESTIONS.

1   Should celebrities have a right to privacy?

2   What are the arguments for and against legalising euthanasia?

3   Have the UK and USA achieved their objectives in relation to Iraq?

4   Some describe membership of the Single European Currency as the most exciting opportunity for Britain in decades, whilst others reject it as doomed to certain failure. Is either of these views correct?

5   'The AIDS epidemic in Africa must surely be the ultimate sign of the developed world's failure to meet their global responsibilities.' Do you agree?

ESSAY PLAN AND NOTES

NATIONAL ADMISSIONS TEST FOR LAW

SAMPLE TEST 3

The test has two separate sections, A and B.

Section A: Multiple Choice

This section is divided into 10 subsections; each subsection has three questions.

You should answer **all** 30 questions in Section A, selecting one of the possible answers and indicating your response on the answer sheet at the back of the section.

Time allowed: 80 minutes

Section B: Essay

This section has five essay questions.

You should select and answer **one** question in Section B. Your answer should be no more than four sides of A4. A page is provided at the back of the section for your essay plan and notes.

Time allowed: 40 minutes

SECTION A: MULTIPLE CHOICE

ANSWER **ALL** OF THE FOLLOWING QUESTIONS.

1　Leisure Time

The introduction of free entry to museums and galleries in England and Wales appears to be achieving the government's objective of widening access, according to MORI research conducted in January 2002. The overall proportion of adults visiting museums and galleries has gone up since similar research was undertaken two years ago from 31 percent to 38 percent.

The profile of visitors to museums and galleries has changed – there is an increase in those attending with children (from 32% to 38%), but especially large increases among the 45–54 age group (31% to 47%) and 55–64 year olds (37% to 46%) – which includes older parents, empty nesters and grandparents. These are people with increased leisure time, increased income, and the majority are well educated (among those who have visited museums, 56% have a degree/Masters/PhD while among gallery visitors, 46% have a degree/Master/PhD). In fact, more people in the 45–54 age group pursue leisure activities now than in 2000 and are the most active age group (+16.3%). Leisure is clearly on the increase however as all the groups show significant increases, although young people aged 15–24 only show an increase of 1.1 percent over two years.

There has been an increase in visitors to museums and galleries across all social grades. However, despite free entry, aimed to allow access to people of all social backgrounds, it seems that at least initially, the increase has been much greater among the wealthy As (up 18%) than among the other social grades. People from both B and C1 social classes are up by 8 percent, C2s are up by 7 percent whereas Ds are up only 5 percent. Looking at museums and galleries separately, the social divide is even clearer, over half of ABs (51%) have visited a museum in the last year, compared with less than one in five DEs (18%). Although more people overall are visiting galleries (ABs 42%, DEs 9%), the gap between the social classes is the same (33%). As more people become aware of the free entry at national museums and galleries, it will be interesting to see whether this gap narrows. Research that MORI conducted for Re:Source (formerly the Museum and Galleries Commission) in 1999 showed that cost was only a very small factor in the reason people did not visit museums and galleries.

Going to the cinema is an extremely popular leisure activity – nearly three-fifths of British adults (57%) have been to the cinema last year. The cinema is especially popular amongst young people with three-quarters (75%) of 15–34 year olds seeing films last year. Cinema going is also by far the most popular cultural activity for low income Brits. Nearly half (43%) of DEs went to the cinema last year, whilst only one in ten (10%) went to a pop or rock concert. Whereas visiting museums and galleries is slightly more popular as an activity in London and the South East than in other areas, going to the cinema is popular throughout Britain. Cinema goers appear to be more technology friendly, three-quarters have Internet access, compared with under a quarter (22%) of those who attend rock/pop concerts.

There has been a slight drop overall in the proportion of people visiting theme parks (from 23.7% in 2000 to 20.4% in 2002), but a significant increase in young visitors, up from under a third of 16–24 year olds in 2000 (29.5%) to over two-fifths of young people in 2002 (43.3%). This would indicate that cost is less of a factor in enticing young visitors – but thrills, and interactive activity are more important. Museums have increasingly been taking interactivity into account in their marketing and new exhibition development – introducing more interactive displays, and experiential activities, child friendly cafes and even cinemas (Imax in the Science Museum) to encourage visitors.

Visiting historic buildings and palaces, as would be expected, is most popular among the middle aged. Nearly two-fifths of all adults (38%) have visited a historic building in the past year. But nearly half of 35–54 year olds (47%) enjoy this activity, and again there is a social divide, people with higher social grades (59% ABs and 45% C1s) are more likely to have visited a historic building than C2s (32%) and DEs (18%). The majority are broadsheet readers (64%). Older people are a group most likely to experience none of these leisure activities (32% of over 55s) along with the poorer DEs (31%).

Despite the new free entry at the national museums and galleries, visiting has not yet reached the peaks seen in 1991. This could be due to increasing demands on people's leisure time and the greater range of leisure activities available over the past decade. Looking beyond demographics at issues such as changing social values will be essential in marketing to potential audiences for leisure attractions in an increasingly competitive environment. Furthermore, the Internet as a marketing channel should not be underestimated.

(Source: 'So much to do, so little time?' by Jane Robinson, MORI, 26 April 2002)

Select one answer for each of the following questions:

1 **Which of the following could not be said to be proved by the research described in the article?**

(a) Those who visit museums are more likely than not to have a degree, Masters or PhD

(b) Those in the 45–54 age group are the most frequent visitors to museums

(c) Those with more leisure time are more likely to visit museums and art galleries

(d) The average visitor to a museum has better educational qualifications than one to a gallery

(e) Young people have been less affected than older people by the government's policy of allowing free admission to museums and galleries

2 **Which of the following cannot be gathered from the passage?**

(a) The main determining factor in deciding whether or not to attend museums and galleries is not money

(b) Cost is less of an issue with visiting the cinema than with other leisure activities

(c) The recent trend is for fewer people to visit theme parks

(d) Rock and pop concerts are beyond the financial reach of many Brits

(e) Older people have a narrower range of leisure interests

3 **Which of the following is stated in the article?**

(a) The increase in visitor numbers at museums and art galleries has been caused by the government's new policy

(b) A majority of those with a degree, Masters or PhD visit museums

(c) An increasing number of younger people are visiting theme parks

(d) Cinema going is more popular amongst those on low incomes than those on higher incomes

(e) The nature of cultural activities is changing

2   Spaces of Consumption

Walter Benjamin's massive torso, The Arcades Project (1999), was one of the first works to actively theorize the relationship between space, aesthetics and consumption. The architecture of the arcade, popularized by the Parisian Haussmann architecture, precedes the late modern aesthetic of consumer space. In the arcade, the goods are on display at the same times as the flâneur is capable of passing through the arcade as an autonomous, enterprising and choosing subject. Consumption becomes an aesthetic experience; space and consumption are merged in the special practice producing spaces of consumption. The visual qualities of the arcade architecture enable a spatialization of the goods, a displacement and spatial distribution in consumer space. Therefore, the arcade is one of the first distinct urban spaces; spaces of production are characterized by rural aesthetics and ethics emphasizing accumulation, the physical transformation of nature. The spaces of production are paradoxically rural spaces located within urban environments. The industrial revolution was orchestrated by the increased productivity in the agriculture sector during the take-off phase. The rural proletariat moved to the urban centers and helped reproduce new forms of rural spaces. The arcade is overturning this assemblage of aesthetics and ethics and makes consumption a spatial practice distinguished from that of the spaces of production. The space of consumption is thus characterized by its loss of facticity; its ontological status is never once and for all determined – a certain degree of uncertainty is always present in consumption because of its symbolic qualities. Alluding to the anthropologist James Clifford, a space of consumption 'is an itinerary rather than a bounded site – a series of encounters and translations'. In addition, the arcades have a distinct quality of 'liminality': they are neither inside (eg proper boutiques), nor outside (eg open street markets); not a building (representing the private sphere), nor a street (representing the public sphere), but passages in-between buildings, a route of transition – spaces of consumption enable goods to be displayed and, at the same time, walking is made possible. Compare with the more recent architectural innovation of the shopping mall. Here, there is no 'liminality', no sense of being 'in-between': the shopping mall is constituting a center of relations in itself. Thus, there is a difference between the architecture of the modern arcade and the late modern shopping mall: spaces of consumption are becoming the center rather than the margin.

Furthermore, the arcades are symbolic spaces; they are spaces where art is becoming a consumer commodity. Although Benjamin has expressed his belief in the revolutionary potential of the mass-production of art, in the arcade, Benjamin argues, art becomes kitsch. Benjamin writes: 'Kitsch ... is nothing more than art with a 100 percent, absolute and instantaneous availability for consumption. Precisely within the consecrated forms of expression, therefore, kitsch and art stand irreconcilably opposed.'

Similarly, Adorno says: '[T]he tension between culture and kitsch is breaking down.' For Eco, kitsch is a 'substitute for art', a supplement: 'As an easily digestible substitute for art, Kitsch is the ideal food for a lazy audience that wants to have access to beauty and enjoy it without having to make much of an effort.' Linstead argues that kitsch is not only a substitute but representative of an anthropocentric, humanist ideology: 'The narcissistic properties of kitsch, and the tendency of the familiar to follow a trajectory of deepening approval from the aesthetic (it is comfortable, pleasing) to the moral (it is approved, advocated, required, the natural way of things) underpin a cosmology which positions humanity at the centre of creation.' Kitsch here represents a certain worldview and a modus vivendi: a form of hedonism. In addition, kitsch shares some important characteristics with the hyper-real. They both go beyond the immediately observable, the 'really real', and they are distinguishing marks of the modern age. For Benjamin, kitsch is debased art; for Eco, the hyper-real conceals the anxieties of the loss of 'the authentic': '[T]he frantic desire for the Almost Real arises only as a neurotic reaction to the vacuum of memories; the Absolute Fake is offspring of the unhappy awareness of present without depth.'

(Source: 'Spaces of consumption: from margin to centre' by Alexander Styhre and Tobias Engberg, in Ephemera (volume 3, number 2, May 2003))

Select one answer for each of the following questions:

4 What is meant in the article by space of consumption?

(a) Where goods are used

(b) Where goods are manufactured

(c) Where goods are bought

(d) Where consumers are in the majority

(e) Where producers are in the majority

5 Which of the following is an unstated assumption made about rural spaces?

(a) They are capable of being moved to urban areas

(b) They represent the principal area of production

(c) They are capable of being contained in arcades

(d) They are totally different in character to urban spaces

(e) Such spaces are specifically linked with individual spaces of consumption

6 **Which of the following is not stated in the passage to be a characteristic of kitsch?**

(a) It is a branch of art

(b) It is popular with consumers

(c) It is commonly found to be pleasurable

(d) It is inherently familiar

(e) It is easily accessible

3   Mental Illness

Population surveys in Britain and elsewhere indicate that people living in rural areas have lower levels of psychiatric morbidity than urban residents. These geographic patterns of mental illness may in part be due to differences in the socio-economic characteristics of people living in different localities. In a recent analysis, half of the excess risk of mental disorder associated with urban residence was explained by the social and economic characteristics of urban residents. Focussing on young (16- to 39-year-old) adults, we analysed data from the Fourth National Survey of Morbidity in General Practice to investigate: (a) whether urban-rural differences in the population prevalence of mental illness in Britain are reflected in differences in patterns of General Practitioner consultation and (b) whether any differences were due to the different socio-economic characteristics of residents of rural and urban areas.

Our analysis shows that rates of consultation for mental disorder by young men and women are lower in rural compared to urban areas. The differences are greatest in men and were more marked than those for overall consultation rates suggesting the importance of factors other than ease of access to GP surgeries in rural areas. Previous analyses of the Fourth General Practice Morbidity Survey have demonstrated strong social class gradients in consultations for psychiatric disorders. While differences in the social and economic characteristics of urban and rural residents explain some of the observed geographical variation in consultation, large differences remain after controlling for social class, housing tenure and marital status. Our findings are in keeping with findings from the National Survey of Psychiatric Morbidity. This found that the odds of psychiatric disorder in 16- to 64-year-olds living in urban compared to rural areas declined from 1.64 ($p<0.001$) to 1.33 ($p<0.05$) after controlling for socio-economic and other differences between the locations. In both these studies the possibility of residual confounding cannot be ruled out. Furthermore, patterns of consultation are only proxy measure of the prevalence of mental disorder as a person must pass through a number of filters/stages between developing mental illness and having a diagnosis of mental disorder made by their General Practitioner. Firstly, many people with mental disorders do not seek help from their GP. The 1993 OPCS National Psychiatric Morbidity study reported that only 35 percent of 'cases' had consulted a GP for mental health reasons in the past year. Secondly, amongst those who did seek help from their GP, many may not have had their mental disorder detected or recorded. The gender differences in the strength of association between rurality and consultation for mental disorder may reflect greater urban-rural differences in the prevalence of mental disorder in males than females. Alternatively, it has been suggested that mental illness is more stigmatised in rural areas and this may lead to a greater reluctance to seek formal health service support; such possible stigmatising effects may be greater in men than women.

There are a number of possible explanations for the apparently lower prevalence of mental disorder in rural areas. First, as discussed above, the finding could reflect the residual effects of socio-economic differences in the residents of rural and urban areas not controlled for in our analysis. Second, rural-urban differences could arise through the drift of those with, or at greater risk of, mental disorder from rural to urban locations. Third, there may be differences in the extent to which people are prepared to report and consult for symptoms of mental disorder in the two locations. Lastly, they may reflect real effects of place of residence on mental health. The two main area characteristics which are thought to be associated with the health and mental health of their residents are social cohesion/social integration and income inequality. It has long been argued, for example, that social integration influences population suicide rates and it is possible that levels of integration are higher in rural compared to urban areas and this leads to the observed area differences. It is of note, however, that recent adverse trends in suicide rates amongst young people have been most marked in rural areas. Further, more detailed, research is required both to explain the observed rural-urban differences in the prevalence of mental disorder in young people and to determine whether recent rises in suicide in rural areas reflect rises in the prevalence of mental disorder in these areas. Such research may have important implications for strategies to improve population mental health.

(Source: 'Patterns of General Practitioner consultation for mental illness by young people in rural areas' by Adrian Gunnell, Health Statistics Quarterly, Spring 2004, www.statistics.gov.uk; Crown copyright material is reproduced with permission of the Controller of HMSO)

Select one answer for each of the following questions:

7   Which of the following is an assertion rather than a stated fact?

(a) Surveys indicate that people living in rural areas have lower levels of psychiatric morbidity than those in urban areas

(b) The stigmatising effect of mental illness may be greater among men

(c) Rates of consultation of GPs about mental illness are lower in rural than urban areas

(d) There are strong social class gradients in consultations for psychiatric disorders

(e) None of the above

8   Which of the following can be inferred to be true?

(a) More people suffer from mental illness than have been diagnosed

(b) Fewer people suffer from mental illness than have been diagnosed

(c) People are more reluctant to consult GPs about mental illness in rural areas

(d) People are less reluctant to consult GPs about mental illness in rural areas

(e) None of the above

9 Which of the following can be gathered to be the main reason for the difference in prevalence of mental illness between urban and rural areas?

(a) Socio-economic differences

(b) The drift from rural to urban areas

(c) The differing reluctance to report symptoms

(d) The differing characteristics of the place of residence

(e) There is insufficient evidence to say

4   Genetic Modification

US researchers have genetically modified mice to be better at learning and remembering. Team leader Joe Tsien, a neurobiologist at Princeton University said simply: 'They're smarter.' Humans also have the added gene, although it is not yet known whether it has the same function in people. But the scientists believe their results show that one day it may be possible to boost human intelligence. The breakthrough will ignite debate about whether such a feat would be ethical but Ira Black, chairman of neuroscience at Rutgers University says: 'It's very exciting and holds the hope of not only making animals smarter but also, ultimately, of having a human gene therapy for use in areas such as dementia.' However, Dr Tim Bliss, head of neurophysiology at the National Institute for Medical Research in London, said: 'When you insert a gene at random into the genome you don't know what might happen. These animals seem to be OK, but there might be all sorts of hidden down sides to having this extra protein. I think it's very unlikely that tinkering with one gene is going to increase intelligence and do nothing else. In my view talk of genetically enhancing human intelligence is nonsense.' However, he said new drug or gene therapy treatments might emerge from the research: 'It certainly raises that possibility, but we are very far away at the moment.'

The research team from Princeton, Washington and MIT universities found that adding a single gene to mice significantly boosted the animals' ability to solve maze tasks, learn from objects and sounds in their environment and to retain that knowledge. The intelligence-boosting effect results from the mice retaining into adulthood certain brain features of juvenile mice. Like young humans, young mice are widely believed to be better than adults at grasping large amounts of new information.

This new strain of mice is named Doogie, after a precocious character on the US television show Doogie Howser, MD. One key feature of learning is the ability to associate one event with another – associating fire with the sensation of pain is a simple example. The research shows that the gene used, called NR2B, is very important in controlling this ability. It is the blueprint for a protein that spans the surface of neurons and serves as a docking point, or receptor, for certain chemical signals. This receptor, called NMDA, is like a double lock on a door; it needs two keys or events before it opens. Studies have shown that in young animals the NMDA receptor responds even when the two events happen relatively far apart, so it is easier to make connections between events and to learn. After adolescence, the receptor becomes less responsive, making learning more difficult. But introducing the NR2B gene kept the Doogie mice's brains 'young'.

Showing that the Doogie mice were more intelligent required a number of tests:

Object recognition – The mice explored two objects for five minutes. Several days later, one object was replaced with a new one. When the mice returned, the Doogie mice remembered the old object, and devoted their time to exploring the new one. The normal mice, however, spent an equal amount of time exploring both objects. The Doogie mice remembered objects four to five times longer.

Emotional memory – The animals received mild electric shocks to their feet. When the mice were put back in the chamber up to 10 days later, the Doogie mice showed much more fear than the control mice.

Learning response – The mice again received shocks and were then placed back into the fear-causing environment, but without the shocks. The Doogie mice were much quicker to resume normal behaviour: they learned faster.

Spatial learning – The mice were put into a pool of water that had a hidden platform where they could climb out of the water. The Doogie mice learned to find the platform after three sessions, while the control mice required six.

(Source: 'Genetic modification', 1999, from BBC News at www.bbcnews.com)

Select one answer for each of the following questions:

10 What fundamental assumption must be made to appreciate the potential benefit of the new technology for humans?

(a) It is possible to alter one gene without affecting others

(b) Intelligence is based partly on genetic factors

(c) Humans share the majority of their genetic characteristics with the mice tested

(d) There are no side effects to such genetic modification

(e) All genes react in a similar way

11 What does the article identify as being the most useful characteristic of NR2B?

(a) It facilitates the learning of new skills

(b) It reverses the effects of ageing

(c) It increases speed of thought

(d) It makes brain receptors less sensitive

(e) It increases memory capacity

12 Which of the following is not stated in the article?

(a) Mice have the ability to learn new skills

(b) It is possible to counteract signs of ageing

(c) The ability to learn declines with age

(d) Memory has a chemical basis

(e) Mice share some genes with humans

5   The True Ultimate

For the religious believer the only true ultimate is God himself. He is the 'bottom line' in any discussion of the significance of the past, present or future. If there is an ultimate hope, an intimate and unfailing care for creation, it can be found only in the eternal faithfulness of the Creator.

That was the point Jesus made in an argument about whether there is a human destiny beyond death. The Sadducees did not believe that there was. They based their religious belief on the Torah, the first five books of our Bible, and they did not think they could find such a hope set forth in its pages. They came to Jesus with a rather ingenious conundrum about a woman who had successively married seven brothers, asking whose wife she would be in the age to come? As he so often did, Jesus cut through the superficial argument and went straight to the real point. He recalled an incident in the Torah, where God speaks to Moses from the burning bush and reminds him that the Lord is the God of Abraham, the God of Isaac and the God of Jacob. Jesus goes on to say 'He is not God of the dead, but of the living' (Mark 12:27). In other words, if the patriarchs mattered to God once, as they certainly did, they matter to him forever. He will not cast them away like broken pots once they have served his immediate purpose. The Lord is eternally faithful in his care for Abraham, Isaac and Jacob, for you and me. And I am sure we can add, for all of creation in appropriate ways. I will return to this last point shortly, but first let me consider whether in this scientific age we can seriously believe that there is an ultimate destiny for human beings beyond their death.

The first question we have to ask is what is the nature of men and women? I have already explained that I think we are psychosomatic unities and that the soul is the 'form' (the information-bearing pattern) of the body. That pattern will be dissolved at death with the decay of my body. Yet it seems to be a perfectly coherent hope that the pattern that is me will be remembered by God and recreated by him in some new environment of his choosing in his ultimate act of resurrection. The Christian hope has never truly been that of the survival of a spiritual component. We are not apprentice angels, longing to rid ourselves of the encumbrance of our bodies. Rather, it is the essence of humanity to be embodied. The Christian hope, therefore, is of death and resurrection, an end and a new beginning.

The 'software' of life cannot run on any old 'hardware' (there is something essential in our specific embodiment, I believe, and I reject a strict computer analogy) but there is surely the possibility of there being a new 'matter' in which we can be re-embodied at our resurrection. Where will this 'matter' come from? I think that it will be the transformed matter of this present world, delivered by God from its destiny to decay. The universe is going to die but, because God cares for it, it will have its resurrection beyond its death, just as we shall have our resurrection beyond our deaths. In fact the two destinies are one. This is the Christian hope, articulated by St Paul, that there is to be a new creation, the redemption of the old creation from its frustration and futility (Romans 8:18–25; 2 Corinthians 5:17), in which we shall all share.

(Source: 'Beyond Science: The Wider Human Context' by John Polkinghorne, Cambridge University Press, 1996)

Select one answer for each of the following questions:

13 What is the main purpose of the extract?

(a) To challenge the traditional view of resurrection

(b) To show that there is life after death

(c) To verify the accuracy of certain biblical passages

(d) To consider whether religion is consistent with science

(e) To explain the nature of humanity

14 What can be inferred to be the writer's opinion of religion?

(a) He does not believe in religion

(b) He believes that religion is consistent with science

(c) He reluctantly accepts the necessity of religion

(d) He believes that religion is vital to everyone

(e) He believes that religion is vital to science

15 Which of the following is least implicit in the writer's description of resurrection?

(a) The existence of heaven

(b) Reincarnation in a different form

(c) Life after death

(d) The existence of God

(e) Life after the end of the universe

6   Global Health

The rancour surrounding the Bangkok AIDS summit of July 2004 has exposed a series of fundamental disagreements surrounding the global politics of public health. These tensions range from access to cheaper lifesaving drugs to disputes over the role of poverty and gender equality in the promotion of sexual health.

The world is now experiencing the most profound public health challenge of the last forty years: we have witnessed the appearance of new diseases such as Ebola, SARS and, in particular, AIDS, combined with the alarming resurgence of diseases previously thought to have been under control, such as malaria and tuberculosis. The AIDS pandemic in particular threatens to devastate entire regions and has already fundamentally altered the life expectancy and demographic profile of many countries in sub-Saharan Africa. Billions of people lack access to adequate sanitation and safe drinking water, and the UN predicts that slums will become the dominant urban form within the next fifteen years.

Yet the very idea of 'public health' sits uncomfortably alongside the current emphasis of bio-medical science on the molecular realm of DNA coding and the development of lucrative Western markets for new pharmaceutical products such as sildenafil (Viagra). The needs of the majority – the global poor – scarcely feature within this tactical alliance between the bio-medical sciences and corporate power. Since most people threatened by AIDS, tuberculosis, unsafe drinking water, and other health threats are poor, they have little or no influence over the global politics of public health.

Making Sense of the Crisis

If we are to make sense of the current public health crisis, we need to explore interconnections between political, economic, and social developments that are ignored by the fragmentary emphasis of the biomedical sciences. The current impetus toward economic globalization is causing widespread social and economic disruption, ranging from wild currency fluctuations to the systematic collapse of viable agricultural systems. The imposition of austerity packages – widely referred to as structural adjustment programmes – in combination with the forcible extension of global markets for Western products is plunging millions of people into poverty and economic dependence. Existing primary health care services in much of the developing world and the former states of the Soviet Union have been drastically cut back, and services that were once freely available are now increasingly beyond the reach of the poor. And these harmful trends also extend even to the wealthiest global cities, such as London and New York, where a combination of poverty, homelessness, and cutbacks in primary health care since the 1980s has contributed toward the spread of tuberculosis and other diseases.

An examination of the social impact of the global public health crisis shows that it is women and children who have been most badly affected. One of the least addressed dimensions to the externally imposed structural adjustment programmes on developing countries is the harmful impact on the sexual health of women caused by their increased economic dependence on men. Sexual health programmes based on abstinence, for example, ignore the difficulties women face in negotiating safer or non-penetrative forms of sex. It is married women in southern Africa and south Asia who make up the largest and most vulnerable group of women, since they are at risk of being infected by their husbands.

A new generation of HIV-positive women activists, such as the Nigerian journalist and AIDS campaigner Rolake Odetoyinbo Nwagwu, are now engaged in a vital struggle to challenge the social attitudes and economic inequalities that have driven the devastating impact of AIDS on women and children in developing countries. The spread of AIDS in more traditional societies is closely linked with patriarchal power structures. The sustenance of these structures is assured by the rise of poverty-fuelled ethnic and religious chauvinism, which undermines the prospects for developing more progressive approaches to social policy. And in regions where war or civil strife prevail, the vulnerability of women and children to sexual violence, economic exploitation, and disease is even greater so that we cannot consider public health questions separately from issues surrounding political stability and social justice.

(*Source: Gandy M (2005) Deadly Alliances: Death, Disease, and the Global Politics of Public Health. PLoS Med 2(1): e4*)

Select one answer for each of the following questions:

16 What is the main idea in the article?

(a) Spending on healthcare in developing countries should be increased

(b) More attention should be focused on the rise of once almost eliminated diseases

(c) There is considerable inequality in the provision of healthcare around the world

(d) The priority should be to tackle the AIDS epidemic

(e) The developed world should not interfere in the affairs of developing countries

17 What of the following comes closest to describing the problem with the focus on bio-medical research?

(a) It is a waste of money that would otherwise be spent on dealing with more prevalent diseases

(b) It leads to certain pharmaceutical companies making large profits

(c) It wastes scarce natural resources needed to produce other drugs

(d) Its effects will only be felt in certain more wealthy countries

(e) It distracts attention away from more fundamental healthcare issues

18 What of the following is not identified as an impediment to improving sexual health?

(a) War

(b) Poverty

(c) Social attitudes

(d) Focus on bio-medical research

(e) Religious beliefs

7   Voting Patterns in America

Voting patterns in America are keenly analysed statistics by party officials. In 1996 the turnout at the general election was 49% which was the lowest turnout since 1924. This was despite a record of 13 million new voters registering to vote in 1992. This could simply have been because so many potential voters considered the result a forgone conclusion rather than America developing a sudden apathy towards politics. However, if the latter is true then the consequences for America in the future could be dire if only a certain section of society involves itself in politics and the rest feel that it is an area they should not concern themselves with. The election result of 2000 replicated the 1996 election in terms of voter participation with only about 50% of registered voters participating and this was in a campaign where there was no foregone conclusion regarding the candidates – Al Gore and George W Bush. The 2000 election was considered to be one of the most open elections in recent years.

Certainly the heady days of 1960 seem somewhat distant now. In 1960 there was a 62.8% turnout at the general election. This was considered high but may have been a result of what is known as the 'Kennedy factor' which could have encouraged voters to use their vote. It is not necessarily true that in 1960 the American public suddenly became more politically aware. Historically, certain groups that have been given the right to vote have taken their time to take up this right. The 19th Amendment of 1920 allowed women the right to vote but their impact on elections took some while to filter in. The 26th Amendment reduced the voting age to eighteen but traditionally less than 50% have turned out at general elections and even less for other elections. Does this signify that the young potential voters of America feel excluded from the political process hence they do not feel inclined to vote?

If this apathy does exist then it is leaving the hard core of voters as the ones who have a vested interest in voting and maintaining the current political set-up – ie the educated white middle/upper class voter. This obviously brings into question the political representation of those groups in America. One problem that has made worse the issue of voter representation is the fact that an individual must initiate voter registration well before election day. It cannot be done immediately before an election and the evidence shows that this is a policy that favours those who wish to involve themselves in the political set-up but acts against those who are less politically motivated. The opposite happens in Britain whereby local government offices initiate the voter registration procedure by sending out a registration form to those who are allowed to vote and then 'chase-up' those who fail to register. If in America a person has a legal right to vote (is an American citizen, over age etc) if he/she has not registered they cannot do so.

Another quirk of American politics is that those who are registered to vote sometimes do not do so. Having gone to the effort of registering, come a general election they simply fail to vote (as would be their democratic right). In 1988, of those who actually registered only 70% voted so that nearly one-third of all registered voters did not vote come the election. In 1993, the 'Motor Voter' Act was passed in an effort to make more easy the procedures someone goes through to register for a vote. It came into operation in 1995. The Act simply allows someone to register when applying for a driving licence. The registration procedure has also been altered to enable the disabled to register with greater ease and the law now states that facilities must be in place to make voting easier for the disabled.

Combined, both the above lead to an extra 5 million people registering by the time of the 1996 general election. But there was a drop of 10 million voters in the 1996 general election compared with the 1992 election. For the 2000 election, just about 105 million people voted – similar to the 1996 figure but still only about 50% of registered voters. However, the 1996 election saw an increase in Black Americans voting. In 1992, the Black vote was 8% of the total electorate. In 1996 it was 10% of the total.

In the 1984 election 92.6 million voted but 84 million potential voters did not. As a result of this, the first major study of voting patterns occurred. There were three main findings to this study:

1   About 20% of the American population is mobile each year and moves about. If you move out of your state you have to re-register within the state you now live in. How many can be bothered to do so?
2   Those groups who have traditionally mobilised voters – such as the trade unions – are in decline.
3   The input of the media (especially TV) has diluted grass-roots face-to-face politics and removed the 'human touch'.

(Source: 'Voting patterns in America' by Christopher Trueman, www.historylearningsite.co.uk)

Select one answer for each of the following questions:

19 What could be inferred to be a result of the 'Kennedy factor'?

(a) It was assumed that Kennedy would definitely win

(b) It was assumed that Kennedy would definitely not win

(c) People were apathetic towards Kennedy

(d) People had strong opinions about Kennedy

(e) None of the above

20 Which of the following could be gathered to be most likely to have the most considerable immediate effect on increasing turnout?

(a) Reducing the age of majority

(b) Extending the electoral franchise

(c) Increasing education about political issues

(d) Increasing facilities for disabled voters

(e) Removing the requirement to register in advance of the election day

21 Which of the following is not identified as a potential explanation of low turnout amongst voters?

(a) Inability to distinguish between different candidates' policies

(b) The complexity of the registration system

(c) Apathy

(d) Belief that the result is a foregone conclusion

(e) Absence of strong characters amongst candidates for the presidency

8   Mysticism and Physiology

For a long time people believed that quasi-mystical experiences such as falling in love were in fact cases of poisoning or contagion. This belief assumed that the interior space of the human body was a kind of forge containing liquid substances that were able to melt and mix with other, possibly alien, substances, a process with often unforeseen and hence dangerous consequences. For many people living in a Cartesian world, with all its logic of purity, it is difficult to understand how literally the physiology of intermingling liquids was taken. However, for many writers in the Middle Ages togetherness in the amorous sense of the word was not only something that belonged to a spiritual real, but also something which implied a 'subtly physiological conditioning with remote effects'. What does it mean when we, post-Cartesians, are expected to take this idea in a literal sense?

Sloterdijk provides us with the example of Marsilio Ficino (1433–1499) who argues that the passion between a particular man and a particular woman is caused by mutual eye-contact. This implies that two persons looking at each other are not at all engaged in an innocent process. Ficino conceives of it as a radiological event during which both partners cast rays towards each other. These rays are, he believes, poisonous, basically because they contain 'subtle and nebulous blood' which is left behind in the heart region of the beloved partner. Once arrived there, it is quickly transubstantiated into less subtle blood with normal thickness. Lovers looking at each other are hence quite literally engaged in a process of contamination. This becomes particularly evident when one realises that blood left behind in the heart region of a partner longs to go back to the vessels it came from. Consequently, this partner develops an unstoppable desire to be with the other, a desire we know as love.

Note, however, that there is more than the intermingling of substances. The imagery invoked by Ficino is also permeated by radiology. The heart is an organ of radiation and emanation, or, as Sloterdijk puts it, it is the sun of all organs. Since the heart is where the soul resides, it is not foolish to argue that the soul also displays certain radiological and emanating properties. Renaissance psychology indeed seems to assume that the soul is a sort of 'radio room for transactions with inspiring others'. Togetherness, Sloterdijk points out, has distinctive radiological aspects.

In a post-Cartesian world, the charm of Ficino's psychology has been somewhat elusive. Where togetherness was once understood as invoking a circulation of high temperatures, that is, where suns, high-energy fusion, and bubbling and boiling liquids were once the dominant metaphors to describe what could be going on between people, somewhere in the 16th or 17th century a massive disenchantment and cooling down of the heart is beginning to impose itself on the minds of people. The rise of anatomic science was crucial for this process. Cutting and opening bodies taught people that they were, if not mentally then at least physically, utterly alone in the cosmos. In the new paradigm, the body came to be understood as an entity in its own right, or, to be more precise, as a functional unit incapable of smoothly entering into relationships with other units. Anatomy, it was believed, provided evidence that the human body was, if anything, an autonomous laboratory. Importantly, this cooling procedure implied a complete redesign of the cardiac function: once a Sun King amidst other organs, it now became a machine, a pump, or, to paraphrase Sloterdijk, the chief clerk in the blood circulation. Subtle physiology was replaced by bureaucratic mechanics. Contagion and poison became illegal and were substituted by organisation and system.

(Source: 'Life between faces' by René ten Bos and Ruud Kaulingfreks, in Ephemera (volume 2, number 3, August 2002))

Select one answer for each of the following questions:

22 What is meant by an 'innocent process' in the second paragraph?

(a) An unintentional one

(b) One involving no physiological changes

(c) One devoid of any impure intent

(d) One which neither party would feel guilty about

(e) One independent of other people

23 Which one of the following is an implicit consequence of Ficino's view?

(a) Rays can transfer blood across a void

(b) Eye contact begins the process

(c) The blood in question longs to return to where it came from

(d) Subtle nebulous blood can be converted into normal blood

(e) People cannot control who they fall in love with

24 Which adjective could not be used to describe Ficino's imagery in the post-Cartesian world?

(a) Metaphoric

(b) Anachronistic

(c) Dated

(d) Superseded

(e) Naïve

9   Time

What is time? 'If nobody asks me,' St Augustine wrote in the fourth century, 'then I know; but if I were to desire to explain it to one that should ask me, plainly I know not.' Some sixteen centuries later the question remains as elusive as ever. Why does time seem to flow like a river? The American physicist John Wheeler once suggested that 'time is what keeps everything from happening at once', a curiously seductive formula, though perhaps no less puzzling than the original question.

In his 'Critique of Pure Reason', the German philosopher Immanuel Kant argued that one could never perceive of or imagine anything existing outside space or in the absence of time. 'These are the subjective conditions of sensibility', he wrote. Much as a prism resolves light into its separate colours, laying them out in order, so does the mind, according to Kant, separate reality along the axis of time. But is time really only an illusion or a result of perception? Did it not exist long before there were any living things and so before there were any perceptions? Today, modern physics traces time's character back to the very origins of the universe and questions its place in the fundamental laws of physics.

Isaac Newton's equations of motion involve time but in a somewhat sterile way. As the Earth orbits perpetually about the Sun, gravitation dictates a calculable change in the Earth's motion in each small interval of time. But this sort of time is merely a bookkeeper's trick, an artifice of accounting. For Newton, both space and time were absolutes: space a thoroughly empty void through which objects can pass, and time a kind of ticker tape running inexorably in the background. Albert Einstein then revealed that time could be stretched and distorted and was affected by matter and energy.

But even if the river of time flows faster in some places than others, and slows down when passing obstacles, this still does not explain what time is or why it has a direction. And experience suggests that time does have direction. Washing machines wear out with use, as do automobiles and shoes and they never return to their former pristine perfection. Mountain peaks crumble into the valley, but never reassemble themselves, and perfume from an opened bottle escapes to fill the room, but never does the reverse. These facts suggest a single direction for time, the direction in which things wear out, spread and erode away, and in which order generally dissolves into disorder.

This tendency also points to a theoretical conundrum. The physics of perfume bottles, mountains and other large-scale things ought to arise out of the workings of their atoms and molecules. But in contrast to the world around us, the atomic realm seems to make no distinction between past and future. Make a movie of a few atoms doing their thing, run it in reverse, and you would see nothing strange – the backward movement would again fulfil the laws of physics. But a movie of scattered rocks miraculously gathering again into a rugged peak would fly in the face of reality as we know it.

So how can the directionless time of the atomic realm give rise to the arrow of time at the larger scale? This is the central question, and its answer has two parts – the first relatively 'easy' and more than a century old, the second rather more difficult, a matter for continuing debate.

(Source: 'What is time?' by Mark Buchanan in 'Big Questions in Science' edited by Harriet Swain, Vintage, 2003; reprinted by permission of The Random House Group Ltd)

Select one answer for each of the following questions:

25 What is implied about time and space?

(a) One cannot exist without the other

(b) Time is more important than space

(c) Space is more important than time

(d) They are both crucial to our understanding of life

(e) Neither can be understood without the other

26 What did St Augustine mean in the piece quoted at the beginning of the passage?

(a) He could precisely define time to himself but could not explain that definition to someone else

(b) It is not possible for anyone to define time

(c) He knew what was understood by time but could not articulate a precise definition

(d) Everyone has a different view of what time is

(e) The definition of time keeps changing

27 Which of the following is not stated in the passage?

(a) Time flows in only one direction

(b) Time is important to the study of physics

(c) Only certain acts are capable of being reversed

(d) Time can only be effectively defined by reference to atoms and molecules

(e) The concept of time has always existed

10   Beauty and Intelligence

Brains and beauty do go together – and that's official. Or it is according to a new academic report by Mensa member Satoshi Kanazawa. Dr Kanazawa, together with co-author Jody Kovar, has just published research findings into the link between intelligence and attractiveness. The paper, 'Why Beautiful People are More Intelligent', was printed recently in the scientific journal Intelligence. In the paper, Dr Kanazawa, a lecturer at the London School of Economics and Political Science, produces a highly technical series of arguments to show how brains and beauty have merged throughout evolutionary history. His case is based on four key assumptions:

1   Men who are more intelligent are more likely to attain higher status than men who are less intelligent.
2   Higher-status men are more likely to mate with more beautiful women than lower-status men.
3   Intelligence is heritable.
4   Beauty is heritable.

As a key part of the argument, Dr Kanazawa demolishes the age-old beliefs that 'beauty is in the eye of the beholder' and 'beauty is skin deep'. And he also explains where the populist 'dumb blonde' tag may have originated. The fascinating report argues that the evolutionary process – both scientifically and genetically – has led to assertive mating, in which partners have been chosen for their strength, good health and even height, all attributes which have given those who possess them a high status.

The report's introduction says 'Empirical studies demonstrate that individuals perceive physically attractive others to be more intelligent than physically unattractive others. While most researchers dismiss this perception as "bias" or "stereotype", we contend that individuals have this perception because beautiful people indeed are more intelligent … If females generally prefer intelligent males because they typically have higher incomes and status, and if most males prefer physically attractive females, then over time these two characteristics will tend to covary.'

… It is worth looking at the report's take on what makes beauty – and why it is neither in the eyes of the beholder or simply skin deep …

The report says that evolutionary psychological research suggests that the standards of beauty might be species-typical because attractive people are genuinely different from less attractive people. Specifically, beauty is an indicator of genetic and developmental health. There is also some evidence that physically attractive people are healthier than physically less attractive people.

But what is our idea of beauty – what makes beautiful people? The report's authors say there appear to be a few features that characterize physically attractive faces: bilateral symmetry, averageness, and secondary sexual characteristics. Attractive faces are more symmetrical then unattractive faces.

And there are, according to the report, good reasons why we have developed these views. For instance, fluctuating asymmetry (FA), which is not found attractive, increases with exposure to parasites, pathogens, and toxins during development. FA also increases with genetic disruptions, such as mutations and inbreeding. Developmentally and genetically, healthy individuals have less FA and more symmetry in their facial and bodily features. For this reason, across societies, there is a positive correlation between parasite and pathogen prevalence in the environment and the importance placed on physical attractiveness in mate selection. This is because, in societies where there are a lot of pathogens and parasites, it is especially important to avoid individuals who have been afflicted with them when selecting mates.

(Source: 'Beauty and intelligence' by Brian Page, Mensa Magazine, September 2004)

Select one answer for each of the following questions:

28 Which of the following cannot be implied from the research?

(a) Less attractive people tend to be less intelligent

(b) There is a correlation between attractiveness and income

(c) Attractive faces share all of the same characteristics

(d) Different societies prioritise different qualities

(e) Men and women look for different things in a partner

29 Which of the following unstated assumptions must be made in order to analyse empirical data on this subject?

(a) All men have the same perception of what an attractive woman looks like

(b) Intelligence is partly genetic

(c) Successful people are always intelligent

(d) Attractiveness can be quantified

(e) A wide range of different levels of intelligence and attractiveness exist in society

30 Which of the following is not stated in the report?

(a) Individuals perceive attractive people to be more intelligent

(b) There is a correlation between health and attractiveness

(c) Attractiveness is the only characteristic used by men to judge a woman

(d) Fluctuating asymmetry can be indicative of poor health

(e) Genetic mutations can decrease attractiveness

MCQ ANSWER SHEET

Leisure Time	The True Ultimate
1	13
2	14
3	15

Spaces of Consumption	Global Health
4	16
5	17
6	18

Mental Illness	Voting Patterns in America
7	19
8	20
9	21

Genetic Modification	Mysticism and Physiology
10	22
11	23
12	24

Time	Beauty and Intelligence
25	28
26	29
27	30

SECTION B: ESSAY

ANSWER **ONE** OF THE FOLLOWING QUESTIONS.

1   Can full gender equality in the workplace ever be achieved?

2   'Criminal law should never seek to punish someone for not doing something.' Do you agree?

3   Have successive governments' policies of privatisation been successful with respect to their aims?

4   Do human beings learn from their mistakes?

5   What do you think should be done to solve the problem of overcrowding on Britain's roads?

ESSAY PLAN AND NOTES

NATIONAL ADMISSIONS
TEST FOR LAW

SAMPLE TEST 4

The test has two separate sections, A and B.

Section A: Multiple Choice

This section is divided into 10 subsections; each subsection has three questions.

You should answer **all** 30 questions in Section A, selecting one of the possible answers and indicating your response on the answer sheet at the back of the section.

Time allowed: 80 minutes

Section B: Essay

This section has five essay questions.

You should select and answer **one** question in Section B. Your answer should be no more than four sides of A4. A page is provided at the back of the section for your essay plan and notes.

Time allowed: 40 minutes

SECTION A: MULTIPLE CHOICE

ANSWER **ALL** OF THE FOLLOWING QUESTIONS.

1   Market Economies

In the market economy, emphasis is laid on the freedom of the individual, both as a consumer and as the owner of resources. As a consumer he expresses his choice of goods through the price he is willing to pay for them. As the owner of resources used in production (usually his own labour) he seeks to obtain as large a reward as possible. If consumers want more of the good than is being supplied at the current price, this is indicated by their 'bidding-up' the price. This increases the profits of firms and the earnings of factors producing that good. As a result, resources are attracted into the industry, and supply expands. On the other hand, if consumers do not want a particular good, its price falls, producers make a loss, and resources leave the industry.

The price system therefore indicates the wishes of consumers and allocates the community's productive resources accordingly. There is no direction of labour; people are free to work wherever they choose. Efficiency is achieved through the profit motive: owners of factors of production sell them at the highest possible price, while firms keep production costs as low as they can in order to obtain the highest profit margin. Factor earnings decide who is to receive the goods produced. If firms produce better goods or achieve efficiency, or if workers make a greater effort, they receive a high reward, giving them more spending power to obtain goods in the market.

In this way the price system acts, as it were, like a marvellous computer, registering people's preferences for different goods, transmitting those preferences to firms, moving resources to produce the goods, and deciding who shall obtain the final products. Thus, through the motivation of private enterprise, the four problems inherent in economising are solved automatically.

In practice the market economy does not work quite so smoothly as this. Nor are its results entirely satisfactory. We speak of 'market failure'.

First, some vital community goods, such as defence, police, justice and national parks, cannot be adequately provided through the market. This is mainly because it would be impossible to charge a price since 'free-riders' cannot be excluded. Indeed, in most advanced countries, the state usually goes further. Thus it may take responsibility for public goods, such as TV programmes and parks, where there is no reduction in the quantity available for others when one person has more, and the cost can be covered by taxation. Moreover, it usually provides a safety net when people are unemployed, sick or old, and gives assistance towards merit goods, such as education, housing, museums and libraries, on which people might otherwise underspend.

Second, the consumers with most money have the greatest pull in the market. As a result, resources may be devoted to producing luxuries for the rich to the exclusion of necessities for the poor. While this is really brought about by the unequal distribution of wealth and income rather than by the market system, the fact is that the latter tends to produce, and even to increase, such inequality.

Third, the competition upon which the efficiency of the market economy depends may break down. An employer may be the only buyer of a certain type of labour in a locality. If so, he is in a strong position when negotiating rates of pay with individual works. The state may therefore have to intervene, eg with minimum-wage requirements, as in agriculture. Similarly, on the selling side, one seller may be able to exclude competitors. This puts the consumer in a weak position because he cannot take his custom elsewhere.

…

Fifth, consumers' sovereignty may be distorted by large firms which use extensive advertising simply to persuade people that their goods are just what they want.

…

Lastly, in a market economy where individuals decide what to produce, resources may remain unemployed because firms as a whole consider that profit prospects are poor.

(Source: 'Mastering Economics' by Jack Harvey, Macmillan, 1994; reproduced with permission of Palgrave Macmillan)

Select one answer for each of the following questions:

1 Which of the following is not an assumption underlying the operation of the market mechanism?

(a) All consumers and producers have perfect information about the state of the market

(b) Consumers and producers wish to maximise their profits

(c) There are no barriers to the mobility of producers and consumers

(d) There is no government interference in the market

(e) Consumers' preferences do not change

2 Which of the following can be inferred to be a reason why it is desirable for the government to invest in merit goods?

(a) Consumers have no incentive to spend on them

(b) They benefit society as a whole

(c) They are not capable of being provided by the private sector

(d) It is more efficient for them to be provided by the government

(e) The government is able to obtain them for a better price

3 Which of the following is an argument in favour of interfering with the operation of the market operation?

(a) It does not promote equality

(b) A perfect market is not achievable

(c) Insufficient merit goods would be capable of being produced

(d) Consumer sovereignty may be distorted by advertising

(e) No public goods can be provided by the market

2   Lutheranism

What exactly is 'revolutionary'? Politically, it is a momentous event that within a short space of time overthrows an established order. Put crudely, it is a major upheaval which usually has important short and long term impacts.

On first examination it would appear that Lutheranism fits this description perfectly. The established order (the Catholic Church) was removed in England, Scotland, Sweden, and northern Germany by a movement called 'Protestantism' which started, though not deliberately, with Luther in 1517. The upheaval was so great that many military conflicts took place post-1517 and the religious break down in western Europe was one of the main causes of the Thirty Years War. Also what occurred took place in a relatively short space of time. The 95 Theses was written in 1517 and by 1521 Luther had developed these ideas and burned the Book of Canon Law and the Papal Bull Exsurge Dominie. Four years in the C20 would be considered relatively quick for the weakening of an established order. The end of the Eastern Bloc did not happen overnight. In the C16 such an occurrence was all but unheard of. However, on closer analysis, arguments against this approach can be forwarded.

Was Luther trying to return the Catholic Church back to its original purity by claiming that salvation could only be achieved through your own goodness and by being truly repentant for your sins? Where in the Bible, on which Luther placed supreme trust, does it refer to a man leading the church living in magnificent splendour, wearing fine clothes etc? Luther may well have argued that it was the Catholic Church that had been revolutionary as it had moved so drastically away from the teachings of Christ and that he was being reactionary (trying to 'turn the clock back') by trying to re-find the purity of Christ as stated in the Bible. Luther's claim that if it was not in the Bible you did not do it was in direct contradiction to the belief that only the Catholic Church could control your destiny and salvation.

Another issue to examine is the 95 Theses. This was not the work of a revolutionary. It was written for a small group of academics to discuss possibly after work at Wittenberg University or during a seminar/discussion group. All these men would have been Catholic and as it was written in Latin it could not have been understood by anyone other than an academic. The 95 Theses in its original state was simply a discussion document for academics – that was all. It was not directed towards those who would be needed if you were targeting overturning the system: the general public. How many revolutions have been won by a handful of academics? If the system is to be overthrown, you need numbers on your side. Quite clearly, Luther's approach did not have this initially. One must doubt whether the document was ever intended to leave the confines of Wittenberg University. From the Catholic Church's point of view it clearly was revolutionary (once thoroughly examined) as it undermined all that the church stood for then and especially would have seriously hampered their finances.

If Lutheranism was revolutionary, why did it receive the support of so many north German princes who would have had a vested stake in keeping society stable? There was no guarantee that Lutheranism, once it had spread, would keep society intact. In fact, during the revolt of 1525, Luther made plain his views on the place of the peasants in society: 'This article (the 12 Articles of the Swabians) would make all men equal ... and that is impossible.' This is hardly the writing of a revolutionary and Luther's approach to the peasants drew him nearer to those who represented the status quo – the princes and state leaders. Luther also commented that slaves can be Christian and he did not condemn slavery within society.

To the Catholic Church, Lutheranism was dangerous and revolutionary. To Luther, the Church was dangerous, as it had conned innocent people for years that they could buy their way into heaven when Luther clearly thought that they could not. Therefore you could maintain a certain lifestyle, buy an indulgence and believe that that was all that was required to get to heaven and then continue leading that lifestyle. Your own naivety in the honesty of the Church would condemn you to Hell and you would never know any difference.

Was money the source of the Church's move away from the purity of the Bible? If so, Luther's stance on this issue is clear and it would have been viewed as revolutionary by the Catholic Church. Finally, if Luther was deemed to be revolutionary, why was he only banned from the Empire after Worms? If he was so obviously a revolutionary, why was he not burned as a heretic?

(Source: 'Was Lutheranism revolutionary?' by Christopher Trueman, www.historylearningsite.co.uk)

Select one answer for each of the following questions:

4   Which of the following would be least likely to fall under the definition of revolutionary?

(a) The overthrow of a government

(b) A military coup

(c) The assassination of a monarch

(d) The outbreak of an AIDS epidemic

(e) A major terrorist attack

5 What conclusion is reached by the writer?

(a) Lutheranism was revolutionary

(b) Lutheranism was reactionary

(c) Lutheranism was not as revolutionary as is often thought

(d) Lutheranism was more revolutionary than is often thought

(e) None of the above

6 Which of the following is an argument in favour of Lutheranism being revolutionary?

(a) The writing of the original 95 Theses

(b) The fact that Lutheranism received support from many north German princes

(c) Luther's attitude towards peasants

(d) Luther's stance on slavery

(e) Luther's views on indulgences

3   Insults in Schools

The word 'gay' is commonly used as an insult in British playgrounds. With homophobia on the increase in schools, should teachers be doing more to stop such name-calling? Calling something, or someone, gay is one of the most popular put-downs in school. A pair of trainers can be gay, so can a broken drinks machine and anyone who does not quite fit in can be deemed gay too. Teachers, health workers and the police are increasingly concerned at the effect the pervasive use of the word gay as a negative term is having on children.

The experience of 16-year-old Jamie (not his real name) shows how anti-gay name-calling can have a disastrous impact if left unchallenged. When he was 14, Jamie joined a new school in north-west England. One girl began to pick on him, calling him a gay boy. Slowly, other pupils picked up on the abuse and Jamie told us how eventually the whole year seemed to be targeting him. A lot of times when the word gay is used it's not used intentionally as a derogatory statement, although it of course has a lot of negative overtones. He said: 'They told me I dropped my gay card, told me I was queer.'

The continual name-calling coupled with family problems and Jamie's own struggle to come to terms with his sexuality eventually led him to attempt suicide. 'I just think I am basically rubbish. So although it has stopped physically, it has not stopped mentally,' he said. Jamie left school as soon as he could, with no qualifications. People who work with young gay men and lesbians say his experience is not rare. One study found 72% of lesbian and gay adults had been regular truants.

That is perhaps understandable when another set of research into school experiences of young lesbians and gays found a marked rise in problems since the early 1980s. The percentage who had experienced verbal abuse rose from around 8% in 1984 to 36% in 2001. 'These days they just think you come out and that is it everything is fine – but it's not'; Mark, teen homophobia victim.

The number who reported being physically assaulted in school had tripled from just 5% to 15%. Turton High School Media Arts College, near Bolton, is one of a small number of schools targeting homophobic language. They began addressing gay and lesbian stereotypes and the effects of name-calling after a survey on bullying found anti-gay abuse second only to insults about weight. Liz Rawsthorne, one of the teachers spearheading the school's work in this area, said colleagues find homophobia far trickier to address than racism. She said: 'If it's racist it's overtly aggressive. A lot of times when the word gay is used it's not used intentionally as a derogatory statement, although it of course has a lot of negative overtones. That makes it much more of an insidious problem – and it's harder to tackle directly.'

Other teachers blame the legacy of Section 28, the controversial education regulation that banned the promotion of homosexuality, for schools' hesitancy. Andrew Mullholland, a health worker in Bolton who has organised workshops on the impact of homophobia among young people, believes the current piecemeal approach to the problem needs addressing. 'With the repeal of Section 28, it is certainly a good opportunity nationally for the government to actually give a clear indication that they need to address this issue in the future.'

(Source: 'Concern over school "gay" insults' by Rebecca Sandles, 30 January 2005, from BBC News at www.bbcnews.com)

Select one answer for each of the following questions:

7 What is identified as being the main difference between homophobic and racist insults in schools?

(a) The intent behind the insult

(b) The effect on the victim

(c) The scale of usage

(d) The accuracy of the insult

(e) The tone of the insult

8 What can be gathered from the fact that inanimate objects are referred to as being gay?

(a) The use of the word is very prevalent

(b) Children do not understand what the word means

(c) Children do not use the word in its literal sense

(d) The word is now used more frequently than in the past

(e) The word is not intended as an insult

9 Which of the following cannot be inferred from the article?

(a) The use of homophobic insults has increased in the last 20 years

(b) Truancy is prevalent amongst homosexual students

(c) Bullying can impede academic progress

(d) Homosexual insults are not dealt with as seriously as racist insults

(e) Section 28 has influenced the educational establishment's approach towards homosexuality

4   The Crucifixion

Recently there have been several articles and TV documentaries on the Crucifixion/Resurrection, suggesting that Jesus Christ was taken down from the cross by Roman soldiers while still alive. I have set aside the traditional view to speculate on what could have happened … if and why Jesus was still alive after the crucifixion.

Highly trained and disciplined Roman soldiers were unlikely to act entirely on their own initiative; they needed to receive orders from a higher authority. They were experienced enough in the 'art' of crucifixion to know when someone was dead and would certainly face punishment if they were lax enough to take down crucified 'criminals' while they were still breathing. So removing Jesus from the cross alive was not an accident on the part of the soldiers – they were following instructions.

After examining the biblical evidence I have come to believe that Pontius Pilate was responsible for saving Jesus, by some lateral interpretation of the facts and events as laid out in biblical texts. We know little of Pontius Pilate; there is only one inscription and a few bronze coins from 29–32AD bearing his name. He was appointed governor procurator of Judea in 26AD, having worked up through the Roman army. There is a legend, originating in Germany, that he had enlisted in the army after committing a murder but as governor of Judea he is said to have been sympathetic to the Christians.

In Jerusalem, Pontius Pilate found allegations against Jesus at the trial to be false. 'I find no case against him' he said and tried to hand judgment firstly to the Jewish authorities and then to King Herod. Pilate made it clear he did not wish to be directly involved but eventually gave way to a crowd baying for execution, reluctantly ordering Jesus to die by scourging and crucifixion. After the scourging part of the process was carried out, a centurion instructed a bystander to assist with the weight of the heavy wooden cross when Jesus became too weak to carry it.

I have read that Jesus was removed from the cross after only six hours, having suffered much loss of blood through scourging and the application of thorns and nails. There are different estimates of how long it takes to die though the tortuous process of crucifixion, varying from a few minutes (through inability to respire adequately) to days. But the biblical record indicates that the Romans at the crucifixion site treated Jesus differently from the two thieves undergoing punishment alongside him – and their actions can be interpreted as being helpful rather than harmful.

When Jesus called for water on the cross, the soldiers offered him a sponge soaked in 'vinegar' also known as posca – a soured wine. But the soaked sponge could have been holding a sleeping potion instead, perhaps with some haemostatic properties. Henbane and mandrake were widely used in Roman medicine as anaesthetics and lemon juice was used as an astringent and haemostat. Thus Jesus could have been heavily sedated while on the cross, to reduce his suffering and to give the appearance of death. The practice of crucifracture (breaking of the legs) was used to hasten the death of those pinned to a cross. Both thieves crucified with Jesus had their legs broken but Jesus did not. According to the soldiers he was already dead or moribund. To demonstrate this, a lance was used to pierce his side and 'blood and water' trickled out, the leakage of water indicating odema and heart failure.

The reference to blood is uncertain but if it was still a red colour it would indicate that life was still present, as at the point of death deoxygenated blood turns black or almost black in colour. Jesus was removed from the cross shortly after this demonstration and his body released to his followers.

(Source: 'Did Pontius Pilate save Jesus from the cross?' by Di Tookey, Mensa Magazine, March 2005)

Select one answer for each of the following questions:

10 Which of the following adds least support to the idea that Pontius Pilate was responsible for saving Jesus?

(a) The fact that Roman soldiers would be unlikely to act on their own initiative

(b) The soldiers were unlikely to have accidentally taken Jesus from the cross while still alive

(c) Those thieves crucified with Jesus had their legs broken whereas he did not

(d) Pontius Pilate was regarded as being sympathetic to Christians

(e) Pontius Pilate initially cleared Jesus of the charges against him

11 Which of the following is not a necessary assumption underlying the theory put forward by the writer?

(a) It is possible to survive crucifixion

(b) There were no independent witnesses to the crucifixion

(c) Jesus was still alive when he was taken down from the cross

(d) The Roman soldiers had been prepared to collaborate with each other

(e) Jesus was removed from the cross relatively quickly

12 Which of the following could be said to be an opinion held by the writer?

(a) The traditional view is correct

(b) The traditional view has been superseded

(c) Pilate was responsible for saving Jesus

(d) There is some support in the Bible for the view put forward

(e) There is merit in reconsidering the traditional position

5   Racism

One of the paradoxes of European racism is that its language seems to be centred on, or engrossed with, the negative characteristics of the Other, blacks (libidinous, dirty, lazy …) or Jews (grasping, parasitical, cunning …), whereas the reverse side of the coin, the construction of European 'whiteness', is strangely absent. The overwhelming concern with the moral and physical features of the Other means that the European is occluded; within most texts white identity and its essential characteristics are implicit, taken for granted, and thus become the unspoken norm, the measuring stick, from which all other racial groups deviate. The invisibility of whiteness, its unstated nature, derives from the fact that in Western culture, through language and representation, whites have an almost universal and central role as the standard of biological and aesthetic excellence. Few Christians take conscious note, let alone realize the significance, of the fact that the predominant Western image of Jesus Christ, a Jewish Palestinian, is of a blue-eyed Aryan, with long, fair tresses. It is only in recent years that scholars have begun to explore more systematically the historical and psychological processes through which 'white' identity has been constructed. This 'self-reflection' by white Europeans is central to an understanding of how racism has historically functioned: as Richard Dyer comments: 'As long as race is something only applied to non-white peoples, as long as white people are not racially seen and named, they/we function as a human norm. Other people are raced, we are just people.'

Racist ideologies are invariably relational and work through binary oppositions between 'Us', the superior group that engages in the process of racialization, and 'Them', the inferior target group. Social psychology suggests that the 'Other' is crucial to the process by which boundaries or frontiers of identity are constructed: 'You know who you are, only by knowing who you are not.' A key feature of racial categorizations of the Other is that they invariably represent a projection and a negative inversion of the central moral, aesthetic and cultural values of the dominant group … when Europeans described blacks as inherently lazy, what they meant implicitly was that white Europeans were naturally dynamic, busy and enterprising. And likewise if blacks were libidinous, dirty, diseased, ugly, thieving, cowardly and superstitious, then Europeans were sexually restrained and monogamous, clean and healthy, fair and beautiful in form, honest and brave, intelligent and moral. Europeans, though racializing the Other, simultaneously racialized themselves. Such rules of binary opposition are common to many types of group boundary definition, from family, tribe and village, to nationalism and ethnicity. Where modern racism differs from these other forms is that it naturalizes difference in absolute biological or cultural terms so that barriers between collectivities are rendered impermeable. The French racist theoretician Vacher de Lapouge typically formulated this by the claim that it was impossible for immigrants to ever become French: 'The Prince can no more make a Frenchman from a Greek or a Moroccan than he can bleach the skin of a Negro, make round the eyes of a Chinaman or change a woman into a man.'

[Here] ... we are concerned with self-referential racism, the processes by which Europeans designated themselves as a superior race, as opposed to hetero-referential racism and the negative stereotyping of inferior Others ... Self-referential racism is of particular interest during the period before the First World War since European society was haunted by the spectre of its own degeneration, while, at the same time, many felt that they had discovered the solution to physical decay in the first scientific methods for the eugenic breeding of a superior racial type. The European racial project had as much to do with technologies for the transformation of its own group biological substance, as it did with the segregation, exclusion of extermination of 'inferior breeds'.

(Source: 'Racism in Europe' by Neil McMaster, Palgrave, 2001; reproduced with permission of Palgrave Macmillan)

Select one answer for each of the following questions:

13 What is meant be 'the Other'?

(a) Blacks and Jews

(b) Europeans

(c) People of a different race from oneself

(d) Westerners

(e) None of the above

14 What unstated assumption is central to the analysis surrounding Jesus being portrayed as a blue-eyed Aryan?

(a) Jesus was the son of God

(b) Jesus did not have blue eyes and long fair hair

(c) Those who depicted Jesus in the way described were not Christians

(d) The image of Jesus described is centuries old

(e) No alternative images of Jesus are used in the West

15 Which of the following is suggested in the passage?

(a) It is not possible to define one race without reference to others

(b) Racialization is more prevalent amongst Europeans

(c) It is impossible for immigrants to ever become naturalised

(d) Racial stereotypes involve a degree of self-reference

(e) Racism in Europe is increasing

6   Leadership

Many of the images associated with leadership have their roots in conflict. It is the stuff of generals who outwit their opponents, politicians who convince and channel groups into action, and people who take control of a crisis. We are directed to special individuals like Gandhi or Joan of Arc; Napoleon or Hitler. The stories around such people seem to show that there are moments of crisis or decision where the actions of one person are pivotal. They have a vision of what can, and should, be done and can communicate this to others. When these are absent there can be trouble. Quality of leadership is, arguably, central to the survival and success of groups and organizations. As The Art of War, the oldest known military text (circa 400 BC), puts it, 'the leader of armies is the arbiter of the people's fate, the man on whom it depends whether the nation shall be in peace or in peril'.

But what is leadership? It seems to be one of those qualities that you know when you see it, but is difficult to describe. There are almost as many definitions as there are commentators. Many associate leadership with one person leading. Four things stand out in this respect. First, to lead involves influencing others. Second, where there are leaders there are followers. Third, leaders seem to come to the fore when there is a crisis or special problem. In other words, they often become visible when an innovative response is needed. Fourth, leaders are people who have a clear idea of what they want to achieve and why. Thus, leaders are people who are able to think and act creatively in non-routine situations – and who set out to influence the actions, beliefs and feelings of others. In this sense being a 'leader' is personal. It flows from an individual's qualities and actions. However, it is also often linked to some other role such as manager or expert. Here there can be a lot of confusion. Not all managers, for example, are leaders; and not all leaders are managers.

In the recent literature of leadership (that is over the last 80 years or so) there have been four main 'generations' of theory:

1   Trait theories.
2   Behavioural theories.
3   Contingency theories.
4   Transformational theories.

It is important, as John van Maurik has pointed out, to recognize that none of the four 'generations' is mutually exclusive or totally time-bound. Although it is true that the progression of thinking tends to follow a sequential path, it is quite possible for elements of one generation to crop up much later in the writings of someone who would not normally think of himself or herself as being of that school. Consequently, it is fair to say that each generation has added something to the overall debate on leadership and that the debate continues.

This fourfold division of 'modern' (management) leadership can go under different titles (eg we might discuss charismatic rather than transformational leadership), and there are other possible candidates eg skill-based approaches and self-management or shared leadership (discussed elsewhere on these pages). However, these four formations can be seen as sharing some common qualities – and we can approach them as variations of the 'classical' model of leadership.

Leaders are people who are able to express themselves fully, says Warren Bennis. 'They also know what they want', he continues, 'why they want it, and how to communicate what they want to others, in order to gain their co-operation and support.' Lastly, 'they know how to achieve their goals'. But what is it that makes someone exceptional in this respect? As soon as we study the lives of people who have been labelled as great or effective leaders, it becomes clear that they have very different qualities. We only have to think of political figures like Nelson Mandela, Margaret Thatcher and Mao Zedong to confirm this.

Instead of starting with exceptional individuals many turned to setting out the general qualities or traits they believed should be present. Surveys of early trait research by Stogdill (1948) and Mann (1959) reported that many studies identified personality characteristics that appear to differentiate leaders from followers. However, as Peter Wright (1996) has commented, 'others found no differences between leaders and followers with respect to these characteristics, or even found people who possessed them were less likely to become leaders'. Yet pick up almost any of the popular books on the subject today and you will still find a list of traits that are thought to be central to effective leadership. The basic idea remains that if a person possesses these she or he will be able to take the lead in very different situations. At first glance, the lists seem to be helpful. But spend any time around them and they can leave a lot to be desired.

(Source: 'Classical leadership' by ME Doyle and MK Smith, Encyclopedia of Informal Education, 2001, www.infed.org)

Select one answer for each of the following questions:

16 What is the main idea in the extract?

(a) There is no theory that adequately explains successful leadership

(b) All the best leaders have led during a conflict

(c) It is impossible to predict whether someone will make a good leader

(d) There are a number of different theories to explain the phenomenon of leadership

(e) There is no merit in attempting to categorise those qualities that make a good leader

17 Which of the following is not suggested in the extract?

(a) Understanding of the theories underlying leadership has increased over time

(b) Conflict gives the opportunity to demonstrate leadership skills

(c) Leadership has traditionally been a prized quality

(d) A good leader does not share any of the qualities of a good manager

(e) Not all leaders share all the same qualities

18 Which of the following could be inferred to be the most likely formula for success in a given society?

(a) One excellent leader

(b) A large number of very good leaders

(c) A balance between good leadership and willingness to follow

(d) A large number of people prepared to follow orders

(e) A good understanding of what constitutes good leadership

7   Adoption

This morning's widespread press discussion of last night's Commons vote to allow adoption by unmarried couples (including same-sex couples) makes much of the political ructions that the issue has caused in the Conservative Party, but there is little reference to public opinion on the issue. The issue is not yet resolved. Separate amendments defining that a couple can be of the same sex or different sex will be voted on next week; and the final bill may still be blocked in the Lords.

The two propositions are bundled together in the bill, but they raise different questions, arouse different responses from the British public, and it is as well to consider them separately. True, most of the British public once found unmarried heterosexual couples and homosexuality alike morally unacceptable; but many now draw a distinction between the two and even those who have no wish to interfere with other people's sexual behaviour in private may have less 'modern' views on suitability of couples to bring up children.

As at least one newspaper reported this morning, a recent NCSR British Social Attitudes survey found 84% of the public would oppose the adoption of children by male homosexual couples. In MORI's last survey on this subject (for the Daily Mail in February 2000: Public Attitudes To Section 28), the majority against was much less overwhelming (55% disagreeing that 'Gay couples should be allowed to adopt children' to 33% agreeing), but a majority nonetheless.

But the position on co-habiting heterosexual couples is very different. MORI research last year for the British Association for Adoption and Fostering (BAAF Survey Shatters Stereotypes Of Potential Adopters) explored the general question of adoption by unmarried couples, as well another related controversial issue (not in question in the present bill), whether children should only be adopted by parents of the same ethnic group. On the latter question, there was a two-to-one majority for the status quo; but opinion was strongly in favour of allowing unmarried couples to adopt.

Approval of adoption by unmarried couples was fairly uniform across all groups – even among the morally conservative older generation, though significantly less supportive than the young, there was a clear majority of more than two-to-one, with 59% of the 55-and-overs agreeing and only 25% disagreeing. Tories were virtually as supportive as everybody else of unmarried couples being allowed to adopt, 64% agreeing that unmarried couples should be able to adopt, and 30% strongly agreeing.

The BSA survey picked out the degree to which the public draws a moral distinction between the two cases. It found that 37% of the public still think that sexual relations between two adults of the same sex are 'always wrong', while

34% think they are 'not wrong at all'. By contrast, only 9% think pre-marital sex between a man and a woman is 'always wrong', 62% that it is 'not wrong at all'. (As a yardstick of comparison, 61% think a married person having sex with someone other than his or her partner is always wrong, and 66% that sex between a girl and a boy who are both under 16 is always wrong.)

But then British attitudes to co-habitation outside marriage are generally much more liberal than perhaps they once were, and there is wide support for extending many of the civil rights that come with marriage to those who are unmarried. The British Social Attitudes survey found strong majority support for an unmarried but stable couple having many of the same legal rights as a married couple: in the case of 'an unmarried couple with no children who have been living together for ten years', three in five thought the woman should 'probably' or 'definitely' have the same rights to claim for financial support from the man as she would have had if they had been married; 92% thought she should have the same rights as a wife to remain after his death living in a house bought in his name; and, if the same couple had had a child, an overwhelming 97% would give the father the same rights to a say in his child's medical treatment as if he had been married to the mother.

If the question in adoption is a practical rather than a moral one (the best interests of the child), opposition to unmarried couples adopting is likely to be equally muted. Only 27% agreed that 'married couples make better parents than unmarried ones', whereas 42% disagreed. On the other hand, 53% agree that 'people who want children ought to get married'.

But in the case of homosexual couples, public opinion is likely to be very different. As we found a couple of years ago when investigating attitudes to the repeal of Section 28, even respondents who claim a generally tolerant attitude to homosexuality become far more cautious as soon as the question involves any contact with children. This change, unlike the other, is likely to be unpopular and the government would be well advised to be prepared to justify it to a hostile audience ...

(Source: 'Adoption: the baby and the bathwater' by Roger Mortimore, MORI, 17 May 2002)

Select one answer for each of the following questions:

19 What can be gathered to be the writer's opinion of how the government should proceed?

(a) Allow adoption by same-sex couples

(b) Allow adoption by unmarried heterosexual couples

(c) Allow adoption by both

(d) Allow adoption by neither

(e) None of the above

20 Which of the following is stated to meet with most public opposition?

(a) A married person having sex with someone other than their spouse

(b) Sex between a girl and a boy both aged under 16

(c) Adoption by lesbian and gay couples

(d) Adoption by unmarried couples

(e) Pre-marital sex

21 Which of the following does the writer suggest that public opinion has shifted least on in recent years?

(a) Adoption by same-sex couples

(b) Adoption by unmarried couples

(c) Rights of unmarried fathers

(d) Rights of unmarried mothers

(e) Rights of cohabiting couples

8   Frontlines

As the 20th century draws to a close, the United States stands as the world's pre-eminent power. Having led the West to victory in the Cold War, America faces an opportunity and a challenge: does the United States have the resolve to shape a new century favourable to American principles and interests? We seem to have forgotten the essential elements of the Reagan Administration's success: a military that is strong and ready to meet both present and future challenges; a foreign policy that boldly and purposefully promotes American principles abroad; and national leadership that accepts the United States' global responsibilities ...

Throughout his journal ... Columbus spoke of the native Americans with ... admiring awe: 'They are the best people in the world and above all the gentlest – without knowledge of what is evil – nor do they murder or steal ... they love their neighbors as themselves and have the sweetest talking in the world ... always laughing.' ... But then, in the midst of all this ... Columbus writes: 'They would make fine servants. With fifty men we could subjugate them all and make them do whatever we want.' And what did Columbus want? This is not hard to determine. In the first two weeks of his journal entries, there is one word that recurs 75 times: GOLD ... He ordered the natives to find a certain amount of gold within a certain period of time. And if they did not meet their quota, their arms were hacked off ... In the [first] Gulf War ... [w]hen Colin Powell was asked about Iraqi casualties he said that was 'really not a matter I am terribly interested in'.

When two brutal regimes clash, they always need as much human cannon fodder as possible. Saddam's policy is to keep his loyal Republican Guards close to him, to protect him from the US/UK invaders ... [w]hile he puts poorly equipped conscripts as cannon fodder to face US/UK forces in the desert, and threatens them with torture of their families should they desert the frontlines. The US has a different arm-twisting technique – to dangle offers of skills training, free college education and health care in the faces of poor Americans in order to get them to sign up ... The sad result is a disproportionate number of 'people of colour' on the US frontlines in the Gulf. During the first Gulf War, over 50 percent of front-line troops were non-white, although people of colour only make up around 10 percent of the overall population. Over 30 percent of US troops are non-white but they make up only 12 percent of officers.

In the summer [of 1999] ... Katherine Harris who was both co-chair of Dubya's presidential campaign and Florida's secretary of state responsible for elections employed a firm of consultants with strong Republican ties, Database Technologies, to clean up the state's electoral rolls. This included removing anyone 'suspected' of being an ex-felon, who cannot vote in Florida. That meant that 31 percent of all black men who have a past felony on their records were prevented from voting. The fact that most black Florida residents vote Democrat – 90 percent of those who were allowed to vote in 2000 voted for Al Gore – was pure coincidence.

US soldiers in Iraq are being asked to pray for President George W Bush. Thousands of marines have been given a pamphlet called 'A Christian's Duty', a mini prayer book which includes a tear-out section to be mailed to the White House pledging the soldier who sends it in has been praying for Bush ... The pamphlet, produced by a group called In Touch Ministries, offers a daily prayer to be made for the US president, a born-again Christian who likes to invoke his God in speeches ... Monday's reads 'Pray that the President and his advisers will be strong and courageous to do what is right regardless of critics'.

(Source: 'Frontline(s)' by Sian Sullivan, in Ephemera (volume 3, number 1, February 2003))

Select one answer for each of the following questions:

22 What does the writer imply to be the reason why ethnic minorities were over-represented on the US front line during the Gulf War?

(a) They were less aware of the potential consequences of war

(b) Many of them felt that they had less to lose

(c) Many were coerced into fighting against their will

(d) Many were enticed by the seemingly generous offers of the US government

(e) Many felt a misplaced loyalty to their country

23 Which of the following cannot be inferred from the passage?

(a) The use of a firm with strong Republican ties to cleanse Florida's electoral rolls was open to criticism

(b) The voters disqualified in Florida would have been allowed to vote had they had a different political allegiance

(c) The reference to 'suspected' felons created an inevitable degree of subjectivity in the application of the policy

(d) The policy implemented by Katherine Harris led to a substantial number of non-whites being disqualified from voting

(e) A majority of those disqualified from voting in Florida were likely to vote Democrat

24 What is the main idea in the passage?

(a) American society discriminates against ethnic minorities

(b) America is faced with an opportunity which it must not waste

(c) America's military policies are no different to those pursued by other countries

(d) The American political system is corrupt

(e) It is crucial for the US population to support George Bush's actions in Iraq

9   Existence of God

The Cosmological Argument

The cosmological argument is the argument that the existence of the world or universe is strong evidence for the existence of a God who created it. The existence of the universe, the argument claims, stands in need of explanation, and the only adequate explanation of its existence is that it was created by God.

Like most arguments for the existence of God, the cosmological argument exists in several forms; two are discussed here: the temporal, kalam cosmological argument (ie the first cause argument), and the modal 'argument from contingency'. The main distinguishing feature between these two arguments is the way in which they evade an initial objection to the argument. To explain this objection, and how the two forms of cosmological argument evade it, I'll use a simple, generic statement of the cosmological argument:

The Simple Cosmological Argument

(1) Everything that exists has a cause of its existence.

(2) The universe exists.

Therefore:

(3) The universe has a cause of its existence.

(4) If the universe has a cause of its existence, then that cause is God.

Therefore:

(5) God exists.

This argument is subject to a simple objection, introduced by asking, 'Does God have a cause of his existence?'

If, on the one hand, God is thought to have a cause of his existence, then positing the existence of God in order to explain the existence of the universe doesn't get us anywhere. Without God there is one entity the existence of which we cannot explain, namely the universe; with God there is one entity the existence of which we cannot explain, namely God. Positing the existence of God, then, raises as many problems as it solves, and so the cosmological argument leaves us in no better position than it found us, with one entity the existence of which we cannot explain.

If, on the other hand, God is thought not to have a cause of his existence, ie if God is thought to be an uncaused being, then this too raises difficulties for the simple cosmological argument. For if God were an uncaused being then his existence would be a counterexample to premise (1), 'Everything that exists has a cause of its existence'. If God exists but does not have a cause of his existence then premise (1) is false, in which case the simple cosmological argument is unsound. If premise (1) is false, ie if some things that exist do not have a cause, then the cosmological argument can be resisted on the ground that the universe itself might be such a thing. If God is claimed to exist uncaused, then, the simple cosmological argument fails.

Each of the two forms of cosmological argument discussed here is more sophisticated than the simple cosmological argument presented above. Each draws a distinction between the type of entity that the universe is and the type of entity that God is, and in doing so gives a reason for thinking that though the existence of the universe stands in need of explanation, the existence of God does not. Each therefore evades the objection outlined above.

The Kalam Cosmological Argument

In the case of the kalam cosmological argument, the distinction drawn between the universe and God is that the universe has a beginning in time. Everything that has a beginning in time, the kalam cosmological argument claims, has a cause of its existence. As the universe has a beginning in time, then, the argument concludes, the universe has a cause of its existence, and that cause is God.

The uncaused existence of God, who does not have a beginning in time, is consistent with the initial claim of this argument: 'Everything that has a beginning in time has a cause.' God's uncaused existence therefore does not give rise to the problem encountered in the discussion of the simple cosmological argument above.

The Argument from Contingency

In the case of the argument from contingency, the distinction drawn between the universe and God is that the existence of the universe is contingent, ie that the universe could have not existed. Everything that exists contingently, the argument from contingency claims, has a cause of its existence. As the universe is contingent, then, the universe has a cause of its existence, and that cause is God.

The uncaused existence of God, whose existence is not contingent but rather is necessary, is consistent with the initial claim of this argument: 'Everything contingent has a cause.' Again, then, God's uncaused existence does not give rise to the problem encountered in the discussion of the simple cosmological argument above.

Each of these two forms of the cosmological argument, then, evades the objection introduced above in a distinct way. The first does so by distinguishing between things that have a beginning in time and things that do not. The second does so by distinguishing between things that are contingent and things that are necessary. In each case it is argued that the universe is of the former kind, that God is of the latter kind, and that the principle that everything has a cause applies only to things of the former kind, and therefore not to God.

(Source: 'The cosmological argument' by Tim Holt, www.philosophyofreligion.info)

Select one answer for each of the following questions:

25 Which part or parts of the statement of the simple cosmological argument could be said to be propositions rather than facts or deductions?

(a) 1

(b) 3

(c) 5

(d) 1 and 3

(e) 2 and 5

26 What assumption must be made in order to follow the kalam cosmological argument?

(a) The concept of time is valid

(b) The universe has a beginning in time

(c) God does not have a beginning in time

(d) All of the above

(e) None of the above

27 Which of the following is stated in the passage?

(a) The simple cosmological argument has an inherent flaw

(b) God exists

(c) God does not exist

(d) The kalam cosmological argument and the argument from contingency receive more support than the simple cosmological argument

(e) The kalam cosmological argument and the argument from contingency are inconsistent with each other

10   Mathematics and Biology

Although mathematics has long been intertwined with the biological sciences, an explosive synergy between biology and mathematics seems poised to enrich and extend both fields greatly in the coming decades. Biology will increasingly stimulate the creation of qualitatively new realms of mathematics. Why? In biology, ensemble properties emerge at each level of organization from the interactions of heterogeneous biological units at that level and at lower and higher levels of organization (larger and smaller physical scales, faster and slower temporal scales). New mathematics will be required to cope with these ensemble properties and with the heterogeneity of the biological units that compose ensembles at each level.

The discovery of the microscope in the late 17th century caused a revolution in biology by revealing otherwise invisible and previously unsuspected worlds. Western cosmology from classical times through the end of the Renaissance envisioned a system with three types of spheres: the sphere of man, exemplified by his imperfectly round head; the sphere of the world, exemplified by the imperfectly spherical earth; and the eight perfect spheres of the universe, in which the seven (then known) planets moved and the outer stars were fixed. The discovery of a microbial world too small to be seen by the naked eye challenged the completeness of this cosmology and unequivocally demonstrated the existence of living creatures unknown to the Scriptures of Old World religions.

Mathematics broadly interpreted is a more general microscope. It can reveal otherwise invisible worlds in all kinds of data, not only optical. For example, computed tomography can reveal a cross-section of a human head from the density of X-ray beams without ever opening the head, by using the Radon transform to infer the densities of materials at each location within the head. Charles Darwin was right when he wrote that people with an understanding 'of the great leading principles of mathematics ... seem to have an extra sense'. Today's biologists increasingly recognize that appropriate mathematics can help interpret any kind of data. In this sense, mathematics is biology's next microscope, only better.

Conversely, mathematics will benefit increasingly from its involvement with biology, just as mathematics has already benefited and will continue to benefit from its historic involvement with physical problems. In classical times, physics, as first an applied then a basic science, stimulated enormous advances in mathematics. For example, geometry reveals by its very etymology (geometry) its origin in the needs to survey the lands and waters of Earth. Geometry was used to lay out fields in Egypt after the flooding of the Nile, to aid navigation, and to aid city planning. The inventions of the calculus by Isaac Newton and Gottfried Leibniz in the later 17th century were stimulated by physical problems such as planetary orbits and optical calculations.

In the coming century, biology will stimulate the creation of entirely new realms of mathematics. In this sense, biology is mathematics' next physics, only better. Biology will stimulate fundamentally new mathematics because living nature is qualitatively more heterogeneous than non-living nature. For example, it is estimated that there are 2,000–5,000 species of rocks and minerals in the earth's crust, generated from the hundred or so naturally occurring elements (Shipman estimates 2,000 minerals in Earth's crust). By contrast, there are probably between 3 million and 100 million biological species on Earth, generated from a small fraction of the naturally occurring elements. If species of rocks and minerals may validly be compared with species of living organisms, the living world has at least a thousand times the diversity of the non-living. This comparison omits the enormous evolutionary importance of individual variability within species. Coping with the hyper-diversity of life at every scale of spatial and temporal organization will require fundamental conceptual advances in mathematics.

(Source: Cohen JE (2004) Mathematics Is Biology's Next Microscope, Only Better; Biology Is Mathematics' Next Physics, Only Better. PLoS Biol 2(12): e439)

Select one answer for each of the following questions:

28 What is the main point made by the writer?

(a) Mathematics will prove to be more important to biology than the microscope

(b) Mathematics will prove to be as important to biology as the microscope

(c) Biology will prove to be more important to mathematics than physics

(d) Biology will prove to be as important to mathematics as physics

(e) The relationship between biology and mathematics is mutually beneficial

29 What can be gathered to be the main similarity between mathematics and the microscope?

(a) Both allow the viewing of previously unseen material

(b) Both allow previously unknown data to be collected

(c) Both were the major scientific advances of their age

(d) Both were comparatively simple discoveries

(e) The full potential of both was not initially obvious

30 Which of the following can be inferred from the article?

(a) Mathematics is more suited to the study of living than non-living nature

(b) Mathematics is more suited to the study of non-living than living nature

(c) Mathematics is equally suited to the study of both

(d) Mathematics is not suited to the study of either

(e) None of the above

MCQ ANSWER SHEET

Market Economies	Racism
1	13
2	14
3	15

Lutheranism	Leadership
4	16
5	17
6	18

Insults in Schools	Adoption
7	19
8	20
9	21

The Crucifixion	Frontlines
10	22
11	23
12	24

Existence of God	Mathematics and Biology
25	28
26	29
27	30

SECTION B: ESSAY

ANSWER **ONE** OF THE FOLLOWING QUESTIONS.

1   Is the House of Lords in need of further reform?

2   Do you think that depictions of sex and violence in the media should be more heavily censored?

3   Which is more important: equality of opportunity or equality of outcome?

4   Should National Service be reintroduced in the UK?

5   'The overriding aim of government policy should be to ensure the greatest happiness for the greatest number of people.' Do you agree?

ESSAY PLAN AND NOTES

NATIONAL ADMISSIONS TEST FOR LAW

SAMPLE TEST 5

The test has two separate sections, A and B.

Section A: Multiple Choice

This section is divided into 10 subsections; each subsection has three questions.

You should answer **all** 30 questions in Section A, selecting one of the possible answers and indicating your response on the answer sheet at the back of the section.

Time allowed: 80 minutes

Section B: Essay

This section has five essay questions.

You should select and answer **one** question in Section B. Your answer should be no more than four sides of A4. A page is provided at the back of the section for your essay plan and notes.

Time allowed: 40 minutes

SECTION A: MULTIPLE CHOICE

ANSWER **ALL** OF THE FOLLOWING QUESTIONS.

1   Racial Stereotypes

Historically stereotypes have played a fundamental role in the way that racial attitudes have been both structured as well as transmitted among both the educated elites and a semi-literate or illiterate public. As social psychologists note, the external world of perception is so immensely complex that the individual, to avoid a kind of sensory overload, is bound to shape and control the chaos of stimuli through imposing simplifying categories or patterns. The mental representations of the world that we all deploy are drawn from a 'vocabulary', a way of seeing, that is transmitted to us through socialization by parents and the wider society. Racial stereotypes, like so many other forms of prejudice (gender, class), have an extraordinary capacity to convey perceptions (and feelings) of the Other which bear little, if any, relationship to external reality. However, these highly distorted images, instead of being recognized for what they are, are understood as real-world entities. So powerfully can stereotypes substitute for reality that the racist can see in both black and Jew, even when they are directly perceived, qualities the very opposite of those that are being observed. Because stereotypes are generally part of a defensive mechanism, to protect established beliefs, they tend to serve a highly conservative function and can be transmitted from one generation to the next, or between classes, and geographically across society, with an astonishing durability. Stereotypes are central to an understanding of racism in Europe and their formation and dissemination, a rich web of signs and references, has been seen by Sander Gilman and others as crucial to the maintenance of prejudice within the wider society. The term 'black' added to any particular context or observation – as in 'The [black] criminal escaped' – has generally carried a complex set of cognitive and affective associations. The mind's eye would not only summon up images of physical appearance (often grossly distorted), but blackness might also activate negative feelings, a mood, a range of preferences. Our aim here is to explore the ways in which the stereotype of black came to constitute a universal feature of European culture, one that existed in all social classes and across the Continent, from the great cities of the West to the most underdeveloped, rural societies of the Mediterranean of Eastern Europe.

It needs to be made clear that contemporary writers often used the term 'black' as the most vague of categories that could include all darker skinned peoples, from Africa to India and New Zealand. During the Indian rebellion of 1857 officers, wishing to express contempt and loathing, consistently referred to Indians as 'niggers'. However, this expression was most commonly deployed by both race theorists as well as within popular discourse as a term for sub-

Saharan Africans, referred to in English as the 'Negro' (in French le nègre, in German the Neger). This categorization did not bear much relationship to the enormous physical and ethnic diversity of African peoples, rather it was a kind of composite being, a caricature that was constructed by reference to exaggerated features, like a crude 'identi-kit' image that constantly used the same simple components. The definition used by the famous Swiss anatomist Georges Cuvier in 1817 is quite typical of the standard formulation: 'The Negro race is confined to the south of Mount Atlas; it is marked by a black complexion, crisped or woolly hair, compressed cranium, and a flat nose. The projection of the lower part of the face, and the thick lips, evidently approximate it to the monkey tribe: the hordes of which it consists have always remained in the most complete state of utter barbarism.'

(Source: 'Racism in Europe' by Neil McMaster, Palgrave, 2001; reproduced with permission of Palgrave Macmillan)

Select one answer for each of the following questions:

1 What does the writer imply to be the main problem with racial stereotypes?

(a) They are often incorrect

(b) They are always used in a derogatory fashion

(c) They are inflexible to change

(d) They become understood as reality

(e) They are overused

2 Which of the following is not identified as being a characteristic of stereotypes?

(a) They do not originate from the truth

(b) They are a simplification

(c) They pass freely through society

(d) They are difficult to change

(e) They can permeate class

3 Which of the following could be inferred to be the principal reason why
   the term 'black' is so widely used?

(a) Ignorance

(b) Efficiency

(c) Laziness

(d) Political correctness

(e) Contempt

2   Home/Work Divide

The distinction between home and work as a principle for social organisation emerged as an 'effect' of the processes of industrialisation which took place during the eighteenth and nineteenth centuries. The change in patterns of behaviour required by the new forms of organisations led to very different conceptions of time and space that have persisted throughout the modern industrial period. Under the feudal system of production the home was the main productive unit within a community; little distinction was made between the activities necessary to ensure the running and maintenance of the domestic residence (the home) and those which led to the production of items which could be exchanged or traded. Although living conditions were often meagre, they were the focus around which an individual's activities took place and activities within the household would often be interrupted by agricultural demands which in turn were determined by the weather or changes in the season. But apart from adjusting their tasks to the vagaries of the climate, people were free to determine how and when they carried out their productive activities.

This close interweaving of work, home and community was disrupted as the burgeoning factory system increasingly meant that production was centralised under the watchful eye of the capitalist. As workers exchanged their labour for wages in a centralised work place, time became firmly equated with money. These changes meant that temporal discipline increased in importance as the labour force was required to adopt a more synchronised approach to their lives. In the mornings they left their homes, spent their days working collectively in factories or offices and then, at the appointed time, were free to return to their individual residences.

A different attitude to the use of space also emerged and led to the clear segregation of activity. Whereas one physical space had previously hosted multiple activities, distinct functions would not each take place within a specifically allocated area. Factories were built for the sole purpose of productive activity and would be inhabited only during set time periods. This spatial distinction occurred not only between but also within places with each part of the labour process being allocated a specific location within the factory. This compartmentalisation of space was also mirrored in the home. Residences that contained separate rooms for eating, sleeping, cooking, bathing and relaxation gradually replaced large communal rooms that had contained all domestic activity.

The newly centralised working environment was portrayed as rational, efficient and alienating, but the home, having become spatially and temporally separated, was seen as something distinct. The wholesome values with which it was associated stood in direct contrast to the activities and values of the modern workplace. But although presenting these as questionable and undesirable, the domestic sphere did not directly challenge the modern organisation of work. Instead it was increasingly portrayed by the bourgeois middle classes as a place to accommodate and temper the vagaries of the modern world, a 'haven in the heartless world'.

Far from being separate and distinct as these descriptions of 'home' and 'work' suggest, the two remained highly interlinked during the industrial period, flowing into and reinforcing each other. The exclusivity and distinctions implicit in the division have never fully been realised; although the home is often portrayed as a private sanctuary, it has never been a complete escape, free from the intrusions of work or the public sphere. In the eighteenth century, legislation was passed permitting entrance to workers' houses to ascertain whether they were pilfering cloth from merchants. In the nineteenth century neither working class homes, which suffered from overcrowding, or middle and upper class homes, which employed maids, gardeners and other servants, offered the individual any privacy. In more recent times the proliferation of email and mobile phones make it difficult to find complete privacy within your own four walls. Such interconnections between the two spheres have been further highlighted in studies of family-run businesses and farming communities. Contrary to the popular portrayal of the differing character of these two spheres, Hochchild's study of females working the 'double shift' of home and work found that it was the workplace that was seen as both the place to escape to and the source of beneficial and satisfying relationships. However, despite these interconnections, the construction of home and work as separate and the differing meanings attributed to each have persisted throughout modernity.

(Source: 'Dialectics of dualism: the symbolic importance of the home/work divide' by Emma Surman, in Ephemera (volume 2, number 3, August 2002))

Select one answer for each of the following questions:

4 Which of the following was not a necessary consequence of industrialisation?

(a) The building of factories

(b) The move away from the home as the main productive unit

(c) The adoption of a more synchronised way of life by the labour force

(d) The division of communal rooms within homes

(e) The equation of time with money

5   Which of the following is not a view put forward in the extract?

(a) It is desirable for there to be a separation been work and home

(b) Total privacy is an unachievable aim

(c) Home and work are different in character

(d) Workers have a free choice as to where they live

(e) Home means different things to different people

6   Which of the following cannot be inferred from the passage?

(a) Industrialisation reduced the influence of the seasons on work levels

(b) Workers had more free time before industrialisation

(c) After industrialisation it became more common for people to be employed by others rather than working for themselves

(d) The middle classes had a degree of self-interest in promoting the home/work divide

(e) Gender accounts for some of the differences in how home and work are respectively perceived

3   Advertising

For advertising types, the pound comes in all sorts of colours. There's the pink pound (free-spending gay shoppers), the green pound (eco-consumers) and the recently-identified brown pound (ethnic minorities have money, marketers have discovered). Before all that was the grey pound – a cliché of the advertising industry since at least the 1970s, according to Reg Starkey, a veteran adman and creative consultant at agency Millennium Direct.

Every creative director knows that the over-50s – currently 20 million strong, and growing fast – hold 80% of the nation's wealth. Trouble is, no one wants to do anything about it: according to a recent Age Concern survey, two-thirds of elderly consumers felt advertising portrays them negatively, and three-quarters simply didn't relate to it at all.

'If you see someone over 40 in an agency, chances are they're either a client or the chairman,' says Jean-Paul Treguer, head of Senioragency, an advertising firm that targets the mature consumer. It doesn't have to be this way. Nor, say advertising professionals, do agencies have to go to traumatic lengths to make their commercials appeal to a broader age-group.

In fact, a few simple rules would suffice:

Don't Just Entertain – Inform

There is a long-established piece of advertising wisdom that says while young people want adverts to make them laugh, older people want hard facts. Like most wisdom, it's only slightly true. Older people are far more rational customers than the flighty young, and need serious persuasion from anyone wanting their money, but they like a laugh as much as anyone.

'Thing is, if there's a hole in an ad, they will spot it,' says John O'Sullivan, chairman of MWO Advertising.

Having often more time and more patience than the young, older shoppers will research their purchases in far greater detail, says Mr Starkey. An effective advert, therefore, has to contribute to that research, rather than simply trying to push the emotional or cultural buttons that turn on the young.

Don't Count Out Celebrities

The use of the famous, or nearly famous, is frequently seen as the last gasp of a copywriter running short of inspiration. In fact, argues Mr Treguer, celebrity role models – what he calls 'generational heroes' – can deliver the goods. In France, advertisers use a range of celebrities d'un certain age, but still with some va-va-voom: Catherine Deneuve, Johnny Hallyday, former cyclist Raymond Poulidor – at 66 still the country's favourite sportsman.

In Britain, meanwhile, the market is sewn up by a small gerontocracy of actors – notably former comic actress June Whitfield, whose perennial reappearance as the face of the elderly provokes cries of despair. 'These are precisely the sorts of ads that are made by the teenage copywriters,' groans Mr Starkey.

Quality Counts

By and large, in fact, the sort of ads that old people like are the sort of ads that everyone likes – the big-budget, cinematic numbers that admen love making and companies hate paying for. In recent years, there has been a rash of these. Pundits pick out a Ford campaign where modern cars were digitally inserted into vintage film milieux alongside Steve McQueen and Dennis Hopper.

Guinness, despite its apparent attempts to court younger drinkers, is another crossover hit, especially for its 'Swim Black' spot, where an ageing strongman discovers his powers are on the wane. 'It's beautifully made, and it brings in images that speak directly to an older audience,' says Martin Smith, managing director of Millennium Direct.

Remember: Old People are Different. Or are They?

The great debate in the industry is over whether it's worth advertising to older people at all. One camp argues that elderly consumers form their tastes early in life, and barely budge after 40 – and almost never in response to advertising. The other camp insists that the old are just as malleable and changeable as the young – they just need special handling.

The second camp seems to be winning out. 'Everyone has misconceptions about being old until they are old themselves,' says John O'Sullivan. 'Anyone who thinks we stop taking in fresh information about products when we're over 50 must be mad.'

In the opposing camp is agency Young & Rubicam. In a controversial report two years ago, Y&R director Simon Silvester argued that consumer tastes are more or less set in stone by the age of 35 – a process of petrification that can be measured by a person's musical tastes.

(Source: 'Ad nausea hits the grey market' by James Arnold, 30 November 2004, from BBC News at www.bbcnews.com)

Select one answer for each of the following questions:

7   What of the following is not stated in the article?

(a) The focus on older consumers is not a new thing

(b) Older consumers are wealthier than younger ones

(c) Older consumers are less trusting than younger ones

(d) It is difficult to make advertisements which appeal to all age groups

(e) Advertisements aimed at older consumers tend to perpetuate a stereotype

8   Which of the following is not identified as being a reason for the tendency to focus advertising on younger consumers?

(a) Their greater disposable income

(b) The typical profile of most advertising agencies

(c) Perception of the reluctance of older consumers to part with money

(d) Perception of younger consumers as impressionable

(e) Perceived constrictions on content of advertisements aimed at older people

9   What is identified as the key difference between an effective advertisement targeted at a younger audience and one targeted at an older audience?

(a) Humour

(b) Use of celebrities

(c) Factual content

(d) Quality

(e) Creativity

4   American Political Parties

Is the whole concept of political parties on the decline in the American political scenario? Is the nation moving away from parties to personalities as elections become more media responsive?

During the Nineteenth Century, the two parties most associated with America had clear and defined roles so that both could be clearly identified as parties with a political function. Both the Republican and the Democrat parties controlled elections, organised Congress and had government offices allocated to them. However, this century saw the peak of their power as since then and more so as the Twentieth Century progressed, their power at a national political level has decreased. The increase in the number of independent voters and the importance of the media have all lead to a decreased role for both parties.

By the end of the Twentieth Century, both parties were using professionals to run their election campaigns and the input of well-meaning party amateurs has been swiftly pushed sideways if only because the stakes are too high in a national election for the tasks involved to be handed to and handled by amateurs. The concept of party does still exist in America but political analysts now refer to 50 Democrat parties and 50 Republican parties as opposed to two extending their power across the nation.

American political parties have to operate within a very diverse society and a federal system of government; they, therefore, tend to be broadly based coalitions of interests organised in a decentralised way rather than tightly disciplined hierarchical structures. The organisation of American parties has traditionally lacked a strong central authority.

In America, politics is often thought to be more based on personalities than policies and party unity. This was probably more true in the 2000 campaign when the Republican Party played on Al Gore's surname, tagging him 'Al Bore'. Likewise, the Democrats retaliated by digging up political dirt on George W Bush's past business life playing on the fact of whether a man with Bush's alleged background in business and earlier lifestyle problems could make a trusted national leader.

An argument in favour of supporting the view that parties remain relevant is that political recruitment of potential government leaders occurs through the political parties. Close ties and a long history of party connections are usually needed to become a candidate to lead the party. The vast majority of the political elite has risen through the party systems.

In America, the national parties play a relatively limited role in electoral politics because over recent years, election campaigns have become candidate-orientated rather than party-orientated. Parties in America used to control elections: candidates were nominated by the party through what was effectively a 'boss' system. Voter loyalty was high and parties concentrated on getting their votes out. There are now more candidate-centred campaigns; activists prefer to work on behalf of individual men and women and are concerned solely with their victories rather than the success of the party ticket as a whole. Often, party workers at state and local levels will distance themselves from a presidential candidate who is unpopular in their state.

Direct primaries have strengthened the grass-roots of the parties at the expense of the centre. They have also encouraged the development of candidate-orientated elections which have helped to undermine party loyalty in Congress. Candidates often have to fight to gain party nomination and they do this with personal organisations rather than using the party. So the advent of the direct primary in America has also added to the apparent lessening influence of the political parties. The parties have lost direct control over the nomination process as more candidates are being selected by the primary process.

National parties in America do not lay down a strong party line because their control of the legislature is insufficiently strong to enable them to enforce the line … Candidate-orientated election campaigns lead to candidate-orientated government. At a presidential level, a candidate, once adopted as the party's candidate, has the freedom to determine policies and the party is expected to get behind these policies and support them.

However, there is evidence that America is still heavily influenced by political parties. With the exception of the support given to Ross Perot and his Reform Party primarily in the 1992 election when he got 19% of the national support (but no success in the Electoral College), independent candidates have not been successful in America. In 2000, Ralph Nader failed to make any dent in the overall result in that the Electoral College only needed to take into account the results achieved by the Democrat Gore and the Republican Bush. Any other party was smothered in the election and the chances of an independent candidate or a different party making any inroads into the electoral structure barely exist.

The electoral system favours only the two main parties and in this sense the concept of party influence is great. Both parties have the ability to fund elections: other parties are severely hampered by their lack of financial backing. Which major backer would financially support a party that had no chance whatsoever of gaining political power? Therefore the major backers support the two main parties and this support gives both parties momentum and political relevance. The two main parties are also capable of adjusting their policies to cope with policies raised by minority parties. By absorbing these policies, the

Republicans and Democrats tend to politically stifle other parties – hence the total dominance of the Republican and Democrat parties in America.

(Source: 'The concept of the party is no longer relevant' by Christopher Trueman, www.historylearningsite.co.uk)

Select one answer for each of the following questions:

10 Which of the following is a cause of the weak party system?

(a) Increased focus on personalities

(b) Use of direct primaries

(c) Distancing of party workers from unpopular presidential candidates

(d) Candidate-centred campaigns

(e) Freedom of candidates to determine their own policies

11 What can be inferred to be the main obstacle to an independent candidate or party gaining power?

(a) Lack of funding

(b) Lack of policies

(c) The Electoral College

(d) Inexperience

(e) Traditional strength of main two parties

12 All of these are arguments supporting the strength of the main political parties except:

(a) The method of recruiting candidates

(b) The federal system of government

(c) The limited success of independent candidates

(d) The major parties' flexibility to incorporate new policies

(e) The financial resources available to major parties

5   Civil Society

The Civil Society Puzzle

According to whose version one prefers, 'civil society' means 'fundamentally reducing the role of politics in society by expanding free markets and individual liberty' (Cato), or it means the opposite – 'the single most viable alternative to the authoritarian state and the tyrannical market' (WSF), or for those more comfortable in the middle ground of politics, it constitutes the missing link in the success of social democracy (central to Third Way thinking and supposedly-compassionate conservatism), the 'chicken soup of the social sciences' – you know those books that provide much-needed comfort without that much substance, so if you can't explain something, put it down to civil society! Adam Seligman, tongue firmly in cheek, calls civil society the 'new analytic key that will unlock the mysteries of the social order', Jeremy Rifkin calls it 'our last, best hope', the UN and the World Bank see it as the key to 'good governance' and poverty-reducing growth, and even the real reason for war against Iraq – to kick-start civil society in the Middle East, according to Administration officials in Washington DC. As a new report from the Washington-based Institute for Foreign Policy Analysis puts it, 'the US should emphasize civil society development in order to ensure regional stability in central Asia' – forgetting, of course, that citizens groups have been a prime cause of destabilization in every society since the Pharaohs.

Some claim that civil society is a specific product of the nation state and capitalism; others see it as a universal expression of the collective life of individuals, at work in all countries and stages of development but expressed in different ways according to history and context. Some see it as one of three separate sectors, others as intimately interconnected or even inter-penetrated by states and markets. Is civil society the preserve of groups predefined as democratic, modern, and 'civil', or is it home to all sorts of associations, including 'uncivil' society – like militant Islam and American militias – and traditional associations based on inherited characteristics like religion and ethnicity that are so common in Africa and Asia?

Are families in or out, and what about the business sector? Is civil society a bulwark against the state, an indispensable support, or dependent on government intervention for its very existence? Is it the key to individual freedom through the guaranteed experience of pluralism or a threat to democracy through special interest politics? Is it a noun – a part of society, an adjective – a kind of society, an arena for societal deliberation, or a mixture of all three? Can you build a civil society through foreign aid and intervention, or is this just another imperial fantasy? What is to be done with a concept that seems so unsure of itself that definitions are akin to nailing jelly to the wall? And in any case, do these questions really matter, except to a small band of academics who study this stuff for a living?

Civil Society – Gaining Some Clarity

When an idea can mean so many things it probably means nothing, so I think the time has come to be rid of the term completely or, now that it has acquired a life of its own, to at least be clearer with each other about the different interpretations in play. Consensus is impossible given the range of views on offer, but clarity is not, and greater clarity can be the springboard for a better conversation about the promise and potential of civil society as a basis of hope and action for the future, and about the pitfalls of using this term as a political slogan or a shelter for dogma and ideology. Recognizing that civil society does indeed mean different things to different people is one of the keys to moving forward, because it moves us beyond false universals and entrenched thinking. And for those who want to discard the term completely my plea would be, not yet – 'don't throw the baby out with the bathwater'. ... [I]deas about civil society can survive and prosper in a rigorous critique.

In part, the fog that has enveloped this term is the result of an obsession with one particular interpretation of civil society as a part of society – the world of voluntary associations – forgetting that there are earlier and later traditions that have just as much to offer. It was Alexis de Tocqueville (the man you probably all remember from your schooldays) that started this craze on his visits across the Atlantic in the 1830s, who saw America's rich tapestry of associational life as the key to its emerging democracy. 'Americans of all dispositions have an incurable tendency to form voluntary associations.' Originally however, civil society, from Aristotle to Thomas Hobbes, represented a kind of society that was identified with certain ideals. And in modern societies, realizing these ideals – like political equality or peaceful coexistence – requires action across many different institutions, not just voluntary associations. Most recently, philosophers have developed a new set of theories about civil society as the 'public sphere' – the places where citizens argue with one-another about the great questions of the day and negotiate a constantly-evolving sense of the 'common' or 'public' interest.

(Source: 'Civil society' by M Edwards, Encyclopedia of Informal Education, 2001, www.infed.org)

Select one answer for each of the following questions:

13 What is the main point made by the writer in the first four paragraphs of the passage?

(a) Civil society is used as a vague term when people are unable to find a more appropriate term

(b) Unrealistic hopes are placed upon the potential success of civil society

(c) Civil society influences business and family life

(d) Civil society is not a feature of all countries

(e) Before any meaningful discussion can be had about civil society, it is necessary to define what is meant by the term

14 Which of the following aims could be inferred to be the least controversial inclusion in a definition of civil society?

(a) Reducing state intervention in politics

(b) Reducing conflict

(c) Improving the quality of a particular society

(d) Promoting democracy

(e) Increasing individual freedom

15 Which of the following views could not be said to be held by the writer?

(a) There is merit in studying different definitions of civil society

(b) There is a common desire to seek more effective models of society

(c) A perfect model of society can always ultimately be found

(d) Different people will always have different agendas in relation to civil society

(e) Co-operation is essential to progress

6   Life in Other Worlds

I need a 'tricorder' – the convenient, hand-held device featured on Star Trek that can detect life forms even from orbit. Unfortunately, we don't have a clue how a tricorder might work, since life forms don't seem to have any observable property that distinguishes them from inanimate matter. Furthermore, we lack a definition of life that can guide a search for life outside Earth. How can we find what we can't define? An answer may lie in the observation that life uses a small, discrete set of organic molecules as basic building blocks. On the surface of Europa and in the subsurface of Mars, we can search for alien but analogous patterns in the organics.

The obvious diversity of life on Earth overlies a fundamental biochemical and genetic similarity. The three main polymers of biology – the nucleic acids, the proteins, and the polysaccharides – are built from 20 amino acids, five nucleotide bases, and a few sugars, respectively. Together with lipids and fatty acids, these are the main constituents of biomass: the hardware of life. The DNA and RNA software of life is also common, indicating shared descent. But with only one example of life – life on Earth – it is not all that surprising that we do not have a fundamental understanding of what life is. We don't know which features of Earth life are essential and which are just accidents of history.

Our lack of data is reflected in our attempts to define life. Koshland lists seven features of life: (1) program (DNA), (2) improvisation (response to environment), (3) compartmentalization, (4) energy, (5) regeneration, (6) adaptability, and (7) seclusion (chemical control and selectivity). A simpler definition is that life is a material system that undergoes reproduction, mutation, and natural selection. Cleland and Chyba have suggested that life might be like water, hard to define phenomenologically, but easy to define at the fundamental level. But life is like fire, not water – it is a process, not a pure substance. Such definitions are grist for philosophical discussion, but they neither inform biological research nor provide a basis for the search for life on other worlds.

The simplest, but not the only, proof of life is to find something that is alive. There are only two properties that can determine if an object is alive: metabolism and motion. (Metabolism is used here to include an organism's life functions, biomass increase, and reproduction.) All living things require some level of metabolism to remain viable against entropy. Movement (either microscopic or macroscopic) in response to stimuli or in the presence of food can be a convincing indicator of a living thing. But both metabolism (fire) and motion (wind) occur in nature in the absence of biology.

The practical approach to the search for life is to determine what life needs. The simplest list is probably: energy, carbon, liquid water, and a few other elements such as nitrogen, sulfur, and phosphorus. Life requires energy to maintain itself against entropy, as does any self-organizing open system. In the memorable words of Erwin Schrödinger, 'It feeds on negative entropy.' On Earth, the vast majority of life forms ultimately derive their energy from sunlight. The only other source of primary productivity known is chemical energy, and there are only two ecosystems known, both methanogen-based, that rely exclusively on chemical energy (that is, they do not use sunlight or its product, oxygen). Photosynthetic organisms can use sunlight at levels below the level of sunlight at the orbit of Pluto; therefore, energy is not the limitation for life. Carbon, nitrogen, sulfur, and phosphorus are the elements of life, and they are abundant in the Solar System. Indeed, the Sun and the outer Solar System have more than 10,000 times the carbon content of the bulk of Earth. When we scan the other worlds of our Solar System, the missing ecological ingredient for life is liquid water. It makes sense, then, that the search for liquid water is currently the first step in the search for life on other worlds. The presence of liquid water is a powerful indication that the ecological prerequisites for life are satisfied.

(Source: McKay CP (2004) What Is Life – and How Do We Search for It in Other Worlds? PLoS Biol 2(9): e302)

Select one answer for each of the following questions:

16 Which of the following is said to conclusively demonstrate the existence of life?

(a) Metabolism

(b) Motion

(c) Either

(d) Both

(e) Neither

17 Which of the following suggestions are not put forward in the article?

(a) No device exists that can detect life forms from orbit

(b) Life is hard to define phenomenologically but easy to define fundamentally

(c) Liquid water indicates the presence of life

(d) Life is a material system

(e) Life is a process

18 Which of the following is a major reason why a definition of life is difficult to formulate?

(a) We are not sure what components life requires

(b) Different life forms do not share characteristics

(c) Life is a process rather than a pure substance

(d) We are not sure which features of life are essential

(e) All forms of life are formed from the same amino acids

7   Ageing

Ageing is a physical phenomenon happening to our bodies, so at some point in the future, as medicine becomes more and more powerful, we will inevitably be able to address ageing just as effectively as we address many diseases today. I claim that we are close to that point because of the SENS (Strategies for Engineered Negligible Senescence) project to prevent and cure ageing. It is not just an idea: it's a very detailed plan to repair all the types of molecular and cellular damage that happen to us over time. And each method to do this is either already working in a preliminary form (in clinical trials) or is based on technologies that already exist and just need to be combined.

The Alternative View

Nothing in gerontology even comes close to fulfilling the promise of dramatically extended lifespan. This means that all parts of the project should be fully working in mice within just 10 years and we might take only another 10 years to get them all working in humans. When we get these therapies, we will no longer all get frail and decrepit and dependent as we get older, and eventually succumb to the innumerable ghastly progressive diseases of old age. We will still die, of course – from crossing the road carelessly, being bitten by snakes, catching a new flu variant etcetera – but not in the drawn-out way in which most of us die at present.

So, will this happen in time for some people alive today? Probably. Since these therapies repair accumulated damage, they are applicable to people in middle age or older who have a fair amount of that damage. I think the first person to live to 1,000 might be 60 already. It is very complicated, because ageing is. There are seven major types of molecular and cellular damage that eventually become bad for us – including cells being lost without replacement and mutations in our chromosomes. Each of these things is potentially fixable by technology that either already exists or is in active development.

'Youthful Not Frail'

The length of life will be much more variable than now, when most people die at a narrow range of ages (65 to 90 or so), because people won't be getting frailer as time passes. There is no difference between saving lives and extending lives, because in both cases we are giving people the chance of more life. The average age will be in the region of a few thousand years. These numbers are guesses, of course, but they're guided by the rate at which the young die these days. If you are a reasonably risk-aware teenager today in an affluent, non-violent neighbourhood, you have a risk of dying in the next year of well under one in 1,000, which means that if you stayed that way forever you would have a 50/50 chance of living to over 1,000. And remember, none of that time would be lived in frailty and debility and dependence – you would be youthful, both physically and mentally, right up to the day you mis-time the speed of that oncoming lorry.

Should We Cure Ageing?

Curing ageing will change society in innumerable ways. Some people are so scared of this that they think we should accept ageing as it is. I think that is diabolical – it says we should deny people the right to life. The right to choose to live or to die is the most fundamental right there is; conversely, the duty to give others that opportunity to the best of our ability is the most fundamental duty there is. There is no difference between saving lives and extending lives, because in both cases we are giving people the chance of more life. To say that we shouldn't cure ageing is ageism, saying that old people are unworthy of medical care.

(Source: 'We will be able to live to 1,000' by Aubrey de Grey, 3 December 2004, from BBC News at www.bbcnews.com)

Select one answer for each of the following questions:

19 **What can be gathered to be the main cause of death in our society at the moment?**

(a) Molecular and cellular damage

(b) Accidents

(c) Disease

(d) None of the above

(e) There is insufficient evidence to say

20 **What does the writer suggest will be prevented by the new technology?**

(a) Death

(b) The effects of ageing

(c) Illness

(d) All of the above

(e) There is insufficient evidence to say

21 **Which of the following cannot be gathered to be a consequence of the new technology?**

(a) A dramatically reduced risk of dying imminently for younger people

(b) A dramatically reduced risk of dying imminently for older people

(c) Better health in old age

(d) An increased life expectancy

(e) A reduced incidence of frailty in older people

8   Population

The Malthusian Theory of Overpopulation

Until the middle of the eighteenth century, the population of Britain grew slowly. But, from then on, growth became more rapid, and in 1798 Thomas Malthus's first essay on 'The Principle of Population as it affects the future improvement of society' made it a major subject of discussion.

Malthus began from two postulates: (i) that the passion between the sexes is necessary and will remain nearly in 'its present state'; and (ii) that food is necessary to the existence of man. Given these postulates, his arguments forced him to conclude that: (i) the population will, if unchecked, double itself every twenty-five years; and (ii) the means of subsistence can, at a maximum, increase by only the same amount every twenty-five years. In other words, while the population multiplies in a geometric progression, food supplies increase in an arithmetic progression.

The first conclusion was based on information collected by Malthus on the populations of various countries. But the second was supported by no evidence whatsoever. In order to substantiate it, Malthus appealed to the 'known property of lan'. Here he was virtually relying on the law of diminishing returns, although that was not precisely stated until some fifty years later.

From these two conclusions the important result followed that the power of population to increase was 'infinitely greater that the power of the earth to produce subsistence for man'. In short, the population would always tend to outgrow its food supply.

Since man cannot live without food, what, Malthus asked, kept population within its means of subsistence? The answer he found in certain 'checks'. First, there were 'positive checks' involving misery – famine, war, disease. Second, there were 'preventive checks' – which, with one exception, all involved 'vice', including contraception. The exception was 'moral restraint', by which was meant deliberately refraining from marrying at an early age. Since this was a remote possibility, the outlook for civilisation was gloomy: in the long run mankind could only expect a subsistence level of existence. Moreover, social policies to alleviate poverty would be self-defeating.

Malthus's 'Blind Spots'

Although at the beginning of the nineteenth century Malthus's views were widely accepted, the final tragedy of starvation, the logical outcome of his two conclusions, has not occurred. Where, therefore, did Malthus go wrong?

First, we must note that to some extent his argument was illogical, for he did not deal with the fact, well known at the time, that, in spite of the rapid increase in the population over the previous fifty years, people on average were no worse off. This showed that the means of subsistence must at least have increased in proportion. Had Malthus possessed a precisely formulated law of diminishing returns, he could have based his argument on a fixed total supply of land which would sooner or later make itself felt as the population increased.

Second, Malthus was preoccupied with people as consumers. He failed to see that, by and large, a consumer is also a producer, for 'with every mouth God sends a pair of hands'. Here again a fixed supply of land with consequent diminishing returns could have overcome this objection.

Third, Malthus did not foresee change. On the one hand the geometric increase in Britain's population did not come about, because of emigration and above all because of the reduction in the size of the family with rising living standards. On the other hand, improved agricultural techniques and the vast increase in imports meant that Britain's food supplies were not limited to increasing in an arithmetic progression.

Thus Malthus's arguments have validity only when there are fixed resources, such as land or energy reserves. It is, for instance, the limited supply of land which brings about a Malthusian situation in the Far East today.

(Source: 'Mastering Economics' by Jack Harvey, Macmillan, 1994; reproduced with permission of Palgrave Macmillan)

Select one answer for each of the following questions:

22 Which of the following can be gathered from the passage?

(a) Malthus's prediction about available food supplies was incorrect

(b) The population did not increase during the period on which Malthus's predictions were based

(c) All consumers are also producers

(d) The historical evidence on which Malthus based his theories was flawed

(e) Malthus's postulates were incorrect

23 What is meant by the suggestion that 'Malthus did not foresee change'?

(a) The two initial postulates were too generalised

(b) The 'checks' envisaged were incorrect

(c) He failed to account for a number of externalities

(d) He failed to consider the law of diminishing returns

(e) He underestimated the supply of available land

24 Which of the following assumptions does the author suggest was being made by Malthus?

(a) The size of the population and the amount of food capable of being produced are not linked

(b) There is an absolute limit to the possible increase in available food

(c) The experience of previous population growth was irrelevant

(d) Methods of farming were likely to change

(e) Not all land is capable of yielding the same amount of food

9   Greek Gods

Pan is a Greek God who lives on the zone between nature and culture, between beasts and humans. He inhabits the space that is neither that of history or community nor that of pure nature: the fields and meadows just outside the city walls are his dominion. He is two-formed and two-natured, human and animal, a man and a goat. When humans live inside the house and beasts in their dens or in their nests, Pan like a herdsman sleeps in a cowshed. And the herdsman is big, tall and a good warrior. He is a messenger between the city and the fields. Plato equates Pan with language; like Pan, language has a snake's tongue; it is good both in lying and in saying the truth. Pan declares all things and he is the perpetual mover of all things. Panic and the disorder that leads to panicking are due to the growing distance between the Gods and men. They destroy or deny communication between the Gods and the human community and between men and lead humans back to bestiality. Pan transforms human being into a gregarious animal and lets the herd instinct proper to humans free so that it is possible to reorganize the community using 'human nature' as a tool in the reorganization. Panic, like terror, has been a privileged instrument in modern politics because it spreads fast without discussions and it is impossible to contest or go against it.

Historically panic functions as a factor of hoarding on a planetary scale. But, despite the gravity of the crises that have punctuated the coming of the New Economy, one cannot avoid being stricken by the weakening of this panic factor.

Let us ask the question then: in the era of the New Economy, what is Pan (God-goat of nature) to which the experience of panic refers, the experience of that occasion of strong anxiety generated by a fear so intolerable as to obstruct the organizing of thought and action, capable of depersonalising, of inducing impersonal behaviour and mass mimetism? What is the 'herd instinct' that produces, brings to light the instinct of 'everything or nothing' that liberates the latent anxiety? 'If Pan is the God of nature "within", then he is our instinct.'

Already the fact that Pan – notwithstanding his mythological 'naturalness' – is a creature that does not exist in the natural world (he is, in fact, half human and half animal), that he is a creature totally imaginable, permits us to define the 'herd instinct' that is within us and that feeds our instincts as a metaphor. As Jung explains, if instinct acts and at the same time forms an image of its action (produces that which is its representation), then 'to be at the mercy of' the depersonalisation that panic brings about constitutes the experience of a behaviour that is simultaneously primary and intelligent. There's a method in panic.

We have come to this paradoxical conclusion studying the genealogy of financial crises, in particular the crisis of 1929, as the explosion of the same rationality of speculation, the activity that, as Keynes has written, consists of foreseeing the psychology of the market, or 'outwitting the crowd'. 'Knowing that our own individual judgment is worthless' – writes Keynes – 'we endeavour to fall back on the judgment of the rest of the world which is perhaps better informed'. That is, we endeavour to conform with the behaviour of the majority or the average. The psychology of a society of individuals each of whom is endeavouring to copy the others leads to what we may strictly term a conventional judgment.

(Source: 'Who killed God Pan?' by Christian Marazzi (translated by Taina Rajanti), in Ephemera (volume 4, number 3, August 2004))

Select one answer for each of the following questions:

25 What does the writer mean by language having a snake's tongue?

(a) Words mean different things to different people

(b) It can be used for different purposes

(c) It is inherently inaccurate

(d) It is inherently ambiguous

(e) It should be used with care

26 What is the paradoxical conclusion referred to at the beginning of the last paragraph?

(a) It is possible to foresee the psychology of the market

(b) We ultimately tend to follow the example set by others

(c) There is order in panic

(d) Instinct forms an image of its action

(e) Panic leads to depersonalisation

27 Which of the following is not a purpose served by the use of the example of financial crises in the last paragraph?

(a) To show that Pan is still relevant in the modern world

(b) To explain the herd mentality

(c) To give an example of panic

(d) To show where Pan's main influence on society is found

(e) To explain how the paradoxical conclusion was reached

10   Foreign Aid

Among the most pressing issues facing our country, according to the British public, are defence, foreign affairs and terrorism on the one hand, and race relations and immigration on the other. Both have been pushed to the fore by the international events of the last few years, though without totally displacing the other important and largely domestic issues of crime, the NHS, education and pensions. International development, overseas aid and poverty are not widely recognised as being important issues facing Britain. But there is evidence to suggest, from young and old alike, that they matter to people – particularly when asked in the context of issues facing developing and Third World countries. In research undertaken by MORI for UNFPA (the United Nations Population Fund) in 13 European countries before the events of September 11, poverty followed the environment to make these two issues the most pressing global problems in the world for Britons. The related issue of famine came third among Britons.

If we compare this with MORI's earlier work for UNFPA in 1996, poverty had increased in importance as a global issue, with 20 percent of Britons citing poverty as one of the most important problems facing the world today in 1996 and 29 percent citing poverty in 2001. When asked to name the most important issues in developing and Third World countries (from a list excluding war and internal conflicts), poverty came top, along with famine/malnutrition, with 61 percent, whilst Third World debt was cited by 48 percent. These sentiments were further echoed in responses to questions about foreign aid – which sent a clear signal to government that their citizens believed assistance to developing countries should be given a much higher priority.

However, there is little understanding about the extent of the British government's expenditure on foreign aid to developing countries, with many Britons overestimating this proportion by a large margin (MORI/UNFPA, 2001). The mean estimate (amongst those expressing a figure) was 9 percent of government expenditure, whilst a plurality of Britons (41 percent) was unable to give a figure at all. People's views on the amount of money their government actually spends on foreign aid to developing countries, which was 0.7 percent of government expenditure (rather than of gross domestic income) in 1999, were also sought. Of note is the fact that most Britons believe this amount to be too little (53 percent). Just 7 percent said it is too much, 9 percent didn't know and 32 percent said it is about right. The results gave a strong indication that assistance to developing countries should be given greater emphasis.

The evidence suggests that young people are also concerned about the developing world. In MORI's annual tracking work for DFID on its schools omnibus of 11–16 year olds, two-thirds said in 2003 that they were very or fairly concerned about many developing countries – where children do not have enough to eat, cannot go to school to learn to read and write, or cannot always get basic healthcare. Concern was highest among 11–13 year olds, girls and children from ethnic minorities. The vast majority believed that poverty in developing countries affects people in the UK at least a little. This proportion (around eight in ten) has been consistent since 2000.

Awareness of developing countries among young people has generally increased in this study, perhaps bolstered by the activity leading up to the Iraq war. Reflecting this, levels of concern have also risen, from an already fairly high base. Regarding possible attainment of the Millennium Development Goals, over half of 11–16 year olds think the government is likely to reach its goal of reducing poverty around the world, representing a four point increase on 2002. However, depth of feeling in 2003 was less strong than a year previously. Furthermore, one in three is sceptical, believing these goals will not be realised.

(Source: 'Foreign aid – the people speak' by Michele Corrado and Andrew Norton, MORI, 30 November 2004)

Select one answer for each of the following questions:

28 Which of the following is suggested by the writer?

(a) Global poverty has increased since 1996

(b) Awareness of Third World debt has increased since 1996

(c) Third World debt is the principal cause of poverty

(d) More people in Britain now support the idea of increasing awareness of foreign aid than in 1996

(e) Britons are becoming increasingly knowledgeable about foreign aid

29 What is the main idea in the article?

(a) Public understanding of the foreign aid situation is generally poor

(b) Not enough money is spent on foreign aid

(c) Younger people tend to be stronger supporters of foreign aid

(d) There is increasing support for a more extensive foreign aid policy

(e) Foreign politics are increasingly being seen as more important than domestic politics

30 From the evidence in the passage, which of the following must necessarily be true?

(a) 11–13-year-olds, girls, and ethnic minorities are equally concerned about developing countries

(b) Increasing government aid to foreign countries would be a popular policy

(c) The most common figure put forward by those surveyed about the proportion of government expenditure devoted to foreign aid was 9%

(d) A majority of people would like to see aid to foreign countries increased

(e) 7% of people would oppose a government policy that involved an increased expenditure on foreign aid

MCQ ANSWER SHEET

Racial Stereotypes		Civil Society	
1		13	
2		14	
3		15	

Home/Work Divide		Life in Other Worlds	
4		16	
5		17	
6		18	

Advertising		Ageing	
7		19	
8		20	
9		21	

American Political Parties		Population	
10		22	
11		23	
12		24	

Greek Gods	Foreign Aid
25	28
26	29
27	30

SECTION B: ESSAY

ANSWER **ONE** OF THE FOLLOWING QUESTIONS.

1 'Preventing the illegal downloading of music and videos from the Internet is neither achievable nor desirable.' Do you agree?

2 Should there be such a thing as a war crime?

3 What are the arguments for and against the present system of jury trial?

4 Is fame a valid aspiration?

5 'Appearance is more important than substance to the modern politician.' Do you agree?

ESSAY PLAN AND NOTES

ANSWERS AND EXPLANATIONS

USING THE ANSWERS AND EXPLANATIONS

A checklist of answers is provided for each of the multiple choice questions in order to allow you to mark your answer sheet. Full explanations are then provided for every question. These consist of a paragraph explaining why the particular alternative is correct, followed by another explaining why the other alternatives are incorrect. For each question, and particularly for the ones that you got wrong, you should consider the explanations and compare them with your own thinking on the subject. This method of learning is generally far more effective than simply reading an explanation of how to attempt particular questions before you have had a chance to think about them, and will help you to spot any weaknesses that you need to work on.

For the essay questions, a few paragraphs of comment are included, identifying the merits or otherwise of answering that particular question, followed by a consideration of some of the key factors that need to be considered. There is then either a sample essay plan or sample essay for you to compare with your own work. The nature of essays is such that there is a considerable degree of subjectivity involved, and there will almost certainly be a number of ways of tackling a particular question. The samples are not, therefore, intended to be definitive, but rather to demonstrate one approach that could be taken. In relation to the sample essays, it should be noted that the length of those included are, for obvious reasons, at the upper limit of what you are likely to be able to write in the time available, and indeed may exceed the specified word limit if this is reduced for subsequent tests. It is not intended that you seek to precisely replicate these, but rather that you aim to include as much as is possible within the constraints which you are working to. Similarly, the sample essay plans are not intended to represent a rigid structure, but rather to give you a framework to work with. If you have time, it would be beneficial to attempt more than one essay from each paper in order to get as much practice as possible. For those essay questions that you are unable to write full essays for, consider just writing down a short plan.

Once you have completed more than one paper, it is often useful to compare your performance in order to see the pattern of any improvement. In doing so, you should consider the wider picture and should not put undue credence just on the numerical mark. The nature of the test is such that papers will always vary in difficulty and it is impossible to compare scores from one to another. Similarly, when it comes to the actual paper, depending on the difficulty level your numerical score may vary considerably within a range. What will not vary so much is your performance relative to other candidates sitting the same paper and this is what admissions tutors will be concerned with.

SAMPLE TEST 1

Checklist of Answers to Multiple Choice Questions

Historical Sources	Freedom of Speech
1 (d)	10 (a)
2 (c)	11 (b)
3 (b)	12 (a)

Opinion Polls	AIDS Research
4 (a)	13 (e)
5 (e)	14 (d)
6 (d)	15 (c)

Defining Intelligence	Life's Destiny
7 (d)	16 (c)
8 (c)	17 (e)
9 (a)	18 (b)

Chess and Gender	Changing Public Attitudes
19 (b)	25 (d)
20 (a)	26 (c)
21 (c)	27 (b)

Quasi-states	American Values
22 (a)	28 (b)
23 (e)	29 (d)
24 (c)	30 (e)

SECTION A: EXPLANATION OF ANSWERS TO MULTIPLE CHOICE QUESTIONS

1   Historical Sources

Question 1

The article considers various aspects of historical sources and their use. For there to be any relevance in considering how sources are used and interpreted, it is necessary to make the assumption that history is based on sources. In the absence of such an assumption the article's whole reason for being would be dramatically restricted. *The correct answer is therefore (d).*

It is stated that historians have an element of choice in how they deal with sources, and it follows from this that different people will attach different value to different sources. It is consequently incorrect to say that this assumption is unstated. *Answer (a) is therefore incorrect.* It is not entirely true to say that it is impossible to be sure of the validity of a source. Even if it is arguably difficult to ever prove beyond doubt that a source is completely true, it is certainly possible to prove that one is false. Either way, such an assumption is not made by the writer. *Answer (b) is therefore incorrect.* Nowhere in the article is it suggested that it is ultimately possible to reconcile all the different sources about a subject and this is certainly not something which is necessary to the writer's arguments. The nature of sources is that there may be a large number dealing with one subject, and it is in no way necessary to the effective use of such sources that they can all be fully reconciled. *Answer (c) is therefore incorrect.* Likewise, it is not suggested that all historians have access to the same sources, and from what we are told about the proliferation of different sources it can be inferred that this is unlikely to be the case. Again, the nature of how sources are used is such that it is not necessary for all historians to have access to the same ones. *Answer (e) is therefore incorrect.*

Question 2

The article considers how sources are used and the relative value attached to different sources. Not only would such discussion be irrelevant if all sources were of equal validity, but the whole concept of using a range of sources would be rendered pointless, as it would never be necessary to consult more than one. *The correct answer is therefore (c).*

The article discusses in some detail the use of sources and as discussed above it can be inferred that all sources are not of equal validity. *Answer (b) is therefore incorrect.* With this in mind, it follows that it is not necessarily the quantity of sources that make a history more accurate, but the quality of the sources. A small number of accurate sources can be of considerably more benefit than a large number of inaccurate ones. *Answer (a) is therefore incorrect.* Although it is true to say that most sources can be interpreted in more than one way, it is not stated in the text that all can, and common sense dictates that this is not necessarily the case as some may only offer themselves to one possible interpretation. *Answer (d) is therefore incorrect.* There is nothing in the extract to suggest that a more specialised history must be a more accurate one, and if any conclusion could be drawn, it is that a more specialised history simply makes for a less diverse set of sources for the writer to consider. The problem of ensuring the accuracy of such sources will still remain. *Answer (e) is therefore incorrect.*

Question 3

The purpose of the article is to discuss the value and accuracy of sources, and throughout it is implied that it is extremely important to take care when using sources. This is a theme that permeates the writing and can be said to be the main idea. *The correct answer is therefore (b).*

Although it may be true to say that anything is capable of being an historical source, this is not an idea which is considered in any detail in the article and it could not be said that this is the main idea. *Answer (a) is therefore incorrect.* The same is true of the suggestion that history is constantly evolving. This may be true and may be implied by what is said, but is very much peripheral to the main idea of the article. *Answer (c) is therefore incorrect.* The suggestions that previous historians' work is one of the most useful sources of information and that it is not possible to investigate every piece of evidence relating to a given subject are not mentioned in the passage and are not necessarily true, let alone the main idea of the article. *Answers (d) and (e) are therefore incorrect.*

2   Opinion Polls

Question 4

It can be seen that there is some link between seats won and votes cast. From the statistics provided, though, it is clear that there is not a directly proportionate relationship between the two. *The correct answer is therefore (a).*

There is insufficient evidence to suggest that one way of predicting an election result is better than another. *Answer (b) is therefore incorrect*. There is no evidence to suggest that Conservative voters are more reluctant to answer opinion polls. *Answer (c) is therefore incorrect*. To say that turnout at elections is declining would require more information than that from just a couple of elections. *Answer (d) is therefore incorrect*. There is nothing to suggest that the opinion polls were not carried out near to the time of the election, and by definition there will always be some period of time in which people will have the potential to change their minds. *Answer (e) is therefore incorrect*.

Question 5

The fact that a similar voting pattern was experienced at the last election shows that there will always be some unpredictable elements involved in opinion polling. Combined with the claim that there was only a small inaccuracy with those polls, it can be said that the writer is trying to play down the truth of newspaper criticism. *The correct answer is therefore (e)*.

There is insufficient evidence provided to say that the results of previous opinion polls are useful in determining the outcome of future elections or that Labour supporters are traditionally less likely to vote. *Answers (a) and (b) are therefore incorrect*. There is no reason why turnout cannot be estimated in the same way as any other variable by way of opinion poll; the word estimate does not imply total accuracy. *Answer (c) is therefore incorrect*. It may be implied that polls carried out by similar organisations will have similar results as result of the identical methods used, but this is very much a peripheral point. *Answer (d) is therefore incorrect*.

Question 6

The writer's principal assertion is that the reason for the inaccuracy in the poll was that Labour voters felt that there was no need for them to vote as the result was a forgone conclusion. For this to be accepted it must be assumed that voters were influenced by other voters' plans; otherwise this argument would be invalid. *The correct answer is therefore (d)*.

It is a general characteristic of opinion polling that some people will not reveal their true intentions to pollsters and there is no reason put forward why this should be a particularly decisive factor with this particular poll. *Answer (a) is therefore incorrect*. Likewise the need to find a representative sample is a key consideration in any poll and not just the one in question, and those surveyed in any poll may always subsequently change their minds. *Answers (b) and (c) are therefore incorrect*. As discussed above, it is incorrect to say that there is no correlation between voting share and actual votes received. *Answer (e) is therefore incorrect*.

3   Defining Intelligence

Question 7

The passage deals with the question of what intelligence is, and the final sentence reads, 'For me, g is what intelligence is all about.' This leads to the conclusions that g is the most valuable indicator of general intelligence. *The correct answer is therefore (d).*

This is not the same as saying that there is more merit in studying g than other forms of so-called intelligence, as such a judgment is relative to what you are trying to achieve from the study. *Answer (a) is therefore incorrect.* That intelligence is an innate quality that cannot be altered is not necessarily a conclusion reached from the research, let alone the main one. *Answer (b) is therefore incorrect.* Throughout the passage a number of different types of intelligence are considered, and it is clear that there is an inevitable variation between different measures of intelligence, but neither of there are the final conclusion reached. *Answers (c) and (e) are therefore incorrect.*

Question 8

At the beginning of the extract, h is defined by the writer as being general cognitive ability. It is later said that Charles Spearman referred to general cognitive ability as g. Although the two may have used slightly different definitions of general cognitive ability, g and h are clearly very closely linked. *The correct answer is therefore (c).*

Emotional intelligence is identified as being different from general cognitive ability and there is no evidence of a strong link between it and g or h. *Answers (a) and (b) are therefore incorrect.* Emotional intelligence and spatial ability are both types of non-cognitive ability and must by definition be linked in some way. The fact that there are a number of different types of non-cognitive abilities, however, means that there is no evidence that they are closely linked. *Answers (d) and (e) are therefore incorrect.*

Question 9

It is said that '[v]ocabulary tests assess the product of previous learning', and on this basis it follows that vocabulary increases as a result of education. In contrast, the definition of the other alternatives is such as to suggest that they are much less likely to be influenced by education. *The correct answer is therefore (a).*

Nowhere in the extract is a strong link suggested between education and spatial awareness, emotional intelligence or general cognitive ability. *Answers (b), (c), (d) and (e) are therefore incorrect.*

4   Freedom of Speech

Question 10

The whole extract is concerned with free speech and considers issues such as its nature and its history. It would be difficult, however, to claim that either of these were the main idea, given that a similar amount of prominence is given to both. In this instance, the best guide to what the writer intends to be the dominant idea comes from an explicit statement that: 'I would like to challenge a number of assumptions that are often and unquestioningly associated with the projection of a dialogical model of free speech into a public place. Specifically, these are the ideas that: there is such a thing as free speech ...' From this, it is clear that the writer's purpose in writing the passage is to challenge the very idea of free speech and associated concepts. *The correct answer is therefore (a).*

It is inconsistent with the idea that he is challenging the very existence of free speech to claim that his purpose is to suggest that it is the best way of regulating government or is the basis of democracy. *Answers (b) and (d) are therefore incorrect.* By including much historical background to free speech, the writer is suggesting that it is not a new concept, but this information is essentially provided to set the debate in context and could not be said to be the main purpose of the passage. *Answer (c) is therefore incorrect.* Consequently, it must be inherently wrong to say that his purpose is to suggest that free speech is underestimated; indeed he is saying the opposite. *Answer (e) is therefore incorrect.*

Question 11

Unlike the other alternatives, which are all fairly absolute requirements for the kind of system of democracy described, how skilled politicians are in the art of oratory will determine more their own success than whether democracy itself is possible. It is said that: '[i]t was therefore the job of politicians, through rhetoric and through dialogue, to convince to the public of the good of a particular decision.' From this, it follows that the less convincing speakers they were, the more difficulty they would have in championing their policies and decisions over those of other politicians. *The correct answer is therefore (b).*

On the other hand, were there nowhere that free speech could be exercised or the lack of a common language in which to communicate, the very basis of the concept would be challenged and it simply would not be possible to have free speech in the way envisaged. *Answers (a) and (e) are therefore incorrect.* Similarly, if there was no requirement on the government to consult or if people were not free to make their own decisions, it would be irrelevant what was discussed. *Answers (c) and (d) are therefore incorrect.*

Question 12

In order to answer this, one first needs to look for a definition of free speech in the passage. At the end of the third paragraph, a situation is described where 'all are in principle free to speak their mind and where critique is thereby assured'. This suggests that everyone should have the right to express their opinion in relation to government policy. Of the alternatives given, the one with the most potential not to satisfy this definition is discussion of government policy in a state owned newspaper, as it is the government that has overall control over what is printed. *The correct answer is therefore (a).*

Although it cannot be said conclusively that there will or will not be free speech in any given situation, it is more likely that there will be in relation to government policy in printed media not controlled by the government itself. *Answers (b) and (e) are therefore incorrect.* In the case of discussions between friends, or a speech by an independent commentator, it is even less likely that there will be any limitations on free speech. *Answers (c) and (d) are therefore incorrect.*

5   AIDS Research

Question 13

For something to be an argument suggesting that a vaccine is likely to be found, it needs to either be something that theoretically suggests that the disease has the potential to be controlled by a vaccine, or something that suggests that there are no practical impediments to the development of the vaccine itself. The inefficiency of sex as a method for transmitting the virus does not fall into either of these categories. It suggests that there is a potential to control the disease, but does not give any guidance as to the suitability of a vaccine or any other method. *The correct answer is therefore (e).*

The fact that some patients have the ability to control the virus suggests that it is possible for the human body to fight the infection, an idea which forms the basis of the concept of vaccination. *Answer (a) is therefore incorrect.* Superinfection by a second viral strain would dramatically reduce the potential for an effective vaccine and the fact that this is described as not being a common eventuality is an argument in favour of a vaccine being potentially found. *Answer (b) is therefore incorrect.* An attenuated live virus is suggested as a likely basis for a vaccine, and the fact that it is theoretically possible to attenuate viruses in this way gives hope for the success of such an approach. *Answer (c) is therefore incorrect.* The fact that it has been possible to provide vaccine-mediated protection against simian immunodeficiency implies that a similar approach could be taken towards AIDS. *Answer (d) is therefore incorrect.*

Question 14

In discussing the strategic plan, the writer says: 'It is my contention that great new ideas are as likely to come from curiosity-driven basic studies as from the mission-oriented approach that is represented by the new proposal. Therefore, the leadership of the Enterprise must safeguard against the kind of "group think" that is so pervasive in large collaborative endeavors of this nature.' This implies that the writer feels that it is important not to limit the scope of the research and to allow scientists the freedom to try new ideas, one of which might ultimately lead to a breakthrough. *The correct answer is therefore (d).*

The likely effect of this narrower focus is that there will be a greater depth of research within the defined areas. *Answer (a) is therefore incorrect.* The discussion focuses on what is being researched rather than the quality of that research, and there is nothing to suggest that the quality would be reduced. *Answer (b) is therefore incorrect.* Likewise, all that is being suggested is that the existing research capacity will be directed more into particular areas. *Answer (c) is therefore incorrect.* There is no reason why this should lead to a change in the quantity of research being carried out, or the speed at which the research is undertaken. *Answer (e) is therefore incorrect.*

Question 15

In talking about the strategic plan, the writer begins by offering praise: 'The scientific strategic plan of the Enterprise is spot-on in identifying the major roadblocks in HIV vaccine development, as well as in establishing the key scientific priorities as we see them today.' He then goes on to consider whether there are any potential downsides to the plan by looking at its limitations. These two components make up a substantial part of the article, and the majority of the other material is ancillary to them. As a result, it can be said that the author's purpose in writing the article is to build on the plan, identifying its strengths and then going on to suggest what else needs to be done. *The correct answer is therefore (c).*

Given this balance between praise and criticism, it cannot be said that the author's purpose is either to solely attack or support the plan. *Answers (a) and (b) are therefore incorrect.* The article does not seek to define the actual nature of the virus in any detail, and focuses more on what can and should be done about it. *Answer (d) is therefore incorrect.* Similarly, the explanation of the challenges faced is provided more to set the rest of the discussion in context and does not form a substantive part of the argument advanced by the writer. *Answer (e) is therefore incorrect.*

6   Life's Destiny

Question 16

In the final sentence of the extract, it is said that: 'Thought is more than the execution of algorithms; computers can do the latter but not the former.' This suggests that there is an inherent difference between silicon- and carbon-based life, which will remain regardless of how much more sophisticated computers become. *The correct answer is therefore (c).*

This is not the same as saying that computers will never be able to perform human functions; they may be able to achieve the same result, but not necessarily through the same process. *Answer (a) is therefore incorrect.* Although the writer challenges some of the opinions put forward by theorists on the subject, and questions the potential for artificial intelligence, he does not say that this would be undesirable, merely implausible. *Answer (b) is therefore incorrect.* It cannot be said that he thinks that people are well informed about the possibilities afforded by artificial intelligence, given that he says that the claims made are implausible. This suggests that he thinks that people are misinformed about the subject. *Answer (d) is therefore incorrect.* Likewise, there is nothing in the extract to suggest that humans are inherently more sophisticated than computers. Although it is said that computers cannot think in the way that humans do, this is not the only measure of sophistication, and it is perfectly feasible that computers could be more sophisticated in other areas. *Answer (e) is therefore incorrect.*

Question 17

The extract starts by posing the question: 'what is the fate of intelligent consciousness to be?' This is a good indicator of the approach to be taken in the rest of the passage, the majority of which seeks to answer that particular question. It follows from this that the writer's main purpose is to consider the evolution of life. *The correct answer is therefore (e).*

Although much of the passage does focus on artificial intelligence, this is in the context of explaining the evolution of life, not vice versa, and could not be said to be the main idea in the passage either in terms of the quantity or purpose of the references to it. *Answer (a) is therefore incorrect.* The issue of thought is considered as a by-product of explaining different forms of life, but only forms a small part of the overall piece. *Answer (b) is therefore incorrect.* Likewise, the writer does refute at least one potential misconception about computers, but this receives only brief mention. *Answer (c) is therefore incorrect.* Parts of the passage could be said to challenge the traditional orthodoxy on the scope of intelligent consciousness, but this does not apply to the passage as a whole, and there is evidence to suggest that the opposite view is being articulated. *Answer (d) is therefore incorrect.*

Question 18

The principle is stated that intelligent information processing must come into existence within the universe. Nowhere is it mentioned how it will come into being and there is insufficient evidence available to suggest that this is an assumption being made by Tipler. *The correct answer is therefore (b).*

The fact that it is said that 'intelligent information processing must come into existence' suggests that the assumption is being made that it does not currently exist. *Answer (a) is therefore incorrect.* Tipler's stated view is that in the final seconds of a collapsing cosmos, infinite information processing would be achieved. *Answer (c) is therefore incorrect.* It is also stated as part of the Final Anthropic Principle that once intelligent information processing comes into existence it will not die out. *Answer (d) is therefore incorrect.* In the final paragraph it is said that the character of life is the processing of information. *Answer (e) is therefore incorrect.*

7   Chess and Gender

Question 19

The analogy with science and the example of the Polgar sisters go to show the advantages of giving children of either gender the opportunity to get involved at an early age. In the field of science it is suggested that getting children involved at a young age created a more level playing field in which either gender had the opportunity to succeed. *The correct answer is therefore (b).*

Having all female tournaments could be seen almost to be counterproductive as the standard of the competition could be implied to be lower and it would not necessarily help to get more women involved with the game. *Answer (a) is therefore incorrect.* A shorter time limit on games would only assist in relation to one of the points raised by the writer, namely that women are unable to sustain concentration for as long as men and little evidence is even put forward to support this idea. *Answer (c) is therefore incorrect.* Changing the general perception of chess could be argued to encourage more girls to become involved, but without additional encouragement there is nothing to demonstrate that this would necessarily be the case, and it may not be sufficient to improve the standard if they were to become involved in the game at an older age than boys. *Answer (d) is therefore incorrect.* Offering women the chance to play in high level competitions would only assist those already involved in the game, and if it is claimed that women are currently not able to compete at as high a level this would be of little use. *Answer (e) is therefore incorrect.*

Question 20

Various reasons are put forward why there may be differences between men and women when it comes to chess. Many of these centre around perception of and access to the game, and there is only a limited and unproven suggestion that the genders may have a different capacity to succeed. For example, although it is stated that men tend to have better spatial awareness than women, it is only an assertion that spatial awareness is a determinant of ability to succeed at chess, and this would be rendered irrelevant if the two genders did not have differing capacities to succeed. At best, it could be said that there might be a difference, but it cannot be gathered that there definitely is a difference for this reason. *The correct answer is therefore (a).*

Although there is every reason to think that they may eventually do as well, there is no evidence put forward to suggest that women will become as good as men and there are a number of reasons cited as to why the opposite may be the case. *Answer (b) is therefore incorrect.* The standard at women's tournaments generally, by implication, must be lower if women are accepted not to be currently as strong in the game. *Answer (c) is therefore incorrect.* It is stated that a lack of physical strength can affect concentration, and implied that the way to reach a good standard is to start at a young age. *Answers (d) and (e) are therefore incorrect.*

Question 21

It is suggested that in the world of science, the genders are much more equal now that both have the opportunity to study the subject from a young age. It is implied that previous assumptions about girls and science, made when opportunities were much less even, were wrong. On this basis, the same could be said about making any judgments about chess until everyone has the same chances. *The correct answer is therefore (c).*

There is no comparison made of the skills required at chess compared with science. *Answer (a) is therefore incorrect.* Although gender differences clearly exist in other areas, the writer does not generalise in this way. *Answer (b) is therefore incorrect.* The perception of women may well have a part to play, but evidence is put forward of a number of other differences that exist as well. *Answer (d) is therefore incorrect.* Although it may well be the case that women become as successful at chess as men, this is not explicitly stated and there is nothing to suggest that they will imminently overtake men. *Answer (e) is therefore incorrect.*

8   Quasi-states

Question 22

The article starts by saying that the 'totalitarian state is easy to define' and that '[n]ot so obliging is what I have referred to as the quasi-state, that elusive entity'. On the basis of this comparison, it can be said that formal states tend to be better defined than quasi-states. *The correct answer is therefore (a).*

Clearly the reverse of this must be false. In the absence of a direct comparison of the aims of different types of states it is impossible to make any claim about one having wider aims than the other. *Answers (b), (c), (d) and (e) are therefore incorrect.*

Question 23

Reference is made to quasi-states contending for power and being states-in-waiting, but there is nothing in the passage to suggest that a quasi-state has to be one that is actually about to assume formal power. It may have, or be about to, acquire power that is not formal in nature, may unsuccessfully seek to obtain formal power or may simply seek to exercise similar influence and challenge the status quo without having any intention of ultimately seizing formal power. *The correct answer is therefore (e).*

It is said that a quasi-state is 'one that repudiates even the minimal codes of accountability' and 'is not defined by physical boundaries that identify the sovereign state'. *Answers (a) and (b) are therefore incorrect.* Quasi-states are also described as mimicking formal states whilst 'lacking the responsibility of governance'. *Answers (c) and (d) are therefore incorrect.*

Question 24

In the second paragraph, the writer talks about the power of fear being indifferent to religion and goes on to compare the brutal regimes of Mariam Mengistu in Ethiopia and Stalin in the former Soviet Union, suggesting that both subjugated their citizens to a similar extent. *The correct answer is therefore (c).*

Although examples are given of the harshness of some religious regimes, nowhere is it suggested that religion is the cause of substantial, let alone most, discontent towards the state. *Answer (a) is therefore incorrect.* Religion may feature in the ideologies of some quasi-states, but there is nothing to suggest that it forms the basis of the ideologies of all such states. *Answer (b) is therefore incorrect.* Similarly, although it may be central to the development of many formal states, examples are given of atheist states and a generalisation cannot be made. *Answer (d) is therefore incorrect*. The rise of quasi-states could be said to increase the significance of religion where that forms part of the state's ideology and either way there is nothing to suggest that its importance is decreased. *Answer (e) is therefore incorrect*.

9   Changing Public Attitudes

Question 25

In the second paragraph, it is said that '... while concern rose alongside an increase in asylum applicants (and after 9/11), it has plateaued at a high level, even as numbers have fallen'. This provides evidence for the fact that concern has remained high while asylum numbers have fallen, but does not provide sufficient evidence to say that the upward trend in applicant numbers has now been reversed. It may simply mean that there have been periods in time since 9/11 when numbers have fallen, but there is no evidence to suggest that this is a general pattern. In order to say that a trend had been reversed it would be necessary to have evidence of what the trend was in the first place and clear evidence from specified subsequent periods showing a change to this trend. *The correct answer is therefore (d)*.

There is survey evidence showing that in 2003, 90% of the public did not think that the government had the issue under control. *Answer (a) is therefore incorrect*. As mentioned above, concern is not directly related to the number of applicants. *Answer (b) is therefore incorrect*. Nevertheless, it is said that concern in the past has risen alongside an increase in asylum seekers and there is no reason to think that this will not happen again. *Answer (c) is therefore incorrect*. It is said that: '[changes in public opinion] ... cannot be dismissed solely as the result of media hype.' Turning this around, it can be said that the changes may partly be caused by the effect of the media. *Answer (e) is therefore incorrect*.

Question 26

Throughout the article, the writer puts forward evidence of how public perception of the issue of immigration differs from reality and how many people hold somewhat irrational views on the subject. He then goes on to explain what actions need to be taken and talks of the need to be realistic about the situation: 'This is extremely sensitive ground, but we need to be able to confront more directly the challenges that increasing diversity brings, as well as simply acknowledging its benefits.' This suggests that it is necessary to look at both sides of the issue and consider the reality behind the perception from a more objective standpoint. *The correct answer is therefore (c)*.

The issue of education is dealt with in two lines at the end of the third paragraph, and although it is suggested that those who are better educated have a clearer impression of the issue, the very limited discussion of this in the passage means that it cannot be suggested that this is the main point being made. *Answer (a) is therefore incorrect.* The same is true of the suggestion that those with personal experiences of other races tend to be less prejudiced, which is dealt with in the same way as the point on education. *Answer (b) is therefore incorrect.* The fact that there are regional differences in opinions on the subject is considered in a couple of places in the article and is used as one piece of evidence for the need to look at the issue more objectively. It is not a sufficiently free-standing idea, or one considered in enough detail, for it to be said to be the main point being made. *Answer (d) is therefore incorrect.* The same is true of different generations' attitudes towards race. It backs up the main argument, but is not itself central to the article. *Answer (e) is therefore incorrect.*

Question 27

It is said that: '… unless more is done to state the facts, by mainstream parties, as opposed to airing the hype, those who revel in talking about it – the BNP – will continue to do better than in the past.' In other words, the failure of mainstream politicians to publicise the true facts about immigration is allowing the hype propagated by the BNP to gain currency and is giving the impression that it is necessary to take the kind of action advocated by the BNP. *The correct answer is therefore (b).*

It is not whether the issue is dealt with at local or national level that is important to the BNP's support, but whether the issue is dealt with effectively, and the involvement of local government is one example of how this could be done. To say that the lack of local involvement is a key factor in the BNP's popularity would be to say that the BNP is better equipped to deal with issues locally than nationally, and that the reverse applies to the main parties. There is no evidence for either of these propositions. *Answer (a) is therefore incorrect.* There is nothing that suggests that all the main parties need to adopt the same approach towards immigration. A successful policy promoted by one would be sufficient to draw support away from the BNP. *Answer (c) is therefore incorrect.* Not only is there no evidence that the BNP is a single issue party, but there is also no evidence that this would be preferred by the public. The fact that a party deals effectively with one issue does not preclude it from considering any other issues. *Answer (d) is therefore incorrect.* One aspect of the liberal consensus is the idea that government interference in the running of the country should be kept to a minimum. It is inconsistent to suggest that this has led to the rise of the BNP, something that would imply a desire for more control. If anything, it could be said that the rise of the BNP is a reaction to the liberal consensus, but this can only ever be secondary to the more immediate factors that have caused a shift in support amongst political parties. *Answer (e) is therefore incorrect.*

10   American Values

The fact that the 'Washington Post' was able to conduct the investigation it did and bring down the leader of the government shows that the government does not always exert an overriding control of the media. Were it to, the suggestion is that the investigation could have been halted. *The correct answer is therefore (b)*.

The example is evidence that the media provides a check on government, but in the absence of any alternative to compare it to, it is impossible to say that it provides the most effective check. *Answer (a) is therefore incorrect*. Although it highlights one example of freedom of speech, this is not sufficient evidence to say that it is an absolute right. *Answer (c) is therefore incorrect*. Both the suggestion that freedom of the media is always a good thing and the suggestion that the media always acts in the best interests of the country as a whole are generalisations and could only be validly made if there were sufficient available comparisons. *Answers (d) and (e) are therefore incorrect*.

In order to establish which of the alternatives is not an assertion, it is necessary to look at which there is evidence to support. It is said that '[r]esearch from the above study also indicated that support for specific freedom of beliefs was much higher among the educated "elite" as opposed to the mass public'. As a result, the statement that education leads to more tolerant beliefs can be said to have a definite factual basis and is not merely an assertion. *The correct answer is therefore (d)*.

On the other hand, in relation to Bill Clinton's experience, it is said that '... a much higher percentage of Black Americans voted for Bill Clinton than Bob Dole presumably as they felt that one through his experience of being president was better able to deliver'. Here the use of the word 'presumably' shows that there is no specific factual evidence to back the point up and that it is an assertion made by the writer. *Answer (a) is therefore incorrect*. Although it is said that in 1996 a much higher percentage of Black Americans voted for Bill Clinton than Bob Dole, this is not evidence for saying that Bill Clinton's policies proved more favourable to ethnic minorities. In addition to the fact that they may not have proved favourable to other ethnic minorities, the reason for Black Americans voting for Clinton is stated to be the perception of his experience, and no conclusion from this can be reached about his policies. *Answer (b) is therefore incorrect*. Similarly, there is no evidence to suggest that Bush's policies were aimed at promoting the interests of men. They may have achieved this purpose without setting out to, or there may have been another reason for the higher proportion of men supporting Bush. *Answer (c) is therefore incorrect*. Although examples are given of where freedom of speech has been overridden due to external circumstances, no figures are given for the percentage of Americans who would support this, and any statement claiming otherwise must only be an assertion. *Answer (e) is therefore incorrect.*

Question 30

The following statistics about communism are given: 'In 1954, 27% of those surveyed in America believed that people had the right to state their support for communism. By 1972, this had increased to 52% and by 1991, to 67%.' These statistics only relate to those people who believe that others have the right to express their opinion about communism and do not give any insight into how many people support the idea of communism itself. On this issue, there is insufficient evidence to form a view. *The correct answer is therefore (e).*

In order to say that support for communism had increased or decreased, it would be necessary to have at least two sets of data to be compared, and to say that a majority were in favour would require a representative sample of the population to be taken on that specific issue. *Answers (a), (b), (c) and (d) are therefore incorrect.*

SECTION B: EXPLANATION OF ANSWERS AND SAMPLES

Question 1: What are the arguments for and against reforming the voting system currently used for parliamentary elections in Britain?

This is a relatively straightforward title and one that most people will be able to write a competent essay on. Nevertheless, it does call for a number of pieces of relatively specific knowledge and it would be a weak answer if there was no analysis of the technicalities of the current system and its practical implications for the political landscape in the UK.

Before any meaningful argument can be advanced as to the merits or otherwise of reforming the voting system, it is important to clearly define what is meant by 'First Past The Post' and how that system operates. Providing this information in a systematic way will provide a solid basis on which to put forward the advantages and disadvantages of each feature of the system, and will ensure that the argument is well grounded. As with any essay title, it is important to be clear exactly what the question is asking, and the fact that 'voting system' could also relate to the way votes are cast, as well as interpreted, should not be overlooked, and some discussion of the potential reforms to traditional paper-based voting should be included. In both cases, it would be desirable to consider the alternatives to the current system and to evaluate their potential effectiveness.

It is impossible to discuss the voting system without making reference to how it affects the political parties, and a good answer will look to capitalise on this by considering not only how reform would affect each party, but also at how the parties have conducted themselves in the past in relation to this issue and what their motivation has been for their policies in this area. A distinction can be drawn between the purely theoretical arguments for reform and the political dimension that affects what happens in practice. There is also the potential to bring in an international element, looking at the experiences of other countries and comparing and contrasting these with the position in Britain.

Sample Essay

British parliamentary elections are at present conducted using what is known as the 'First Past The Post' (FPTP) voting system. Under FPTP, the country is divided into a number of constituencies, currently 659, each of which comprises a similar number of voters and returns one MP to Westminster. To win an election, a candidate must simply secure more votes than any of the other candidates, regardless of whether they achieve an overall majority of the votes. The government is then formed from the party that secures the largest number of seats in parliament. Although it has been around in various guises for many centuries, during which time a number of reforms have been made, FPTP is regularly criticised for a number of reasons. In addition, there are frequent calls for different methods to be introduced for casting votes in order to make the voting system more accessible and to increase turnout. I shall therefore be considering the arguments for and against the present system and the merits of some of the main alternatives, as well as looking at the political and historical factors which have affected this area.

One of the main advantages of FPTP is its simplicity and the fact that it is clearly understood by the majority of the electorate, something which is crucial to a democratic system. Voters are faced with a simple choice between two or more candidates and are just required to indicate their preference by placing a cross in the appropriate box on the ballot paper. This means that the results can be counted very quickly and cheaply and the potential for any confusion or uncertainty regarding the result is minimised. Perhaps even more importantly, there is just one elected representative for each constituency and each voter is therefore aware of who is representing their interests, something which is not a feature of many alternative systems.

The 'winner takes all' nature of FPTP, whilst sometimes seen as a disadvantage by opponents of the system, is, in many ways, its greatest strength as it dramatically reduces the potential of a minority government and avoids the need for ever-changing coalitions to be formed as tends to be the case in countries like Italy, which use a system of proportional representation. This promotes greater stability, something that is generally seen as a virtue for government. The argument could also be raised that the fact that FPTP reinforces the 'two party' system is good in ensuring that extremist parties are unable to gain a foothold in parliament, although obviously there is a strong counter-argument to the effect that this is not always desirable.

A final argument in favour of FPTP is the fact that in the considerable time in which it has been used for parliamentary elections in Britain, few if any major problems have arisen with it. Although this may be a weak argument conceptually, practically it could be said to be the most important consideration with a voting system and is one that ought not to be overlooked. Certainly, since the 1832, 1867 and 1884 Reform Acts eliminated some of the absurdities so vividly described by Charles Dickens in *Pickwick Papers*, such as 'rotten boroughs' often containing only one voter, few could argue that there has been relatively strong and representative government in Britain with few, if any, of the allegations of electoral corruption that have dogged many countries.

This could of course be down to cultural differences, and opponents of FPTP are keen to point out that other voting systems could retain many of the advantages of the current system whilst eliminating some of the less fair aspects. It is this lack of fairness that forms the central thrust of the argument against FPTP, with there being no fixed correlation between the number of votes won by a party and the number of seats that they receive in Parliament. For example, in the 1997 general election, the victorious Labour Party won 43.2% of the votes cast, which translated into 63.6% of the seats at Westminster, whilst the Conservative Party and the Liberal Democrats, who between them received 47.5% of the vote, only received 32.1% of the seats. This is a typical result of FPTP, with no government since 1935 having received a majority of the public vote, and leads to what Lord Hailsham once described as an 'electoral dictatorship' with powerful governments able to push through legislation regardless of the views expressed by opposition parties. An inevitable consequence of only one MP being elected from each constituency is that those votes cast for the other candidates will be wasted, meaning that the preference of all those voters is effectively disregarded. It is suggested that a knock-on effect of this is that voters who perceive their vote as likely to be wasted will not bother voting at all, which will discriminate against the minority parties. Eliminating this wastage of votes is where the strength of alternative voting systems, based on proportional representation (PR), lies.

PR in its purest form involves seats being allocated strictly in proportion to the number of votes received, usually by reference to a national list of candidates put forward by each party. The difficulty with this is that there is not the same sense of local representation, thereby often outweighing the advantage of the fairer voting system. Most of the systems proposed by opponents of FPTP are therefore something of a hybrid, retaining some elements of the traditional concept of a constituency. The most similar to FPTP is the Additional Member System (AMS), which is currently used for elections to the Scottish Parliament and Welsh Assembly. Here, voters cast two votes, one for a constituency MP in the same way as under FPTP and one for their favourite party. Additional members are elected from a list on the basis of these additional votes in order to ensure that the result in each region is roughly proportional. Another alternative is a system called Single Transferable Vote, currently used for elections to the Northern Ireland Assembly. This utilises larger constituencies consisting of several MPs, with voters casting their votes in order of preference. These preferences are then added up to determine which candidates are elected, thereby ensuring an approximately proportional result. A number of other systems such as the List System and Alternative Vote have also been suggested, combining elements of the systems already mentioned.

To examine the theoretical merits of any voting system in isolation would be to miss arguably the most important issue, that of how it is affected by political factors. In the same way that it follows that FPTP has created what is essentially a two party system in Britain, then it follows that it will be most popular with those two parties. The strongest support for FPTP comes from the Conservative Party who are the ones to have benefited by being in power for so much of the 20th century, whilst the biggest supporters of change are the Liberal Democrats who are most disadvantaged by the present system. In the 2001 general election, for example, the Liberal Democrats gained 19% of the total vote, which on a strictly proportional basis would have given them 120 seats in parliament, whereas they won 52 seats. There is a certain degree of circularity about this argument as it is the party or parties in power that have the greatest influence on any reforms to the voting system, yet by definition they have been elected using it. Nevertheless, public awareness of this issue is now at a higher level than at any time in the past, and this may be sufficient to see independent public pressure being placed on the government of the day by opponents of FPTP.

There have also long been calls for changes to the way in which votes are actually cast, and these have increased as a result of technological advances and the advent of widespread Internet use. This is of significance particularly in the context of reversing the trend of declining turnout at elections, something which undermines the democratic legitimacy of those elected. Initial calls for reform in this area centred around having voting stations in more accessible places, such as supermarkets and post offices, but now tend to focus on the potential to allow voting by way of an electronic medium. On a theoretical level, it is difficult to criticise any measure that increases access to democracy. Those concerns which do exist relate largely to security and ultimately it is likely to be the potential to resolve practical concerns of this nature that will determine the scope of any reform. Whilst it is beyond the scope of this essay to consider the merits of such a change, it should be noted that this drive to increase participation in elections has also led to some calls for the age of majority to be lowered from 18 to 16 years of age, although such a move currently attracts less public support than the other reforms discussed.

In conclusion, there are compelling arguments for and against making any reforms to the voting system. Assuming that democracy is an ideal to be aspired to, I would tend to suggest that the decisive factor is the need for access to, and fair representation in, the political system. PR, by its nature, must offer the fairest representation, but would be unlikely to allow the same kind of access given the lack of a local representative in the same way as under the present constituency system. On balance, therefore, I believe that limited reform, moving to a system such as AMS, which retains the best features of the existing system whilst also introducing a number of positive improvements, would be the most desirable outcome. Combined with the implementation of new methods of voting, such as online polls, the AMS would increase both access to, and confidence in, the British political system. Ultimately, whether any changes will be made depends on their receiving support from the major political parties, something which has in the past been a handicap to reform. The fact that the weakness of the Conservative Party in recent years has led to more of a three party system developing in Britain may, however, be the impetus for change that is required, with opinion polls now showing a higher level of support for electoral reform than at any point in the past.

Question 2: Is religion a good thing?

This is a much more philosophical and abstract essay title than the majority of which you will encounter and this brings with it a number of advantages and disadvantages. On the plus side, having less constraints imposed by the question allows you more freedom to demonstrate your ability to write incisive and informative prose. On the minus side, the fact that there is nothing by way of guidance in the question as to the structure required can leave you very exposed to producing a confusing answer. The bottom line is that you should only choose a question like this if you are confident that you can do it justice. To attempt it otherwise, particularly if your motivation is the fact that it requires less specific factual knowledge, would be an unnecessary risk.

The key question, before you even begin to discuss the merits of any arguments either way, is what is actually meant by religion. This is something that you could write an entire book, never mind an essay, on and will require considerable thought as to the best way of defining it. The definition is not something that should simply be a couple of lines in the introduction; it merits at least a paragraph on its own. For the main section of the essay, the outline structure should be arguments for religion being a good thing, followed by arguments against, or vice versa. How you arrange the material within these sections is very much a matter of personal taste and will be determined by the approach you choose to take to the question.

A really first class answer will get right to the heart of each of the terms and consider not only what is meant by religion and how this varies amongst different individuals and groups, but also what is meant by 'good'. This is a very subjective word and you need to consider whether it is possible to settle on a meaning that everyone would agree with or, if not, whose opinion is relevant in determining whether something is good. It may be of interest to consider how the importance and perception of religion has changed and how it is likely to evolve in the future.

Sample Essay

Very few things both divide and unite society in the way religion has done in the past, and continues to do today. Almost every culture in every area of the world has developed some sort of religion or faith. Hinduism, Sikhism, Islam, Christianity and Judaism, along with many other religions, have been a fundamental part of people's lives for hundreds or thousands of years. Clearly, religion, or faith, is something that some people find important and upon which many people rely in one way or another. This essay will argue that in a great many ways religion is a good thing, but that in other ways it seems to have been the cause of great strife and upheaval. Because religion has been such an important part of society for so many years, I believe it is impossible to assess whether the things that religion provides to society, both good and bad, could be found in or caused by anything other than 'faith'.

In order to assess whether religion is a good or a bad thing, we must have some understanding of why some people are religious. There are many reasons for religion, perhaps most importantly for those who believe that our creators should be thanked and worshipped. This sort of attitude can only really be explained by a true belief in the existence of some higher being. Wherever this belief comes from, it exists in a great many people and this belief is probably the main rationale behind 'religion' as we know it. On a more psychological level, it could be said that people need something to believe in – something to hope for and something to trust in. A great many terrible things happen in the world and these things can prove a lot for people to deal with. When people lose family members or suffer difficult times, faith provides them with something to believe in and hope for. With regard to people who have died, it is a great help to those who survive them to believe that the dead person has 'gone to a better place' or to heaven, and that they will one day see them again. Similarly, the idea of reincarnation prevails in some religions.

In this way religion is a good thing, and it is very difficult to see any other mechanism by which people could be made to feel better about death and about the terrible things that happen in the world. The only real alternative, and that which is adopted by atheists (people who are not believers in any religion or any God), is to accept that there is no superior being looking down on the world and orchestrating events that occur. From this comes, almost necessarily, an acceptance that death is the end of a person's consciousness and that nothing follows except the purely physical breakdown of the body. Further, there must be acceptance that prayers are of no practical use and that the bad things that happen in the world simply have to be accepted and dealt with.

It is clearly the case that many people rely on religion as a method of coping with difficult circumstances. Many people say that it is only their faith that gets them through difficult times. In providing this sort of support to people, religion certainly is a good thing. More importantly, this sort of help is provided by religious groups and organisations generally organised around places of worship, such as churches and temples. Another purpose of religion seems to be to provide society with some sort of agreed and organised set of moral standards. Each religion has its own set of moral standards and its own way of disseminating and implementing them. Almost all religions have one or more texts upon which the beliefs of that religion are based. Many of these religious texts contain what people interpret as being a codified set of moral rules. In this way, religion can be seen to be a good thing, particularly today when religion seems to have become less important to society and, perhaps as a result, society seems to be on some sort of moral decline.

An argument against religion being seen as a good thing in relation to moral standards might be that people should be allowed to adopt their own moral standards rather than having them legislated in the way religion seeks to. Further, the differing moral standards required by each of the religions are sometimes contradictory and this leads to a great many problems in the world. For example, one of the greatest debates in the world at the moment is the pro-life versus pro-choice debate surrounding abortion. Devout followers of the Catholic faith are staunchly opposed not only to the use of methods of contraception, but also to women being allowed to have abortions. The strongest believers in this point of view are opposed to any woman having an abortion in any circumstances. The question must then be asked, is it ever right that one person should be able to impose their religious and moral principles on other people who are not believers in those principles? In my view the answer must be no, but many people do not feel that way and it is these differences that have led to numerous instances of persecution, which reflect religion in a poor light.

Unfortunately, there are also numerous other problems in the world that are arguably caused by religion. It is always likely to be the case with such an emotive subject, particularly when it is part of human nature to be apprehensive about that which is different or that which is difficult to understand. This causes a particular problem because there are so many different religions in the world and, indeed, so many different splinter groups from each of the main religions. There are innumerable examples of strife caused by the differences between religions. Closest to home is the fighting in

Northern Ireland, which has been going on for many years; the main division in Ireland is between Catholics and Protestants. This is far from the only example: there is also the continuing strife in Palestine, the persecution of Sikhs throughout their relatively short history and also, perhaps the worst example of persecution of a single religion – the Holocaust – in which 6 million Jewish people were killed. All of these are or were caused to a greater or lesser extent by religious differences.

Can it really be said that a device that has led to so many wars and deaths and so much persecution is a good thing? It is certainly arguable that if no religion existed there would be no religious differences between different races and cultures and there would be one less thing to cause disagreements and unrest. Further, there would be no religious extremists to take their beliefs beyond all reasonable bounds and to use their religion as an excuse for committing terrible acts of violence. Having said all this, it could also be said that people will always disagree and fight and some people will always find some reason or excuse to carry out atrocities. I have to say that I do not find that to be a particularly compelling argument. The faith and belief that some people have in their religion is a faith that goes beyond all reason. I think these are beliefs that go so far as to convince people that, if they act in a certain way, it will please the superior being in their religion to the extent that they will receive special treatment in the afterlife. Without religion, I do not think that people would become fanatical with the same frightening regularity that seems to be the case in the world at the moment. For this reason, I do not think religion is a good thing.

Religion is also a bad thing because it allows people to pass on the responsibility for their actions. People can often blame bad things which have happened on God; they say 'God moves in mysterious ways' and 'the good Lord sends these things to try us' and sometimes people think that God is punishing them. In my opinion this does not encourage a healthy attitude to life and it fails to encourage people to take responsibility for their own lives and the things that happen in them. It is also the case that, in the wrong hands, religion allows the weak to be taken advantage of by the unscrupulous and those who seek power or money. This criticism can be made at a number of levels, one example might be people who sell fake 'holy water' and other fake religious symbols to people who are sick or badly off and need something to believe in. On a larger scale, monarchs, such as Henry VIII, used religion as a political tool to ensure he could marry who he wished and so that he could take the wealth of the Church and use it for his own ends. Even nowadays there are religious sects who persuade people to part with all of their money, convincing them that if they do so they may be able to benefit from the communal belief created by some extremist religious fanatic.

At the end of the day, it is impossible to assess whether religion is a good thing or a bad thing. There are many good things that have come about as a result of religion, but there are also a great many bad things that seem to have religion as their root cause. The problem is that religion has been around in all societies for thousands of years, and for this reason one cannot possibly tell whether the good things, which religion provides, would have been found in some other way if there was no religion. In precisely the same way, it is impossible to tell if the bad things, which are seemingly caused by religion, would have happened anyway, even if there had never been any religion in the world for people to blame the bad things on.

Question 3: 'Prison is no more than a school for criminals.' Discuss.

This is a question that allows for an in-depth discussion of social and political issues, and therefore offers the potential to write a relatively unique and thought-provoking response. To do so requires a good understanding of the criminal justice system in its present form and, equally as importantly, some ideas as to what could be done to reform it.

The starting point when answering a question containing a quotation should always be to explain what you understand the phrase to mean; otherwise it is impossible to meaningfully evaluate it. Where the quotation is not attributed to anyone in particular, it is useful to explain who might have said it and whether it is indicative of a widely held view or whether it represents more of a minority opinion. Once the question has been put in context, you can then put forward arguments for and against the suggestion made, before coming to a conclusion. It is perfectly valid, and indeed desirable, for such a conclusion to include a degree of personal opinion, provided that this is backed up by some factual knowledge.

On top of this basic structure there are a number of ways in which the essay could be developed into a more advanced piece of writing. First, some discussion could be included on whether the situation has always been as it is now and whether it is likely to change in the short or long term future. Secondly, you could introduce some of your own ideas by considering what could be done to improve the situation and what effect such measures would have on each of the problems that you have identified. Thirdly, you could include a comparison of how this situation relates to other social issues and whether any concerns raised over the prison system could be said to be symptomatic of other problems in society. Throughout the essay, it is desirable to compare and contrast the position in the UK with that in other countries, pointing out the relative strengths and weaknesses of our system.

Sample Essay Plan

1 Introduction

  ➢ explanation of quotation (meaning, possible source, support for view)

  ➢ how you intend to structure answer

2 Arguments supporting view

  ➢ criticism of leniency of prison system

  ➢ rate of re-offending

  ➢ experiences of young offenders

  ➢ drug abuse in prisons

3   Arguments against view

>   potentially difficult argument to counter directly (may be best to concentrate on other positives about prison)

>   rehabilitation

>   lack of alternatives (practical rather than theoretical argument)

4   Alternatives

>   education

>   community service

>   curfews/tagging

>   victim confrontation schemes

>   monetary damages

>   corporal/capital punishment

5   Other issues

>   comparison with other countries (rates of re-offending, size of prison population)

>   change over time (increasing prison population, changing crime rates)

6   Conclusion

>   evaluation of prison system

>   comparison with alternatives

>   potential improvements

Question 4: Which do you believe is more important in explaining human development: nature or nurture?

This is an interesting scientific debate and one that has run for many years with no firm conclusion being reached. It can be answered either in a very scientific way or from a more general theoretical point of view depending on your preference, although, clearly, there is a basic threshold of knowledge that must be reached in order to be able to write a good answer.

It should not be assumed that the reader will know precisely what you understand by the terms 'nature' and 'nurture' and these should be clearly defined at the beginning of the essay. The most obvious way to proceed would then be to look at the case for saying that nature plays a more important part, followed by the case for nurture, or vice versa, although it would be possible to go through it on an issue by issue basis explaining how each contributes to one side of the debate or the other. Evidence from research, such as that into the differences between fraternal and identical twins, is key to showing what the conventional thinking on the subject is, although it is perfectly acceptable to challenge such research, providing that you have grounds for doing so.

The question specifically asks what you believe to be most important, and a top-rate answer will develop a well-reasoned personal viewpoint in response to the evidence that has been put forward. It would also be desirable to go more deeply into the ideas of nature and nurture and consider what each comprises and whether or not each of the elements is of equal importance.

Sample Essay Plan

1   Introduction
    ➤   basis of the two theories
    ➤   context/relevance of debate
    ➤   approach to question

2   Case for nature
    ➤   inheritance of physical and other characteristics
    ➤   talent displayed from a young age (before any tuition or encouragement)
    ➤   life-long characteristics displayed (which are impervious to change)
    ➤   link between separated identical twins

3   Case for nurture
    ➤   differences between close relatives
    ➤   similarities between adopted children (without same birth parents)
    ➤   people changing as they get older
    ➤   role of education and other external influences

4   Conclusion
    ➤   evaluation of evidence (including acknowledgment that much of the evidence can be viewed either way)
    ➤   personal opinion (with explanation of reasons)
    ➤   overall view

Question 5: 'Scottish and Welsh devolution was a weak compromise that has satisfied no one.' Do you agree?

This is a question likely to be attempted by relatively few candidates given the fairly specialised knowledge that is required to produce a detailed answer. For those who have studied the area, however, it is a good question to choose as it offers the potential not only to demonstrate a strong factual knowledge, but more importantly to demonstrate an understanding of the political and social reasons behind the policies adopted.

This question can, and should, be split into three sections when writing your answer. It is easy to overlook the need to clearly explain what Scottish and Welsh devolution consisted of, but this temptation should be avoided as such detail is crucial to understanding the subsequent analysis. The next part of the question is to consider whether the devolution was a weak compromise, and the final part is to discuss how it was received by the various interested parties. It is important to deal with each of these parts separately as the question is relatively specific and is not simply calling for an overview of everything you know on the subject.

Continuing with the theme of how to achieve clarity, the way the question is worded leaves open the potential to examine the language in even more minute detail, looking for examples as to whether the compromise was weak and whether anyone was satisfied. You should try to demonstrate an appreciation of the fact that different groups will have had different agendas which means that their opinion may differ from an objective view of the situation. In stating your own opinion, you should seek to exploit these differences to highlight the difficulty in formulating a policy in this area.

Sample Essay Plan

1　Introduction
  ➢ background to devolution
  ➢ context of the debate
  ➢ structure of essay

2　The policy
  ➢ Scottish devolution
  ➢ Welsh devolution

3　Arguments in favour of the proposition
  ➢ extent to which devolution a compromise (strong or weak)
  ➢ devolution did not go far enough to satisfy nationalists
  ➢ unpopular with Unionists
  ➢ differences between position in Scotland and Wales
  ➢ anomalous situation with Scottish and Welsh MPs at Westminster

4　Arguments against the proposition
  ➢ extent to which devolution a compromise (strong or weak)
  ➢ success of policy (economic, social, political)
  ➢ lack of viable alternatives

5　Support for the policy
  ➢ Scottish National Party
  ➢ Plaid Cymru
  ➢ UK-wide parties (Conservative, Labour, Liberal Democrats)
  ➢ public reaction

6　Conclusion
  ➢ weigh up arguments for and against proposition
  ➢ comparison with alternatives and what could have been achieved

SAMPLE TEST 2

Checklist of Answers to Multiple Choice Questions

Cultural Relativism	Speeding
1 (d)	10 (c)
2 (e)	11 (b)
3 (c)	12 (e)

Trade and Health	Community Cohesion
4 (c)	13 (a)
5 (a)	14 (e)
6 (b)	15 (e)

Hieroglyphs	Democracy
7 (d)	16 (a)
8 (b)	17 (c)
9 (c)	18 (b)

Unemployment and Health	Einstein
19 (a)	25 (d)
20 (e)	26 (a)
21 (e)	27 (e)

Dreams	Nature of Intelligence
22 (d)	28 (e)
23 (c)	29 (d)
24 (b)	30 (d)

SECTION A: EXPLANATION OF ANSWERS TO MULTIPLE CHOICE QUESTIONS

1   Cultural Relativism

Question 1

Cultural relativism is defined as being the view that 'all ethical truth is relative to a specified culture' and it is said that 'it allows us to hold fast to our moral intuitions without having to be judgmental about other societies that don't share those intuitions'. By this definition, societies are entitled to lay down rules for themselves, but not to seek to impose these moral judgments on other societies. A group of countries that impose rules on other countries are breaching this principle in a way which is inconsistent with cultural relativism. *The correct answer is therefore (d).*

A country laying down laws for its own citizens is clearly perfectly consistent with cultural relativism, as is one laying down laws for foreign visitors. The latter situation is sometimes incorrectly thought to be different, but in reality accords perfectly with the principle that a society can decide how to control itself, as the foreign visitors have made the choice to enter that society. *Answers (a) and (b) are therefore incorrect.* Similarly, groups of countries that impose rules upon themselves and a religion that does the same are in accordance with cultural relativism. *Answers (c) and (e) are therefore incorrect.*

Question 2

It is specifically said that '[t]he strength of cultural relativism is that it allows us to hold fast to our moral intuitions'. By not having to judge other countries that do not comply with our beliefs, it makes it possible to follow a consistent set of principles. *The correct answer is therefore (e).*

Far from allowing for exceptions, the fact that there may be times when cultural relativism does not allow us the flexibility to condemn other societies is highlighted as a weakness: 'Cultural relativism excuses us from judging the moral status of other cultures in cases where that seems inappropriate, but it also renders us powerless to judge the moral status of other cultures in cases where that seems necessary.' *Answer (a) is therefore incorrect.* Cultural relativism does not imply that objective standards are invalid as it allows people to follow such standards by justifying the resulting inconsistencies. *Answer (b) is therefore incorrect.* It is said that cultural relativism allows us to avoid judging what has happened in the past, which is in no way the same as saying that the past is irrelevant. *Answer (c) is therefore incorrect.* Nowhere is it stated that it is wrong to describe actions as being morally inferior to others. It is said that 'there is no pressure on us to hold others to our moral standards at all', but this does not judge whether or not it is right or wrong to do so. *Answer (d) is therefore incorrect.*

Question 3

The basic strength of cultural relativism is identified as being the fact that there is no need to judge others by the standards that we set for ourselves. This can be said to promote understanding of other societies: we may think that what they do is wrong by our standards, but we accept that by their standards it is not. *The correct answer is therefore (c).*

This principle flies in the face of morality as we know it as it allows actions that would otherwise be condemned as immoral to be tolerated. *Answer (a) is therefore incorrect.* The fact that different standards are applied to different societies means that equality cannot be said to be promoted. *Answer (b) is therefore incorrect.* The fact that there is no need to judge people from other societies does not mean that it is necessary to go as far as empathising with their actions; it is sufficient to understand their right to act in that way. *Answer (d) is therefore incorrect.* Whether or not such understanding fosters prosperity is highly subjective and there is insufficient evidence to make a judgment on the issue. *Answer (e) is therefore incorrect.*

2   Trade and Health

Question 4

Two conditions are stated to limit the right to restrict trade to protect health: the restriction is applied in a non-discriminatory way and the restriction is based on recognised scientific evidence. It is then later stated that '[t]he process also makes it difficult to regulate inappropriate production methods which do not lead to problems in the end product but may be of public health concern', and that '[t]he short shrift given to precautionary measures to protect health, where existing scientific evidence is deemed insufficient, reflects a further inbuilt priority given to trade'. This clearly shows that the fact that little attention is paid to future health risks is a serious concern, and the quantity and tone of references to this particular concern mark it out as being of greater importance than other concerns also mentioned. *The correct answer is therefore (c).*

The fact that decisions are made by trade experts, rather than health experts, is highlighted as a flaw with the dispute resolution procedure. This is not, however, to say that all decisions on health are made by trade experts, and it could also be argued that it would be less of an issue who the decisions were made by if a clear procedure was established for taking into account future health risks. *Answer (a) is therefore incorrect.* The question is posed in the last sentence of the extract as to '[w]hether the public health community will be able to argue successfully to protect health, when pitted against the vast resources of a multi-billion dollar industry, remains to be seen'. Although this is identified as being a potential concern, it could not be the main concern due to the fact that it is not conclusively found to be a problem, and because it could be argued that the financial resources of the respective industries would be rendered irrelevant if the regime laid down was strong enough. *Answer (b) is therefore incorrect.* The fact that genetically modified organisms (GMOs) are not adequately regulated is an example of the problem that future health risks are not taken into account, and is not a separate factor in itself. *Answer (d) is therefore incorrect.* Likewise, the fact that there are only limited regulations on tobacco is only one specific example of a much larger issue. *Answer (e) is therefore incorrect.*

Question 5

At the beginning of the third paragraph of the article, it is said that 'there are greater tensions than ever before between promoting trade and protecting health because of globalisation'. The rest of the article then goes on to consider the relationship between trade and health and how a balance can be found between the two. The fact that this is an idea that is mentioned on a number of occasions right through the article leads to the conclusion that it is the main idea. *The correct answer is therefore (a).*

Although it is suggested that health concerns should not be subordinated by trade issues, the article does not go as far as suggesting that the reverse should be the case. *Answer (b) is therefore incorrect.* In addition to the suggestion that globalisation has created new tensions, it is said that 'trade has raced ahead of corresponding measures to protect health'. This is, however, an idea limited to one paragraph and is used to introduce the main part of the article, which focuses on achieving a balance between trade and health. *Answer (c) is therefore incorrect.* It is suggested that there are a number of vested interests involved in this area, but this is only a small part of the article and is used as an example of the difficulty in establishing an appropriate balance between trade and health. *Answer (d) is therefore incorrect.* Although there is some suggestion that trade was more important than health in the past, evidence is also given of steps taken to protect health, and in any case this is again only used as an introduction to the main part of the article. *Answer (e) is therefore incorrect.*

Question 6

Although the writers quote the view of public health advocates who have argued that tobacco should be subject to special restrictions, they also put the alternative viewpoint. With this in mind, it cannot be said that they have stated a view that tobacco products should be subject to a stricter health regime. *The correct answer is therefore (b).*

It is stated at the beginning of the third paragraph that globalisation has created new tensions between promoting trade and protecting health. *Answer (a) is therefore incorrect.* It is said in the penultimate paragraph that the jury is still out in relation to GM crops. *Answer (c) is therefore incorrect.* It is said at the beginning of the penultimate paragraph that various restrictions imposed on health grounds could constitute barriers to trade and market access, which would be in contravention of the principles put forward earlier in the article. *Answer (d) is therefore incorrect.* The discussion of GM crops, also in the penultimate paragraph, lays down the principle that the focus is on proven health concerns rather than on techniques used in production. *Answer (e) is therefore incorrect.*

3   Hieroglyphs

Question 7

In the extract, there is mention of the priests 'sustaining the myth of their professionalism'. If their professionalism was in part a myth then it follows that they were not as professional as sometimes claimed. *The correct answer is therefore (d).*

It is not suggested that the general populace did not understand the purpose of hieroglyphs, and it can be inferred that people understood that they were a language used by the priests. *Answer (a) is therefore incorrect.* What the majority were not able to do was to draw and interpret hieroglyphs themselves. Nowhere is it suggested that the priests were not well respected in the times described, and indeed the mention of 'reinforcing their power among the practitioners of the old beliefs' suggests that they were respected by the general populace. *Answer (b) is therefore incorrect.* It is suggested that the priests made hieroglyphs complicated so that they were the only ones who could understand them. *Answer (c) is therefore incorrect.* Nowhere is it implied that they themselves were not able to understand them, or that they did not in fact make them more complicated. *Answer (e) is therefore incorrect.*

Question 8

At the end of the penultimate paragraph, it is said that 'the pictorial turn from the hieroglyph to the portrait should be visualised as a sort of "picto-hieroglyph" ... or a suturing of the image/word divide'. This suggests that the writer regards portraits as a type of hieroglyph. *The correct answer is therefore (b).*

This is the opposite to saying that there was an increasing difference between pictures and words, but does not go as far as saying that the two had become completely interchangeable. *Answer (a) is therefore incorrect*. The whole article is about portraits and hieroglyphs, and the similarities and differences between them, and it would be illogical to say that there is no relevance in studying how words are different from pictures. *Answers (c) and (d) are therefore incorrect*. The phrase in question is used in the specific context of portraits and hieroglyphs and no generalisation can be made from that as to how images are used in other languages. *Answer (e) is therefore incorrect*.

Question 9

In the fourth paragraph, it is said that '[t]he portraits have filled a gap the newly acquired alphabetical language has created, by its linearity, by its effacement of the visual incorporated in the hieroglyph'. This, in conjunction with the other descriptions of the function of hieroglyphs and portraits, suggests that the use of portraits was largely to convey sentiments not capable of being expressed by alphabetical language. *The correct answer is therefore (c)*.

Although the difficulty of using hieroglyphs is made clear in the extract, there is no suggestion that it was any easier to create portraits. *Answer (a) is therefore incorrect*. Likewise, although hieroglyphs were established to have a very clear link with religion, there is nothing to suggest that the same could not be true of portraits. *Answer (b) is therefore incorrect*. There is no suggestion that portraits were less time consuming to create than hieroglyphs, or that they were any easier to understand. *Answers (d) and (e) are therefore incorrect*.

4   Speeding

Question 10

The fact that the writer goes on to question the logic of the roads having to be piled high with casualties before the speed limit can be enforced shows that he feels that the threshold for the installation of speed cameras is too high. *The correct answer is therefore (c)*.

The use of inverted commas does little to highlight the change in policy and, even if it did, there would be no logic for only placing one word inside the punctuation. *Answer (a) is therefore incorrect*. To suggest that the number of crashes required before a speed camera is installed is too low is to contradict what the writer says immediately afterwards. *Answer (b) is therefore incorrect*. The writer does not discuss alternative criteria for the situation of speed cameras: from what is said, all that can be inferred is that he believes that the threshold is too high, not that the number of crashes should not be taken into account at all. *Answer (d) is therefore incorrect*. The tone of the paragraph is such as to suggest that speed cameras should be more readily available and, with this in mind, it is incorrect to suggest that the writer disagrees with their use. *Answer (e) is therefore incorrect*.

Question 11

The explanation put forward for why this new policy is being pursued is public perception of the government's approach toward speeding. Such views are outlined at the beginning of the article and a further reference is made to the issue in the concluding sentence. Given that the explanation of such perception and the explanation of the problems with the resulting policy occupy the majority of the article, this can be said to be the main idea. *The correct answer is therefore (b).*

It is said that motorways are the safest type of roads and that the application of the system of variable penalties would be appropriate, but nothing in this suggests that it would be safe for speed limits to be increased. *Answer (a) is therefore incorrect.* It is said that the penalties for speeding should not be reduced, but nowhere is it suggested that they should be increased. *Answer (c) is therefore incorrect.* Although there is the potential to infer that this would have positive consequences, given the negative consequences of the reduction, this cannot be said to be the main idea of the article in the absence of so much as one explicit reference. The evidence of the consequence of speeding in built-up areas focuses on the difference between driving at 35mph and driving at 40mph. Both are some way above the current speed limit, and no argument is put forward by the writer that the speed limit should be reduced to below 30mph, merely that the current limit should be enforced. *Answer (d) is therefore incorrect.* An inference can be made that increasing the number of speed cameras would increase road safety, but this is not explicitly discussed and does not form a central enough part of the article to be regarded as the main idea. *Answer (e) is therefore incorrect.*

Question 12

It is specifically said that it is almost certain that there would be no change to the existing enforcement threshold, which is stated earlier in the article to be 35mph in 30mph zones. Given this, motorists driving at this speed would not be prosecuted or fined under either regime, and the introduction of the new rules would make no difference. *The correct answer is therefore (e).*

In view of the lack of enforcement action, it could not be said that drivers would be fined more or less under the new rules. *Answers (a) and (b) are therefore incorrect.* The new legislation only affects the penalties and enforcement of speeding and by definition there can be no difference in the likelihood of having an accident. *Answers (c) and (d) are therefore incorrect.*

5   Community Cohesion

Question 13

The tone of the second paragraph, where it is said that 'a lack of community cohesion is not simply seen as a "race" issue', and the fact it is said that '[r]ace is often used as a shorthand for these [other] problems', suggests that race is the most commonly cited cause of a lack of community cohesion, even if it is not the actual cause. *The correct answer is therefore (a).*

Employment, housing and education are all mentioned as other potential causes, but it is suggested that these are often all thrown together under the label of race. There is insufficient evidence to say which is actually the main cause, but the writer implies that race is cited as such. *Answers (b), (c), (d) and (e) are therefore incorrect.*

Question 14

There is insufficient evidence to make a judgment on this issue for two reasons. First, the survey only deals with the overall change in perception in comparison with 10 years ago, and does not provide any insight into what happened in the intervening time. Secondly, it relates only to the perception of race relations and does not use an objective measure of racially-motivated incidents, or similar, during the period. *The correct answer is therefore (e).*

In order to prove any of the first three alternatives to be correct, it would be necessary to have the kind of evidence mentioned above. *Answers (a), (b) and (c) are therefore incorrect.* In order to prove the fourth one correct, it would be necessary to have evidence of how important people thought the issue as a whole was, rather than just how they thought that relations had changed. *Answer (d) is therefore incorrect.*

Question 15

The evidence quoted does not prove that none of those surveyed correctly estimated the percentage of ethnic minorities present in the country. Rather, it shows that, on average, people thought that the percentage was higher. This could either be due to everyone giving a higher estimate, or some giving a correct or lower estimate, and others giving a much higher estimate. *The correct answer is therefore (e).*

The fact that it is said that '[t]hose who are dissatisfied with their area are most likely to overestimate the population', combined with the average estimate being too high, suggests that many people have a negative view of ethnic minorities on a locality. *Answer (a) is therefore incorrect.* The fact that the average estimate was so unrealistically high suggests that perception of race is not always based on reality. *Answer (b) is therefore incorrect.* From what is said above, it can be inferred that the state of race relations affects how people view their community. *Answer (c) is therefore incorrect.* It is stated that people of all ethnic minorities overestimate the percentage of the population that is made up of ethnic minorities. *Answer (d) is therefore incorrect.*

6   Democracy

Question 16

Direct democracy is defined in the extract as being the right of every citizen to become involved in the political process, and it is said that it requires full participation from those allowed to participate. This can be contrasted with other forms of representative democracy where most people's involvement in the political process goes no further than voting in elections. With this definition, it cannot be said that the creation of a small panel leads to direct democracy as it does not involve an element of mass participation, and at best could only be said to be representative of the rest of the electorate. *The correct answer is therefore (a).*

The fact that the participants were chosen randomly is only relevant to determine how representative the panel is, as is the fact that they do not form a cross-section of society. *Answers (b) and (c) are therefore incorrect.* The fact that the panel is not consulted on all issues and has limited influence could be said to affect the quality of the democracy, but this is of no importance if direct democracy does not exist in the first place. *Answers (d) and (e) are therefore incorrect.*

Question 17

The assertion that democracy is the most valued political term in the world, combined with the comparison between Britain as a democratic state and other countries as undemocratic, suggests that democracy is an ideal that Britain lives up to and other countries do not. The fact that those countries that are labelled undemocratic receive this label as a result of failing to live up to certain standards implies that democracy is in some way superior, and the preserve of only certain countries. *The correct answer is therefore (c).*

Implicit in this is the fact that certain requirements must be met in order to qualify as democratic, but there is no discussion of whether these requirements are widely accepted or not. *Answer (a) is therefore incorrect.* To suggest that the definition of democracy was somewhat arbitrary would require it to be shown that it was not capable of being applied consistently and no evidence is put forward in the extract as to whether this is the case. *Answer (b) is therefore incorrect.* Whilst Britain is held up as an example of democracy, to claim that Britain is the birthplace of democracy or that it is the arbiter of democracy is going well beyond what is actually said in the passage and if anything could be said to be based on preconceived stereotypes. *Answers (d) and (e) are therefore incorrect.*

Question 18

All five of the alternatives could be seen as flaws within direct democracy, and the group can be divided into theoretical and practical difficulties. The only one that could be said to fall into the former class of difficulties is ignorance amongst citizens as this is not a difficulty that relates to the ability of the system to operate on a practical level, but rather one which goes to the question of whether direct democracy is a good idea in theory. It is also a more fundamental difficulty as it is not something that can be resolved by increasing resources in the short to medium term, and possibly not at all if education and other policies prove unsuccessful. *The correct answer is therefore (b).*

The other four alternatives can each be clearly identified as practical difficulties, all of which would make the operation of direct democracy difficult, but not fundamentally impossible. The size of the population means that it would be difficult for everyone to be involved, but this is not absolutely impossible. *Answer (a) is therefore incorrect.* Insufficiently advanced technology may mean that it is more difficult to involve everyone in the political process, but there are alternatives to such technology and in any case technology is rapidly improving and may eventually be suitable. *Answer (c) is therefore incorrect.* Again, a lack of time does not render direct democracy impossible, but is a practical difficulty that must be circumvented. *Answer (d) is therefore incorrect.* Likewise, a lack of suitable meeting places is very much a practical issue, and one that could be resolved without the need to examine the theory underlying direct democracy. *Answer (e) is therefore incorrect.*

7   Unemployment and Health

Question 19

It is said that 'there is evidence that the unemployed were more likely to report themselves as retired or permanently sick when unemployment rates were high'. This implies that, at all times, not everyone who is unemployed reports themselves as such. *The correct answer is therefore (a).*

Although it may well be the case that not everyone who is sick reports themselves as such, this is not considered in the article. *Answer (b) is therefore incorrect.* From what has already been said, it follows that it cannot be true that more people report themselves as unemployed than actually are, and that there is insufficient evidence to claim that more people report themselves as sick than actually are. *Answers (c), (d) and (e) are therefore incorrect.*

Question 20

In order to determine where in the UK had the worst overall health, it would be necessary to have overall figures for each of the regions to compare. In the absence of such evidence, it is impossible to make a judgment. *The correct answer is therefore (e).*

It is stated that '[e]ach of the seven main occupational classes had higher rates of poor health in Wales, the North East and North West of England'. All that this shows is that poor health in these regions was not limited to particular social classes, but no evidence is provided as to how poor the overall heath was. *Answer (a) is therefore incorrect.* The largest gap between classes is said to be found in London and Scotland, but again this does not provide any evidence of overall health. *Answers (b), (c) and (d) are therefore incorrect.*

Question 21

A number of pieces of evidence are put forward in the last paragraph of what is described as 'ecological effect modification', showing that the most negative health consequences arise where there is variation from the norm. For example, it is said that the suicide rate for members of ethnic minority groups is lower in areas where they represent a larger proportion of the population and that in areas with low unemployment, being unemployed for a long time may be perceived as an 'aberrant and personally stigmatising situation'. *The correct answer is therefore (e).*

Although it could be inferred that there is a link between poverty and ill health, this is not specifically explored in the extract, and is not identified as a significant factor. *Answer (a) is therefore incorrect.* Location and unemployment are both highlighted as significant factors, but both can be included in the category of variation from the norm which is the underlying issue in both cases. *Answers (b) and (d) are therefore incorrect.* Similarly, ethnic origin is most relevant where this represents the biggest departure from the norm. *Answer (c) is therefore incorrect.*

8   Dreams

Question 22

Nowhere is it suggested that it is possible to control what one dreams. Indeed, such an idea would undermine Freud's theory given that this was based on unconscious thoughts, which had been repressed by waking thought. *The correct answer is therefore (d).*

The fact that Freud attributed mental illness to repression leads to the inference that he thought it was a fundamentally bad thing. *Answer (a) is therefore incorrect.* The tension between conscious and unconscious thought is mentioned and it is central to Freud's theory that there is a link between the two, given that he believed that by studying unconscious thought it was possible to gain an insight into conscious thought. *Answer (b) is therefore incorrect.* Given that his work was based on finding out the content of dreams and building on the results of this, it follows that he must have regarded there to be a benefit to discussing dreams; was there not, his work would be irrelevant. *Answer (c) is therefore incorrect.* Freud's theory was based on the idea of a three-dimensional mind, and it follows that he must have believed there to be a number of different aspects to the mind. *Answer (e) is therefore incorrect.*

Question 23

To develop a scientific theory of dreaming without believing there to be a scientific basis to dreaming would be a nonsense, and it follows that Freud must have started with the premise that there was such a basis. *The correct answer is therefore (c).*

It is not suggested that the theory requires everyone to dream, and there is no particular reason why this should be the case. Although a case could be made for saying that people with certain characteristics are more disposed to dreaming, there is nothing to stop this being taken into account in the theory and it would certainly be quite possible to carry out research on those that did dream. *Answer (a) is therefore incorrect.* For the same reason, it is not vital that everyone be able to remember the content of their dreams, provided that some are able to. *Answer (b) is therefore incorrect.* Whether or not everyone is honest in recounting dreams simply affects the accuracy of the research and does not preclude a theory from being developed. *Answer (d) is therefore incorrect.* Nowhere is it suggested that a fixed meaning was attributed to particular dreams and there would be nothing to prevent a researcher from taking into account characteristics of a particular person in order to interpret what they had dreamt. *Answer (e) is therefore incorrect.*

Question 24

In order to infer that we are now able to more accurately understand dreams than in the past, evidence would need to be put forward, first, of our present ability to understand dreams and, secondly, of our previous ability to do so. Not only is no such evidence put forward, but the very nature of dreams, as described in the passage, is such that this is very hard to quantify. *The correct answer is therefore (b).*

From the tone adopted in the first paragraph it can be inferred that people think that they can learn about themselves from their dreams. *Answer (a) is therefore incorrect.* Evidence is put forward of Francis Bacon's view that dreams are meaningless and Freud's view that they have a deep meaning. From this, it can be inferred that different people attach a different significance to dreams. *Answer (c) is therefore incorrect.* Likewise, it follows that the term 'dream' means different things to different people, as some regard it as meaning an expression of unconscious thought, whilst others see it as a meaningless jumble of ideas with no basis. *Answer (d) is therefore incorrect.* Although it can be said, on the basis of Freud's theory, that the content of dreams is based on our conscious thoughts and acts, there is no suggestion that it is possible to exert any control over which such acts translate into dreams. *Answer (e) is therefore incorrect.*

9   Einstein

Question 25

'Ether' is only mentioned in the context of introducing the experiments carried out by Michelson and Morley. The subsequent analysis goes on to consider some of the results arising from these experiments, but does not consider whether or not they demonstrated the existence of 'ether'. On this basis, this cannot be said to be something either challenged or accepted by the writer. *The correct answer is therefore (d).*

It is specifically stated that the Michelson-Morley results were invalid and it is said that 'their beautiful experiment was in fact useless'. *Answer (a) is therefore incorrect.* It is made clear in the introduction that the article seeks to challenge Einstein's Theory of Relativity. *Answer (b) is therefore incorrect.* Again, it is specifically said that Newton's laws were not beaten. *Answer (c) is therefore incorrect, as must be answer (e).*

Question 26

From what is said in the passage, it can be inferred that an emission is something that is sent out without a tangible object being moved (as would be the case, for example, with a bullet fired from a gun). Heat, like light, falls within this definition as it is emitted away from its source but is not something that is simply moved from the source to the destination. *The correct answer is therefore (a).*

By contrast, water is merely an object and steam is simply a different state of water. *Answers (b) and (d) are therefore incorrect.* Both are capable of being propelled from one point to another, but do not have the requisite properties of an emission. Fire is a state and is consequently clearly different in nature. *Answer (c) is therefore incorrect.* A column of smoke falls into the same category as steam, and again is unlike an emission in that it is capable of being moved from one point to another such that an identifiable part that is moved no longer remains in the original place. *Answer (e) is therefore incorrect.*

Question 27

The last part of the article considers whether light is an emission or a standard projectile and outlines some of the differences between the two. At no point is a comparison made about which of the two travels faster as a general principle, or which of the two is easier to measure. *The correct answer is therefore (e).*

Experimental or other evidence considering the speed of travel or the potential to measure would need to be advanced before any of the first four alternatives could be found to be the answer. *Answers (a), (b), (c) and (d) are therefore incorrect.*

10   Nature of Intelligence

Question 28

The link between intellectual and emotional intelligence is described as follows: 'Just because someone is deemed "intellectually" intelligent, it does not necessarily follow they are emotionally intelligent ... Highly intelligent people may lack the social skills that are associated with high emotional intelligence ... However, high intellectual intelligence, combined with low emotional intelligence, is relatively rare and a person can be both intellectually and emotionally intelligent.' From this, it is impossible to infer a sufficient relationship between the two for any of the first alternatives to be necessarily true. *The correct answer is therefore (e).*

For any of the other alternatives to be true, a more definite relationship between the two intelligences would need to be stated, or statistical evidence would need to be provided from which such a relationship could be deduced. *Answers (a), (b), (c) and (d) are therefore incorrect.*

Question 29

It is stated that the fact that black children adopted into white middle class families score significantly higher on average than those in working class families implies a cultural slant to tests. This shows that IQ tests are not a perfect test for raw intelligence. *The correct answer is therefore (d).*

This does not show that intelligence is not genetic, at least in part, as it does not consider whether such adopted children do as well as the natural children of the families who they are adopted by. *Answer (a) is therefore incorrect.* Similarly, the absence of such a comparison makes it impossible to determine whether the social environment is the main influence on intelligence. *Answer (b) is therefore incorrect.* Although it shows that children from non-white families who are brought up by white families do better in IQ tests than they would otherwise, it does not provide any evidence of whether non-white children do better or worse than white children. *Answer (c) is therefore incorrect.* It could not be said that children raised in middle class families always do better unless much evidence was put forward of research with a much wider scope, taking into account a spread of different types of family. *Answer (e) is therefore incorrect.*

Question 30

The only comparison of gender is where it is said that '[i]t is impossible to devise questions without some cultural or gender bias; boys tend to do better in spatial tests whereas girls score higher on linguistic tests'. This does not give any indication of which gender is better at intelligence tests overall, and therefore which gender has a higher average intelligence. *The correct answer is therefore (d).*

On the other hand, the example of black children adopted into white families suggests that social background is a determinant of intelligence. *Answer (a) is therefore incorrect.* The research into identical twins suggests that there is a genetic link to intelligence. *Answer (b) is therefore incorrect.* It is suggested that depression and feelings of rejection can reduce the ability to perform well in IQ tests, implying a lower utilisable level of intelligence, at least temporarily. *Answer (c) is therefore incorrect.* Race is mentioned a number of times in the article as being linked to intelligence, whether genetically or through social factors. *Answer (e) is therefore incorrect.*

SECTION B: EXPLANATION OF ANSWERS AND SAMPLES

Question 1: Should celebrities have a right to privacy?

This is a very topical issue in the light of recent cases involving celebrities such as Naomi Campbell and the Beckhams, and is one which most people are likely to have an opinion on. The question itself is a good one to attempt as it offers the chance to combine everyday knowledge with an understanding of the underlying law. You would not be expected to have a detailed knowledge of all of the case law on the subject, but it would be necessary to know sufficient information so that you could comment on what the current law is before discussing whether or not this is the correct position.

Indeed, such an explanation ought to feature near the beginning of your essay in order to lay the foundations for the subsequent arguments that you will be putting forward. The essay is best structured in a simple way with the arguments for celebrities having a right to privacy followed by the arguments against, or vice versa. In forming a view on which of these positions is more tenable, you should consider what the extent of this right should be and whether any exceptions are necessary.

From the outset it is necessary to clearly define what you mean by celebrities and this should involve distinguishing the different ways in which people can become famous and how this might impact on their right to privacy. For example, there is potentially a stronger case for affording a right to privacy to someone who has not sought fame than to someone who has continually courted the attention of the media. It would then be desirable to consider the practical side of the issue and consider how any right to privacy might be policed and whether this should be a consideration in the debate. In addition, there is the potential to look at privacy in a global context and to bring in some details of how the area has evolved in other countries.

Sample Essay

Although Britain does not have a specific privacy law in the way some other states do, everyone has a right to respect for a private and family life under Article 8 of the European Convention for the Protection of Human Rights and Fundamental Freedoms, incorporated into English law by the Human Rights Act 1998. Thus, it is generally accepted in our society that, within reason, people have rights to privacy, save in certain exceptional circumstances, for example where the law abrogates these rights to allow investigation into criminal or other unlawful activities. The question is whether celebrities should be treated as having forfeited or waived some or all of these basic rights. This essay will argue that celebrities, some of whom are famous through no deliberate act/s on their part, have done nothing to waive this fundamental human right and that, in all circumstances, they deserve the same protection from breach of their right to privacy as everyone else. Of course, as with all rights and corresponding duties, there is always a certain amount of balancing to do. Against people's right to privacy must be weighed the right to freedom of expression, which is every bit as important to society as the right to privacy. I will also argue that in some circumstances there may be justification for treating those who purposely seek public attention differently to those who are unwillingly or unintentionally celebrities.

Before I turn to examine whether celebrities have waived their rights to privacy, it is important to consider what we understand by the term 'celebrity'. Crucially, if we are to decide that celebrities have fewer rights to privacy than non-celebrities, then it is important to be able to point to as clear as possible a definition of a celebrity so that certainty and consistency are ensured. The word 'celebrity' comes from the same root as the word 'celebrate'. The original meaning of 'celebrate' was to gather in large numbers. Thus, a celebrity is a person who is known by many or, to put it more simply, is famous. The problem with this definition is that there are a very large number of people who could be described as 'famous' and they have become famous in a great many different ways. These could include politicians, royalty, television personalities, sports personalities, famous criminals or people who have been in the news for any reason. Further, people who are friends and relations of celebrities can easily gain a certain amount of celebrity simply as a result of being close to a famous person. This leads to the conclusion that trying to draw a rigid line in such circumstances is almost impossible, but it is something of a fool's errand given the multiplicity of reasons why a person may be well known. Ultimately, the most realistic approach is to give celebrity the wide meaning that it seems to have acquired in society, and refine the definition by considering the nature of people's fame.

There are arguments in favour of depriving celebrities of their rights to privacy. The first is that some people actively seek media attention and put themselves in the public eye. It must be remembered that some people are famous because they want to be, while other people, such as children of celebrities for example, become famous quite by accident and quite often wish they were not famous. Two interesting examples of celebrities are David and Victoria 'Posh Spice' Beckham. David Beckham became famous because he is a professional football player. He and numerous other people are famous simply as a result of doing the job that they do. At the start of her career Victoria could have been classified in the same way – she was famous because she was a singer in a famous girl group – that was her job. Now, however, the position is slightly different. Victoria Beckham is often now accused of creating a 'brand' out of the Beckhams and courting publicity by trying to sell this brand. Other people have had similar accusations levelled at them. For example, Jodie Marsh, Tara Palmer-Tomkinson and Tamara Beckwith are all people who are not famous because of their jobs or because of something particular that they have done. Essentially these people are all famous for being famous.

Celebrity can be a difficult thing to cope with, but along with the downsides there is also the chance of making considerable amounts of money. Celebrities have a wealth of opportunities to make money from their personalities. Prime examples of this are 'Celebrity Big Brother', 'Celebrity Fit Club' and 'I'm a Celebrity, Get Me Out of Here!'. Where people court publicity in this way, so that they can be shown on our television screens day in day out, it is very difficult to be sympathetic when they complain that their right to privacy is being breached on other occasions. Arguably, where a person is happy to be shown on the television all the time doing all manner of ridiculous things, they should be seen as having impliedly waived their right to privacy in other situations.

I could not disagree with this more strongly. As with a great many things in life, loss of the right to privacy can only be acceptable if the holder of that right consents to that loss. Take another fundamental human right, that of free speech. Would it ever be said that simply because someone did not exercise their right of free speech, that if they later wish to use it they could not because they have waived it. This is a ridiculous argument and in my view it is equally ridiculous to suggest that because a celebrity sometimes waives his or her right to privacy they can be said to have waived it in other situations too.

Some would argue that some jobs bring a certain amount of fame and attention and that if a person chooses to do that job then they must accept the media attention. On many occasions that job might make the person a role model for youngsters. One such example is Sven Goran Eriksson: the media has used his job and the fact that he is a role model as reasons to expose elements of his private life, despite his actively seeking to keep his private life separate from his job. It is very difficult to come to a firm conclusion as to where this sort of view is acceptable; however, I would argue that the requirement for a balance between the right to free speech and the right to privacy must hold the answer.

Numerous celebrities have been the victims of quite serious breaches of their privacy, among them are Princess Diana, Jamie Theakston, Naomi Campbell, Michael Douglas and Catherine Zeta Jones, David and Victoria Beckham and Geri Halliwell. Some of the breaches have led to legal action. In *Douglas v Hello!*, the Court of Appeal held that the right to privacy has to be balanced against the right to free speech and only where the right to privacy outweighs that to free speech would publication of such information be restrained. In my view, this is an ideal and extremely sensible way of dealing with problems like this. In almost all cases it will be necessary to weigh the right to privacy against the right to free speech. Further, it may be that in more cases involving celebrities than in cases involving non-celebrities, the right of free speech will outweigh the right to privacy. That would be an unfortunate by-product of celebrity, but it is a necessary result of the balancing of privacy and free speech. It must be borne in mind that at no time was it found that because Catherine Zeta Jones and Michael Douglas are celebrities they had no right to privacy. The court did find that because they had sold the rights to publish photos of their wedding to another magazine they had less privacy remaining for the court to protect. As a matter of fact, this must be correct; however, it would be the same rule for everyone, whether they are celebrities or not. Further, if celebrities choose to jealously guard their privacy then the courts should protect them against breaches of their right to privacy.

In conclusion, we must remember that magazines only publish what sells and while the public continue to be interested in celebrities the media will continue to do all that they can to get information about them and to publish it in magazines and to show in television programmes. In this way, celebrities will always have a greater weight of freedom of expression to weigh against their right of privacy and for that reason they will always have more difficulty protecting their right. In my view, however, in cases where a person is unintentionally and unwillingly famous, the courts should do what they can to protect their privacy rather than weighing the right of free speech against it so heavily because there is far less justification for invading these people's privacy than there is for those who intentionally court public attention for their own financial gain.

Question 2: What are the arguments for and against legalising euthanasia?

This is one of the most straightforward essay titles you are likely to encounter and is the kind of moral dilemma that you are likely to have thought about even if you haven't specifically studied it. It tends to be the case with questions structured like this that it is not overly difficult to write a reasonable answer, but it is fairly difficult to really excel, as the question does not leave much room for interpretation. Nevertheless, the fact that there are so many ethical issues involved with euthanasia means that you have plenty of opportunity throughout your answer to introduce some of your own thinking and interpret existing ideas in different ways.

The starting point of your answer should be to explain what the law is as it stands, providing some context about the debate for reform. The logical way to structure the main part of the essay is to run through all the arguments for legalising euthanasia followed by all those against, or vice versa. A more unusual approach is possible, but would run the risk of not fully answering the question and is likely to be more difficult to develop in the time available.

A subtlety that is easy to overlook, but which must be appreciated in order to write a top-class answer, is what is actually meant by euthanasia, as the term could be used to refer to a so-called mercy killing in a passive sense or may involve an active element. Throughout your essay you should keep in mind what an emotional subject this is, and your arguments should also reflect the practical, as well as theoretical, issues at stake. It is also worth comparing and contrasting the experiences of other countries, as the laws on euthanasia vary considerably.

Sample Essay

The term 'euthanasia' has traditionally been used to refer to the hastening of a suffering person's death or 'mercy killing'. Active euthanasia involves an intervention in respect of a terminally ill or severely debilitated person that is administered to that person to cause death; for example, a lethal injection. Passive euthanasia is where lifesaving treatment is withheld from a dying patient. There is a distinction between voluntary and involuntary euthanasia, the former requiring a positive act, and the latter only an omission. Passive euthanasia is already lawful in the UK, in certain carefully regulated situations, but active euthanasia is outlawed in its entirety. This is in contrast to countries such as the Netherlands, where voluntary euthanasia is already legal in certain circumstances, and there presently exists the somewhat anomalous situation where people have travelled abroad to die because of the stricter regime in the UK. In this essay I will concentrate on the emotive subject of whether active euthanasia should be allowed, considering the arguments for and against its use, which are so passionately put forward by campaigners for both sides.

The main argument against euthanasia is that life is the most precious thing that we have and killing is not acceptable in any circumstances. Of course, there is force in this argument and for a long time this was reflected in the fact that even suicide was regarded as both a moral and a legal crime. Such a view is deeply founded in religion, but even wholly secular societies respect life with a special reverence and regard it as something to be cherished and protected. To take this argument further, some suggest that because God gives the gift of life, only he should be able to take it away and that to kill oneself or another will always be a terrible crime against God. The fact that this view transcends religion, and extends to so many non-believers, shows the strength of the argument, albeit there are those that oppose it purely on the basis of its religious overtones.

Many opponents of euthanasia are also concerned that people who give up hope are in a worse position than those who still have hope. They also think that people who opt for euthanasia might later have changed their minds if they had hung on. It is certainly a possibility that there will be people who, if given the choice of euthanasia, would take it, but might later have changed their minds about it. This would more likely be the case if people are not properly apprised of their options nor given proper counselling before they make the decision. Linked to this is the argument that if euthanasia was never an option then people would never consider it. They would know they had to fight on and that would be the end of it. Although this argument is a sensible one, it clearly does not reflect the true facts of the situation. Even now, while voluntary euthanasia is illegal in the UK, people still want it and there are still occurrences of it. Sometimes a person's life is simply so desperately unbearable that all they want to do is end it.

It is certainly a problem that the legalisation of euthanasia could be open to abuse. People could be put under duress and forced to sign agreements that they want to die, for example by unscrupulous relatives who want their inheritance or in innumerable other circumstances. Considering cases such as that of Dr Harold Shipman, who might actually have killed more than 200 people in his time as a doctor, it is clear that there are people in the world who suffer some sort of psychosis that leads them to kill and kill again. Unless voluntary euthanasia is properly organised and regulated then any law legalising it might prove to be a 'murderer's charter'.

Another argument against legalising euthanasia might be that there is no need to. There have been recent occurrences of voluntary euthanasia carried out by husbands and wives and doctors and when these cases go to court, the judge will often exercise his discretion to give a very much reduced sentence to the person who carried out the act of euthanasia. One example is that of the ex-policeman who helped his terminally ill wife to die. The court gave him a two-year suspended sentence. Perhaps the best way to keep euthanasia to a minimum and ensure that it does not become a 'murderer's charter' would be to refuse to legalise it and allow the courts to use their discretion to deal with those who commit euthanasia.

There are, of course, a great number of arguments in favour of euthanasia too. First, and perhaps most compelling, is that a person's life is their own and if they choose to end it they should be allowed to do so. It is not fair to hold everyone up to the moral standards of those who believe life is a gift which should never be given up. Law is not in existence simply to create moral standards and in my opinion it is an unduly paternalistic approach to forbid people to choose to have their own lives ended. People can choose their own moral standards and if they think euthanasia is wrong then they can refuse to accept it for themselves; however, it is not right that people should seek to impose their own standards on others who cannot bear their own suffering. This argument is backed up by the fact that people obviously do not see euthanasia as such a bad thing anymore: the recent example discussed above, of the former policeman who helped his wife to die and received a two-year suspended sentence for killing her, is evidence that euthanasia is not universally condemned by society anymore, in fact it seems that more people accept it than do not. Very few would think that a man who was begged by his wife to end her suffering should go to prison because he helped her to die.

If able-bodied people decide that they want to commit suicide then no one can stop them. Why should the situation be different just because someone is unable to do the act themselves? In my opinion it should not be different. Whether a person lives or dies is their own choice and under the current system where voluntary euthanasia is illegal, people are forced to turn to their loved ones to suffocate them with pillows or subject them to other such terrible deaths. If euthanasia was legalised it would minimise the suffering of the dying person's loved ones, as well as ensuring the death was quick and painless. Some people have to put up with terrible indignity, pain and suffering; if there is a way for them to avoid that suffering then should they not be allowed to choose it? It is my view that there can be times when life is so painful that it would be better not to live it. Suffering animals are put to sleep every day, even though they cannot have a choice in the matter; since humans are intelligent enough to make that decision, they should be allowed to make it.

It has been shown in the Netherlands that people who know they have euthanasia as an option often hang on to life longer than they would have done without it because it gives them the hope and the safe knowledge that if the pain gets too much for them then they can escape it. If giving people a way out improves their length and quality of life then I can see very few compelling arguments against giving them that option. Voluntary passive euthanasia is legal in the UK. No one can force a person to accept treatment for their illness. Involuntary passive euthanasia is also legal under English law. The families of people who are in a vegetative state often have to make the decision to turn off life support machines. The arguments in favour of this are that the person is unable to make the decision for themselves, they won't ever recover and their brains are dead, so the person who they used to be has effectively already gone forever. Further, although it might seem heartless to consider the cost, the expense of running a life support machine to keep a brain-dead, but otherwise healthy, body alive for 20, 30 or 40 years would be a massive drain on the National Health Service's already suffering resources.

In conclusion, the debate about euthanasia is a very emotive one and there is no easy answer. It is my view that if the law is to allow people to refuse treatment, so that they will necessarily die, then they should be enabled to die painlessly and with dignity if they so choose. The parallels between the euthanasia debate and the abortion debate are highly evident. Simply put, the debate is pro-choice versus pro-life. Campaigners on both sides feel very strongly about this issue and although it is my opinion that people, should not be able to enforce their own moral standards on other people, it seems that, for now at least, this will continue to happen. Of course, if active euthanasia were to be legalised then it would have to be highly regulated and those who wanted it would have to undergo proper tests and counselling to ensure they were truly competent to make the decision to die.

Question 3: Have the UK and USA achieved their objectives in relation to Iraq?

This is the kind of question that everyone has some knowledge of as a result of the extensive media coverage that surrounded the conflict with Iraq. The danger of this can be that it is all too easy to think that this is a straightforward question and jump straight into writing a fairly generic answer, which does not demonstrate your full ability. This is not intended to dissuade you from answering what is potentially a very good question to choose, but rather to warn of the need to have a good depth of knowledge on the subject, such that it is possible to provide meaningful analysis rather than just a chronology of events.

The first and most crucial, although all too often overlooked, step when dealing with questions mentioning objectives is to set out what those objectives were. It is logically unsatisfactory to simply discuss the merits of actions in respect of vague and unstated aims, as such an approach makes it impossible to get to the heart of what the question is asking. Setting the aims out at the beginning of the essay provides a solid structure, as the results of the UK's and USA's actions can then be compared either result by result with the aims, or separately in relation to each aim. In forming a conclusion, it is likely that different aims will have met with different levels of success. Considering these together will allow an overall view to be taken on the success of the actions.

In relation to the original aims, a further question arises, namely whether the stated aims of the UK and USA were the same as the actual aims of the two countries. A good answer will consider what forces, political and otherwise, were at play in formulating the policy to attack Iraq, and whether there is any difference as to the level of success achieved in relation to these two potentially different sets of aims. Arguments could be put forward as to whether such a difference matters, conceptually or actually, to the debate over the success of the war, bringing in where possible an historical dimension and considering whether this was typically the case with government foreign policy.

Sample Essay Plan

1 Introduction
   - background of Iraq situation
   - necessity of evaluating success with respect to aims
   - aims and approach of essay

2 Aims of the UK and USA
   - difference between stated and unstated aims (the latter more speculative by definition)
   - removing Saddam Hussein's regime
   - reducing terrorism (possible link with Osama bin Laden and Al Qaida)
   - protecting oil supplies (lessons learned from Kuwait conflict)
   - political motivations (contrasting UK and USA position)

3 Analysis of success in relations to aims
   - consideration of each of the above aims

4 Other issues
   - consequent loss of life
   - instability
   - financial cost
   - potentially dangerous precedent set for future

5 Conclusion
   - global consequences
   - domestic consequences
   - which aims achieved and by whom
   - were there any alternatives?

Question 4: Some describe membership of the Single European Currency as the most exciting opportunity for Britain in decades, whilst others reject it as doomed to certain failure. Is either of these views correct?

Given the enormous media attention that has surrounded virtually every aspect of the Single European Currency, the majority of people will have an opinion one way or another as to its merits. This question demands an appreciation of both views and an ability to articulate the rationale behind each. It also demands an in-depth understanding of the workings of the currency and an understanding of how it has fared so far in other countries. In this way, the question is likely to appeal most to those who have studied economics, and it should be treated with some care by those who have only read about the subject on a superficial level without going into the kinds of intricacy that tend to be ignored by the press.

Having begun by briefly explaining some of the background to the debate, the essay should be split into three sections: arguments in favour of the first proposition, arguments in favour of the second proposition, and any alternative views that may be more accurate. It is easy to ignore the last of these, but given how diametrically opposed the two views expressed in the title are, it is likely that there will be some kind of compromise that you can advance. The question refers to opinions held by different groups of people and you should consider who is likely to hold these views and the reasons why, in order that you have some basis on which to build a discussion of the merits of each position.

The best essays on the subject will take this idea a stage further and consider the divergence between the theoretical arguments for and against the currency and peoples' perception of the situation. Following on from this, it would be useful to consider how this divergence arose and how the perception of people in other countries differs. It is impossible to fully answer the question without looking at the political aspects of the issue and the role played by the government. In this regard, it is useful to consider whether it has been the government that has determined public opinion or whether it has simply been following the opinion of the voters.

Sample Essay Plan

1 Introduction

> ➤ background to the Single Currency (history and development)
> ➤ Britain's current position (tests laid down by government; public opinion; likelihood of joining)
> ➤ context of the debate (supporters and opponents of the Single Currency)
> ➤ proposed structure and approach of essay

2 Arguments in favour of joining the single currency

> ➤ closer links with the rest of the EU (politically and economically)
> ➤ stability (no exchange rate fluctuations; traditionally lower interest rates)
> ➤ promotion of trade and investment
> ➤ convenience (for businesses and individual travellers)
> ➤ experience of other countries (success of currency so far)

3   Arguments against joining the Single Currency

➤ loss of control over interest rates (controlled by central bank)

➤ tradition (hostility to change)

➤ strength of Sterling (which advantage would be largely lost after membership)

➤ lack of convergence of economic cycles (historically different interest rate patterns and trade cycle in Britain)

➤ lack of flexibility (difficulty in correcting local fluctuations)

➤ experience of other countries (difficulties in achieving convergence)

4   Conclusion

➤ weigh up both sides of the argument

➤ difference between reality and perception of the debate (and which is more important)

➤ an exciting opportunity even if not the most exciting one

Question 5: 'The AIDS epidemic in Africa must surely be the ultimate sign of the developed world's failure to meet their global responsibilities.' Do you agree?

This is a less mainstream question, and one that is likely to be answered by fewer candidates. Providing that you have a sufficient knowledge of the subject to be able to write a meaningful answer, this gives you the opportunity to set yourself apart from the larger number of candidates answering some of the other questions.

When tackling a question like this, it is crucial to start by defining exactly what is understood by the expressions used. It is insufficient to assume that the reader will have a clear idea what the AIDS epidemic in Africa involves, and this should be explained at the outset, where possible using statistics to back up what you are saying. An analysis should then be put forward of the developed world's role in the AIDS epidemic and other global scenarios and a conclusion reached on how the AIDS epidemic compares to other responsibilities.

There are more aspects to this question than may be immediately obvious and in order to write a really excellent essay it is necessary to think laterally. One of the main areas to focus on is how responsibility is apportioned between the developed country and the African nations involved. Whilst it is a perfectly tenable conclusion that the AIDS epidemic is more serious than any other global crisis, there is a strong argument for saying that various African governments should have played a much more active part in dealing with the problem. The success of any policies implemented by developed countries should be evaluated in relation to what could reasonably be achieved, and mention should be made, first, of the overall difficulty of combating an epidemic of this magnitude and, secondly, of the difficulty of taking any action from outside the countries concerned with potentially limited co-operation from those in power locally. Throughout the answer, it is necessary to keep in mind the enormous cultural differences between African countries and other more developed countries, another factor which potentially limits the help which can be given.

Sample Essay Plan

1 Introduction
- ➢ AIDS problem generally
- ➢ specific problem in Africa
- ➢ how the question is to be approached

2 The problem itself
- ➢ how the disease has reached epidemic proportions (lack of education; lack of availability of condoms)
- ➢ comparison with the position in other countries (confined to sections of society; never reached predicted levels; better education)

3 What has been done
- ➢ by developed countries
- ➢ by developing countries

4 What could be done
- ➢ role of developed countries (providing education and healthcare; difficulties of providing aid to distant countries; cultural differences)
- ➢ role of developing countries themselves (lack of experience and resources)

5 Global responsibilities
- ➢ extent of obligations to foreign countries (domestic needs; limited resources)
- ➢ other global obligations (natural disasters; conflicts; other health problems; economic problems)

6 Conclusion
- ➢ extent of problem
- ➢ extent of responsibility
- ➢ degree to which this responsibility has been fulfilled
- ➢ limits on further help
- ➢ balance with other global responsibilities

SAMPLE TEST 3

Checklist of Answers to Multiple Choice Questions

Leisure Time	Genetic Modification
1 (b)	10 (b)
2 (d)	11 (a)
3 (e)	12 (e)

Spaces of Consumption	The True Ultimate
4 (c)	13 (d)
5 (b)	14 (b)
6 (a)	15 (a)

Mental Illness	Global Health
7 (b)	16 (c)
8 (a)	17 (e)
9 (e)	18 (d)

Voting Patterns in America	Time
19 (d)	25 (d)
20 (e)	26 (c)
21 (a)	27 (d)

Mysticism and Physiology	Beauty and Intelligence
22 (b)	28 (c)
23 (e)	29 (d)
24 (b)	30 (c)

SECTION A: EXPLANATION OF ANSWERS TO MULTIPLE CHOICE QUESTIONS

1   Leisure Time

Question 1

The only statistic provided about 45–54 year olds' attendance at museums is that the proportion has increased from 31% to 47%. This is the largest increase mentioned, but it is not possible to say that this group are the most frequent visitors to museums unless the overall percentages from the other age groups were included. *The correct answer is therefore (b).*

It is said that 56% of museum visitors have a degree, Masters or PhD. *Answer (a) is therefore incorrect.* The people who are now more likely to visit museums and art galleries are described as being people with 'increased leisure time, increased income, and the majority are well educated'. *Answer (c) is therefore incorrect.* The statistics quoted are that only 46% of gallery visitors have a degree, Masters or PhD, compared with 56% of museum visitors. *Answer (d) is therefore incorrect.* The fact that the groups that have shown the largest increases in visitor numbers to museums and galleries since the introduction of the government's new policy have been older people suggests that young people have been less affected. *Answer (e) is therefore incorrect.*

Question 2

Although it is said that only one in 10 low income Brits attend such concerts, it is not possible to deduce from this whether they cannot afford to or whether they simply have a preference for other leisure activities. *The correct answer is therefore (d).*

It is specifically said that that '[r]esearch that MORI conducted for Re:Source … in 1999 showed that cost was only a very small factor in the reason people did not visit museums and galleries'. This is a view backed up by much of what is discussed in the article. *Answer (a) is therefore incorrect.* The fact that cinema going is described as the most popular cultural activity for low income Brits suggests that cost is not such a major issue. *Answer (b) is therefore incorrect.* It is stated that '[t]here has been a slight drop overall in the proportion of people visiting theme parks (from 23.7% in 2000 to 20.4% in 2002)'. *Answer (c) is therefore incorrect.* It is said that '[o]lder people are a group most likely to experience none of these leisure activities', suggesting that they pursue a narrower range of leisure activities. *Answer (e) is therefore incorrect.*

Question 3

It is said that '[m]useums have increasingly been taking interactivity into account in their marketing and new exhibition development – introducing more interactive displays, and experiential activities, child friendly cafes and even cinemas ...'. This is an example of how cultural activities are changing in nature. *The correct answer is therefore (e).*

Nowhere is it stated that the increase in visitor numbers at museums and art galleries has been caused by the government's policy and, indeed, some of the evidence about factors influencing attendance suggests that this may not be the case. *Answer (a) is therefore incorrect.* It is said that a majority of those visiting museums have a degree, Masters or PhD. No statistics are given for how many people have such a qualification, and what proportion of people with such a qualification visit museums. *Answer (b) is therefore incorrect.* It is stated that an increasing number of young people are visiting theme parks. *Answer (c) is therefore incorrect.* It is said that cinema going is the most popular leisure activity for low income Brits, but it is not stated that cinema going is more popular amongst those on lower incomes than those on higher incomes. Statistics for both would need to be provided in order to make a comparison. *Answer (d) is therefore incorrect.*

2   Spaces of Consumption

Question 4

The following description is given of spaces of consumption: 'In the arcade, the goods are on display at the same times as the flâneur is capable of passing through the arcade as an autonomous, enterprising and choosing subject. Consumption becomes an aesthetic experience; space and consumption are merged in the special practice producing spaces of consumption.' This talk of consumers being able to choose from goods on display leads to the conclusion that an arcade is where goods are bought. *The correct answer is therefore (c).*

The element of choice mentioned above suggests that goods are being purchased rather than used, and the reference to consumers suggests that this is not where goods are being manufactured. *Answers (a) and (b) are therefore incorrect.* No evidence is put forward to suggest whether consumers or producers are in the majority; indeed, it is possible that another group, such as retailers, are. *Answers (d) and (e) are therefore incorrect.*

Question 5

It is said that '[t]he spaces of production are paradoxically rural spaces located within urban environments', and a number of references are made to new or moving forms of rural spaces. Given that such references feature in a discussion about production, the assumption must be made that rural spaces represent the principal area of production, otherwise the logic of the argument is lost. *The correct answer is therefore (b).*

As mentioned above, it is stated that rural spaces are capable of being moved to urban areas, and this cannot be said to be an unstated assumption. *Answer (a) is therefore incorrect.* It is suggested that consumption takes place within the arcades, not production. *Answer (c) is therefore incorrect.* Although it may be the case, it is not a necessary assumption to make that rural spaces are totally different in character to urban spaces. *Answer (d) is therefore incorrect.* No fixed link between rural spaces and individual spaces of consumption is suggested or assumed. *Answer (e) is therefore incorrect.*

Question 6

It is not suggested that kitsch is a branch of art, as it is not a distinct form of expression in the way that impressionism or modernism could be said to be. Rather, it is described as being a characteristic of a range of different types of art, and a characteristic that can ultimately distinguish it from all art. *The correct answer is therefore (a).*

It is also described as being comfortable and pleasing, and its familiarity is commented upon. *Answers (b), (c) and (d) are therefore incorrect.* It is said that '[k]itsch … is nothing more than art with a 100 percent, absolute and instantaneous availability for consumption'. This suggests that it is easily accessible. *Answer (e) is therefore incorrect.*

3   Mental Illness

Question 7

It is stated that 'it has been suggested that mental illness is more stigmatized in rural areas and this may lead to a greater reluctance to seek formal health service support; such possible stigmatising effects may be greater in men than women'. The use of the word 'may' and the absence of any evidence to back up this specific point mean that this is an assertion rather than a fact. *The correct answer is therefore (b).*

The statistics provided from the National Survey of Psychiatric Morbidity show that 'the odds of psychiatric disorder in 16- to 64-year-olds living in urban compared to rural areas declined from 1.64 (p<0.001) to 1.33 (p<0.05) after controlling for socio-economic and other differences between the locations'. Given the survey evidence used, this can be said to be a fact rather than an assertion. *Answer (a) is therefore incorrect.* Similarly, it is said that '[o]ur analysis shows that rates of consultation for mental disorder by young men and women are lower in rural compared to urban areas'. *Answer (c) is therefore incorrect.* It is said that '[p]revious analyses of the Fourth General Practice Morbidity Survey have demonstrated strong social class gradients in consultations for psychiatric disorders', suggesting that this finding is based on fact rather than merely being an assertion. *Answer (d) is therefore incorrect, as must be answer (e).*

Question 8

The following findings are stated in relation to the rate of consultations: 'The 1993 OCPS National Psychiatric Morbidity study reported that on 35 percent of "cases" had consulted a GP for mental health reasons in the last year. Secondly, amongst those who did seek help from their GP, many may not have had their mental disorder detected or recorded.' This suggests that more people suffer from mental illness than have formally been diagnosed as such. *The correct answer is therefore (a).*

With this in mind, it must by definition be incorrect to say that less people suffer from mental illness than have been diagnosed as such. *Answer (b) is therefore incorrect.* Although it is suggested that due to the stigmatising effects of mental illness there may be a greater reluctance to seek formal health service support in rural areas, no facts are included to back this up. Consequently, such an assertion cannot be inferred to definitely be true. *Answer (c) is therefore incorrect, as must be answers (d) and (e).*

Question 9

Socio-economic differences, the drift from rural to urban areas, the differing reluctance to report symptoms and the differing characteristics are all put forward as potential explanations for the difference in prevalence of mental illness between urban and rural areas. No comparison is made of the relative importance of each, and in the absence of such evidence it is impossible to say which is the main reason. *The correct answer is therefore (e).*

It is stated that '[f]urther, more detailed, research is required ... to explain the observed rural-urban differences in the prevalence of mental disorder in young people ...'. Some method of establishing the relative significance of each would need to be found in order for any of the other alternatives to be said to be true. *Answers (a), (b), (c) and (d) are therefore incorrect.*

4   Genetic Modification

Question 10

If intelligence is not based on genetic factors, then a technique based on altering a gene would have no relevance to a person's intelligence. By definition, this must be a fundamental assumption made in order to appreciate the potential benefit of the new technology. *The correct answer is therefore (b).*

With this in mind, any of the other alternatives would be of little importance unless the technique had any theoretical chance of working and arguably it would be irrelevant whether or not such assumptions were made. It may not matter whether it is possible to alter one gene without affecting others, providing that the effects can be controlled. *Answer (a) is therefore incorrect.* Likewise, it may not be necessary for humans to share the majority of their genetic characteristics with the mice tested, as what would be important is whether they shared the particular characteristics that were influenced by the technology. *Answer (c) is therefore incorrect.* Whether or not there are any side effects to the genetic modification will not necessarily affect the usefulness of the technology and this is something that would need to be investigated in detail rather than making a blanket assumption. *Answer (d) is therefore incorrect.* It is also not necessary for all genes to react in a similar way, only those which are being influenced by the technique. *Answer (e) is therefore incorrect.*

Question 11

The key advantage of NR2B is identified as being the fact that it makes things easier to learn by allowing the connected events to occur further apart. This clearly facilitates learning. *The correct answer is therefore (a).*

It is stated that NR2B can keep mice's brains young, but this is not the same as saying that it reverses ageing; at most it is the equivalent of saying that it stops ageing. *Answer (b) is therefore incorrect.* Nowhere is it suggested that the speed of thought is increased by the gene, simply the speed at which things can be learned. *Answer (c) is therefore incorrect.* If anything, it is suggested that it makes the brain receptors more sensitive not less. *Answer (d) is therefore incorrect.* It is not suggested that NR2B has any function in increasing memory capacity. *Answer (e) is therefore incorrect.*

Question 12

Although by implication it could be said that mice must share some genes with humans in order to make the research of any relevance, this is not actually stated in the article. *The correct answer is therefore (e).*

It is stated in some form in the text that mice have the ability to learn new skills, that it is possible to counteract signs of ageing, that the ability to learn declines with age and that there is a chemical basis to memory. *Answers (a), (b), (c) and (d) are therefore incorrect.*

5   The True Ultimate

Question 13

Throughout the extract, the writer articulates a number of religious views and considers whether various pieces of scientific thinking are consistent with them. For example, the writer says 'let me consider whether in this scientific age we can seriously believe that there is an ultimate destiny for human beings beyond their death'. Given the prevalence of this theme, it can be said that the main purpose of the extract is to consider whether religion is consistent with science. *The correct answer is therefore (d).*

There is nothing to suggest that the traditional view of resurrection is being challenged. It is simply being viewed in the context of modern scientific thinking. *Answer (a) is therefore incorrect.* Although it is suggested that there is the potential for life after death, this is an example of how science is consistent with religion, and is in itself not as fundamental to the passage. *Answer (b) is therefore incorrect.* The writer's purpose is more to consider the overall consistency of religion and science than to verify the accuracy of specific biblical passages. *Answer (c) is therefore incorrect.* It could be said that the discussion in the extract goes some way towards explaining the nature of humanity, but this is very much a by-product and is not the main purpose of the extract. *Answer (e) is therefore incorrect.*

Question 14

As mentioned above, throughout the extract, the writer weighs up religious views and arguments involving science, and at no time is any inconsistency raised. For example, in the last paragraph, he says that '[t]he universe is going to die but, because God cares for it, it will have its resurrection beyond its death, just as we shall have our resurrection beyond our deaths'. From this, it can be inferred that he believes that religion is consistent with science. *The correct answer is therefore (b).*

From what has been said above, it appears that the writer does believe in religion, and there is nothing to suggest that this agreement is in any way reluctant. *Answers (a) and (c) are therefore incorrect.* He does not go as far as saying anything which suggests that religion is vital to everyone or that religion is vital to science. He merely suggests that it is possible for everyone to follow it and that believing in scientific explanations for phenomena does not preclude you from believing in religion. *Answers (d) and (e) are therefore incorrect.*

Question 15

In considering resurrection, the writer says the following: 'The "software" of life cannot run on any old "hardware" ... but there is surely the possibility of there being a new "matter" in which we can be re-embodied at our resurrection.' Depending on your interpretation of this concept of resurrection, it may suggest reincarnation into another form of earthly life rather than a heavenly one. Either way, heaven is not mentioned in the article, and it does not follow from what the writer has said that heaven must, or is even likely to, exist. *The correct answer is therefore (a).*

As discussed above, the writer's concept of resurrection involved reincarnation into a different form. *Answer (b) is therefore incorrect.* This is clearly a form of life after death, and one which relies on the existence of God. *Answers (c) and (d) are therefore incorrect.* It is stated that although the universe is going to die out, 'because God cares for it, it will have its resurrection beyond its death'. *Answer (e) is therefore incorrect.*

6   Global Health

Question 16

The article is introduced by comparing the horrendous consequences of disease in some parts of the world with the 'current emphasis of bio-medical science on the molecular realm of DNA coding and the development of lucrative Western markets for new pharmaceutical products ...'. This is a theme continued throughout the article, and one that can be summed up by the fact that there is said to be considerable inequality in the provision of healthcare around the world. *The correct answer is therefore (c).*

Although it could be said that the increase of spending on healthcare in developing countries would alleviate many of the difficulties faced, this is not a particular point pursued in the article. Instead, the need to change attitudes and focus on the politics of global health is highlighted. *Answer (a) is therefore incorrect.* The resurgence of diseases previously thought to be under control is mentioned as being a problem, but there is only one fairly limited reference to this, and it is used more as an example of a wider problem than as an overriding theme in itself. *Answer (b) is therefore incorrect.* The same is largely true of the references to the AIDS epidemic, albeit that the AIDS epidemic is mentioned more frequently. Nevertheless, it is only one of a number of examples used, and could not be said to be the main idea. *Answer (d) is therefore incorrect.* It is suggested that more attention should be paid to some of the affairs of developing countries, not that the developed world should not interfere. *Answer (e) is therefore incorrect.*

Question 17

It is stated that the idea of public health sits uncomfortably alongside bio-medical science and that '[t]he needs of the majority – the global poor – scarcely feature within this tactical alliance between the bio-medical sciences and corporate power'. This, combined with the references to the health problems suffered by so many people around the world, suggests that attention is being distracted away from more fundamental healthcare issues. *The correct answer is therefore (e).*

It cannot be said that bio-medical research is a waste of money, which would otherwise be spent on dealing with more prevalent diseases, as it is said that much of this money comes from big corporations, and there is little to suggest that such companies would otherwise offer financial support to deal with more fundamental healthcare issues. *Answer (a) is therefore incorrect.* It may be the case that certain pharmaceutical companies make large profits, but this is a very insignificant problem in comparison with the suffering of millions of people affected by disease. *Answer (b) is therefore incorrect.* There is no suggestion that a lack of natural resources is likely to hinder the provision of healthcare. *Answer (c) is therefore incorrect.* It cannot be said that the effects of bio-medical research will only be felt in more wealthy countries, and, in any case, the major problem is identified as being access to fundamental healthcare, not the more advanced techniques that are being researched. *Answer (d) is therefore incorrect.*

Question 18

Although the focus on bio-medical research is highlighted as being a problem in respect of public health in general, it is not one of the factors identified as being an impediment to the improvement of sexual health. *The correct answer is therefore (d).*

War is stated to provide such an impediment: 'And in regions where war or civil strife prevail, the vulnerability of women and children to sexual violence, economic exploitation and disease is even greater …' *Answer (a) is therefore incorrect.* Poverty, social attitudes and religious beliefs are similarly identified as problems: 'The spread of AIDS in more traditional societies is closely linked with patriarchal power structures. The sustenance of these structures is assured by the rise of poverty-fuelled ethnic and religious chauvinism, which undermines the prospects for developing more progressive approaches to social policy.' *Answers (b), (c) and (e) are therefore incorrect.*

7   Voting Patterns in America

Question 19

The 'Kennedy factor' is identified as being a reason for a high electoral turnout. The only one of the alternatives that would encourage a high turnout is the fact that people had strong opinions about Kennedy. If this were the case, people would be keen to vote whether it be for or against him. *The correct answer is therefore (d).*

If it were to be assumed that Kennedy would definitely win or definitely not win, this would act as a disincentive to vote as there would be little to be gained from doing so. *Answers (a) and (b) are therefore incorrect.* Similarly, if people were apathetic, they would be less likely to go to the effort of voting. *Answer (c) is therefore incorrect, as must be answer (e).*

Question 20

Evidence is provided that more people registered to vote following the introduction of the Motor Voter Act. This suggests that many people were previously put off by the registration procedure, and implies that were it even easier, there would be likely to be a further increase in participation. Combined with the fact that it is stated that around 20% of the population is mobile and may be discouraged from voting by the difficulty in having to register in advance, it follows that removing the requirement to register in advance of the election day is likely to have a positive effect on turnout. Such an effect would, almost by definition, be immediate in relation to the next election as there is inherently no time lag involved. *The correct answer is therefore (e).*

Reducing the age of majority is suggested not to have had a major impact in the past, and by nature is likely to take some time to have an effect as it would require a changing of attitudes amongst young people. *Answer (a) is therefore incorrect.* The same is largely true of extending the electoral franchise as it is unlikely that all those with a new-found right to vote would do so without some additional form of encouragement. *Answer (b) is therefore incorrect.* Increasing education about political issues, whether or not it was effective, would by definition not be particularly immediate as education is a gradual process. *Answer (c) is therefore incorrect.* Increasing facilities for disabled voters is unlikely to make much of a further difference and by definition would only affect a small part of the population. *Answer (d) is therefore incorrect.*

Question 21

Nowhere in the passage is the issue of deciding between candidates' policies considered and there is nothing to suggest that this is a factor in the low turnout at elections. *The correct answer is therefore (a).*

Several references are made to the effect of the registration system in discouraging participation in elections. *Answer (b) is therefore incorrect.* In the first paragraph, apathy is raised as a potential explanation of the low turnout, even though its role is played down. *Answer (c) is therefore incorrect.* Similarly, the fact that the result is a foregone conclusion is identified as a factor in the first paragraph: 'This could simply have been because so many potential voters considered the result a foregone conclusion ...' *Answer (d) is therefore incorrect.* A comparison is drawn between the turnout resulting from the so-called 'Kennedy factor' and the turnout for the very open contest between Al Gore and George Bush. This suggests that where there is a particularly strong character in the running, turnout may be higher. *Answer (e) is therefore incorrect.*

8　Mysticism and Physiology

Question 22

Ficino is said to conceive of mutual eye contact as being 'a radiological event during which both partners cast rays towards each other'. This is contrasted with an 'innocent process', suggesting that the latter must be one in which there is not the kind of physiological change envisaged by Ficino. *The correct answer is therefore (b).*

It is not stated that the process envisaged by Ficino is an intentional one, so the opposite view does not necessitate it being an unintentional process. *Answer (a) is therefore incorrect.* Similarly, in either case, intent may or may not be present, at least on a conscious level. *Answer (c) is therefore incorrect.* Whether or not either party would feel guilty about eye contact depends on the individual situation and is not necessarily altered by the nature of the process. *Answer (d) is therefore incorrect.* Both processes are capable of taking place independently of other people. *Answer (e) is therefore incorrect.*

Question 23

By Ficino's reasoning, once the process described has taken place, the person involved 'develops an unstoppable desire to be with the other, a desire we know as love'. If the process takes place between people who had not intended it to take place, the implicit consequence would be that they would have had no control over whom they had fallen in love with. *The correct answer is therefore (e).*

Ficino is said to have believed that rays can transfer blood across a void, that eye contact begins the process, that the blood in question longs to return to where it came from, and that subtle nebulous blood can be converted into normal blood. None of these are, however, consequences; they are factors that, when taken together, lead to the consequence in question. *Answers (a), (b), (c) and (d) are therefore incorrect.*

Question 24

Something is described as being anachronistic when it is attributed to the wrong period; for example a modern car appearing in an old film or a very old car being portrayed as new in a modern film. The view put forward by Ficino may be seen as being out of date, but it is not being attributed to the modern age and could not therefore be regarded as an anachronism. *The correct answer is therefore (b).*

The imagery used could be said to be a metaphor for falling in love, and that is the most likely way of viewing it in modern times. *Answer (a) is therefore incorrect.* It is said that, '[i]n a post-Cartesian world, the charm of Ficino's psychology has been somewhat elusive' and various developments are cited as leading to this. It follows that this idea would be described as dated, given that advances over time have rendered it less relevant. *Answer (c) is therefore incorrect.* By the same token, it has been superseded by other views. *Answer (d) is therefore incorrect.* Judged by our standards, there is a considerably naïvety about Ficino's view, given the number of unfounded assumptions required to be made in order to support it. *Answer (e) is therefore incorrect.*

9   Time

Question 25

The concepts of time and space are mentioned or alluded to a number of times in the passage in explaining our perception of life. For example, it is said that 'Kant argued that one could never perceive of or imagine anything existing outside space or in the absence of time', and Newton is said to have believed that 'both space and time were absolutes'. This suggests that both are crucial to our understanding of life. *The correct answer is therefore (d).*

Nowhere is it stated that one cannot exist between the other, and no comparison is made of the relative importance of each. *Answers (a), (b) and (c) are therefore incorrect.* Although the way that space and time are described suggests that there may be a link between the two, no evidence is put forward in the extract to suggest that neither can be understood without the other. *Answer (e) is therefore incorrect.*

Question 26

St Augustine's response to the question of 'what is time?' is quoted as having been: 'If nobody asks me … then I know; but if I were to desire to explain it to one that should ask me, plainly I know not.' This suggests that in the absence of a specific need to define time he understood what was meant by it and it was not something that would concern him. On the other hand, he would not be able to provide a definition to someone else, if asked, because he was unsure himself precisely how to define it. *The correct answer is therefore (c)*.

This is different to him being able to define it precisely to himself and simply not explain it to others. The point is that he knew what he understood time to be, but was unable to formulate this into a definition. *Answer (a) is therefore incorrect*. The fact that St Augustine was unable to define time does not preclude anyone else from being able to do so. *Answer (b) is therefore incorrect*. There is nothing in what he said which suggests that everyone necessarily has a different view of what time is. *Answer (d) is therefore incorrect*. Although many people may have difficulty defining it, they may all be thinking of it as the same thing. Similarly, the quotation gives no guidance as to whether the definition of time does keep changing or not. *Answer (e) is therefore incorrect*.

Question 27

Reference is made to the atomic realm in the last two paragraphs, but nowhere is it said that it is only possible to define time by reference to atoms and molecules. *The correct answer is therefore (d)*.

On the other hand, it is stated in the fourth paragraph that time only flows in one direction: 'And experience suggests that time does have direction.' *Answer (a) is therefore incorrect*. It is said that time is important to the study of physics, as it is described, at the end of the second paragraph, as having a place in the 'fundamental laws of physics'. *Answer (b) is therefore incorrect*. A number of examples are given of acts that cannot be reversed: 'Washing machines wear out with use, as do automobiles and shoes and they never return to their former pristine perfection. Mountain peaks crumble into the valley, but never reassemble themselves, and perfume from an open bottle escapes to fill the room, but never does the reverse.' However, examples are also given of things that are capable of being reversed: 'Make a movie of a few atoms doing their thing, run it in reverse, and you would see nothing strange – the backward movement would again fulfil the laws of physics.' This suggests that only certain acts are capable of being reversed. *Answer (c) is therefore incorrect*. It is said that 'modern physics traces time's character back to the very origins of the universe and questions its place in the fundamental laws of physics', suggesting that the concept has always existed. *Answer (e) is therefore incorrect*.

10   Beauty and Intelligence

Question 28

Although there tend to be a number of qualities found in attractive faces, this is not the same as saying that attractive faces share all of the same characteristics, as that would be to imply that all attractive people look the same, which is obviously incorrect. *The correct answer is therefore (c)*.

It is said that 'If females generally prefer intelligent males because they typically have higher incomes and status, and if most males prefer physically attractive females, then over time these two characteristics will tend to covary'. From this, it can be extrapolated that less attractive people tend to be less intelligent and that there is a correlation between attractiveness and income. *Answers (a) and (b) are therefore incorrect.* It is suggested that in some societies the need to avoid pathogens and parasites is of paramount importance. This is not the case everywhere and provides an explanation for why different societies prioritise different qualities. *Answer (d) is therefore incorrect.* The whole basis of the research is that men look for beauty and women look for intelligence, suggesting that different genders seek different things in a partner. *Answer (e) is therefore incorrect.*

Question 29

The answer to this question would be almost the same regardless of the subject matter, given that analysis of empirical data will always require the variable to be quantifiable. It is fairly well accepted that intelligence can be quantified, but it is also necessary to assume that attractiveness can. *The correct answer is therefore (d).*

There is nothing to say that tastes do not vary between individuals and this does not disprove the findings of the research. *Answer (a) is therefore incorrect.* The fact that intelligence can be inherited is stated to be an assumption made by the researchers. *Answer (b) is therefore incorrect.* It is not necessary to assume that successful people are always intelligent without exception, or that there are a range of different levels of intelligence and attractiveness in society, as the nature of such an analysis is that a range of different values will be considered. *Answers (c) and (e) are therefore incorrect.*

Question 30

Crucial to the research is the fact that men judge women at least in part by how attractive they are. Nowhere in the text is it stated that this is the only characteristic, however. *The correct answer is therefore (c).*

That individuals perceive attractive people to be more intelligent, that there is a correlation between health and attractiveness, that fluctuating asymmetry can be indicative of poor health and that genetic mutations can decrease attractiveness are all stated in some form in the text. *Answers (a), (b), (d) and (e) are therefore incorrect.*

SECTION B: EXPLANATION OF ANSWERS AND SAMPLES

Question 1: Can full gender equality in the workplace ever be achieved?

This is one of the more abstract and open-ended questions that you will encounter, and as such offers greater potential for bringing in your own ideas and opinions. This freedom will suit many people, but will not appeal to everyone and before answering the question you should consider whether you will find it a handicap to have a less specific question to work with. It is not a question that is designed to test factual knowledge, but will nevertheless require some specific information, ideally including statistical trends, if your arguments are going to be totally convincing.

The question itself is based on a major assumption, namely that there is currently not gender equality in the workplace. Although this may be taken for granted by many people, it is vital to identify this assumption and not simply take it for granted. Having done this, your arguments are likely to be split into those in favour of the proposition and those against, or vice versa. In putting each argument forward you should bear in mind the need to constantly relate back to the question and you should ensure that every point you make advances your arguments and is not simply set down in isolation.

To lift your essay into the category of really excellent, you need to show a deeper level of understanding about what it is that the question actually means and you should look to challenge terms like equality, considering what kind of equality you are discussing. There is also the potential to challenge the traditional view, which is that where there is a lack of gender equality it is in favour of men, by pointing out various instances of reverse discrimination and professions where women are seen as having an advantage. You should also look at the debate in a wider context and look at other areas of life where there could be said to be gender inequality, as well as considering how the position has already changed and how it is likely to change further in the future.

Sample Essay

Gender equality means that people of different sexes, but with otherwise similar credentials, should be treated the same way in recruitment, in pay and bonuses, in promotions and job opportunities and generally in the workplace. In today's society, it seems hard to believe that gender inequality is ever allowed to prevail, but, unfortunately, there are still clear-cut instances where a woman doing exactly the same job as a man is paid less. There are also instances of gender discrimination against men, an issue of equal concern, although this essay will concentrate on discrimination against women. I will argue that equal rights between different genders in the workplace are something that modern society should strive to achieve, and that there should never be a situation where a person is treated differently from others simply based on their gender.

Whether we will ever be able to ensure that all workplaces are gender equal is dependent on the views of society as a whole, the views of some individuals within the society and the attitude of the government to gender equality in the workplace. In my view, it can and should be achieved, but it will not be easy and it will not be done quickly. It seems that the main thing that gets in the way of gender equality in the workplace is that men and women are very different. Men are, on the whole, physically stronger than women, there is some suggestion that men have better spatial awareness than women and it is generally thought that men are less emotional than women. Women, on the other hand, are better at empathising with the positions of others, they are generally considered to be better at multi-tasking and are more caring than men. On the whole, therefore, it can be suggested that men and women are good at different jobs.

This is, of course, something of a generalisation. It must be borne in mind that there are some women who are stronger than some men and some men who are more caring than some women. Everyone is different and for that reason the fact that the different sexes are good at different things is irrelevant to this debate. The point is that all people are different, all people are good at different things, and so the generalisations that can be made about men and women make no difference to the point that there should be gender equality in the work place and that strict checks on inequality should prevent its occurrence.

There is one very specific problem which must be dealt with if gender equality in the workplace is ever to be achieved. That problem is pregnancy. It will always be women who are pregnant and have to take time off work to have babies; this is a fact of life. Somehow, workplaces must develop gender equal ways to accommodate it. Unfortunately, research published by the Equal Opportunities Commission in February 2005 showed that 30,000 women every year are sacked, made redundant or otherwise forced to leave their jobs every year because they are pregnant; that is 7% of all working women who fall pregnant. Overall, 45% of pregnant women felt that they had been discriminated against in some way at work because of their pregnancy. The government's approach to the 'problem' of pregnancy has been to rule that employers must pay women Statutory Maternity Pay for 26 weeks if they are in that employer's employment in the 15th week before the baby is due and have been employed by that employer for at least the last 26 weeks at that point. Statutory Maternity Pay is 90% of the woman's normal wage for the first six weeks (with no upper limit) and roughly £100 per week or 90% of the woman's wage (whichever is the lesser amount) for the last 20 weeks.

Unfortunately, as things stand, the government places the responsibility to pay this money on the employer. This hits small businesses particularly hard for obvious reasons. If a large employer has 1,000 staff, then paying for one member of staff who is not actually working is unlikely to cause terrible hardship. This is not the case with a small business, which has, for example, only four employees. Having to pay 90% of the wage of a person who is no longer working and having to pay for a replacement is crippling when it is such a large percentage of the wages budget. Statistically, 50% of the GDP of the UK is provided by 95% of the small businesses (that is those with 15 or fewer employees). While the government approach to dealing with maternity pay results in the crippling of small businesses with the resultant damage to the UK economy, there is no chance of gender equality in the workplace. Although it is unlawful under EU law to discriminate on grounds of sex when hiring employees, it is possible to get around this rule if the employer does not advertise. For this reason, many small businesses now operate a policy of head hunting their employees rather than advertising available positions. This allows them to avoid hiring women of child bearing age. It is unacceptable that this is allowed to happen, but whilst the government forces the obligation of maternity pay on small businesses it will continue. In my view, gender equality in the workplace can certainly not be achieved until the government takes back the responsibility for paying maternity pay.

Other evidence of gender discrimination in the workplace is the still unacceptably high number of situations where gender has an effect on wages, despite the fact that parties are equally qualified and doing precisely the same job. Reduction of the gender pay gap is very important and can be helped by 'job desegregation', an EU policy to counter the concentration of men and women in certain jobs. Gender-based pay inequality is objectively very easy to spot and should be easily stamped out as long as those who are discriminated against assert their right to equal pay. In my view, the non-discrimination provisions of EU law have gone a long way to assuring gender equality in the workplace. EU law is particularly successful in this vein because it prevents not only direct discrimination, but also indirect discrimination – that is discrimination that is not directly based on gender, but which is nevertheless likely to affect one gender more than the other. For example, any law that discriminates against part-time workers is likely to be found to discriminate against women because women are more likely to work part-time than men. These EU rules are an excellent progression towards gender equality in the workplace because they require direct and indirect equality all over Europe, and the European Court of Justice are able to adjudicate any appeals or legal questions that national courts are unable to answer. On a national level, issues of gender equality in the workplace are adjudicated in the first instance by employment tribunals, which are accessible and inexpensive and which strive not to be intimidating to people who bring claims. The existence of these legal routes against employers who fail to promote gender equality go a long way to ensuring that one day full gender equality in the workplace will be achieved.

Laws are a good way to ensure gender equality, but, in my opinion, if full gender equality in the workplace is ever truly going to be achieved then it will be necessary to change the attitudes of many people in society. Prejudice is extremely difficult to stamp out because it is so easily hidden; women can be refused jobs and overlooked for promotions and even paid less than men and as long as a reasonable explanation is put on it the decision-maker will be able to refute allegations of discrimination. It will only be when we are able to change peoples' preconceptions of the roles of men and women that true gender equality can be achieved. This seems like a difficult prospect today, when discrimination in the workplace is seemingly still rife, but over the coming years I have no doubt that slowly but surely peoples' attitudes will change and eventually there will be full acceptance of gender equality.

In conclusion, the fact that men and women are different does not mean that they should not be treated equally. All people are different and they should all be treated equally. This is a necessary objective for employers and it can and must be met. Full gender equality in the workplace can be met as long as society continues to evolve towards a deeper acceptance of equality, and in the long-term that peoples' biases and prejudices are stamped out. Proper regulation of employers by our domestic and European legal systems will also help to ensure gender equality in the workplace. Finally, the government will have to accept some responsibility for maternity pay, which is an issue that will otherwise continue to stand in the way of full gender equality in the workplace, particularly for small businesses. In short, full gender equality in the workplace can be achieved as long as people are properly educated in the long-term in respect of the issues and a zero tolerance stance is taken by the courts.

Question 2: 'Criminal law should never seek to punish someone for not doing something.' Do you agree?

The majority of essay titles are likely to avoid any direct connection with law, but it is possible that there will be questions that allow you to demonstrate some specific legal knowledge. Providing that you have the requisite knowledge, such a question is likely to be a good thing, given the aim of the essay. There is, however, the danger, where you are not entirely certain of the material, that you will simply expose a weakness and this is a danger that should be avoided.

The quotation has quite a specific meaning and it is important to identify the reference to 'omissions' as part of the introduction and explain early on in the essay what is meant by this. Although the purpose of the essay is to analyse and evaluate, rather than describe, some explanation should be made of the current law, considering the situations where criminal law does punish people for doing things. This will allow you to argue for and against both the general statement in quotation and the law as it currently stands, potentially forming a conclusion in favour of some middle ground.

The main thrust of your answer must be to consider the position under English criminal law, but this is an area of law that varies dramatically from one country to another and it is impossible to provide a full answer without looking at the situation elsewhere. The broader question, which also arises, is how other areas of law deal with omissions and whether they do, and should, take a different approach.

Sample Essay

On the whole, criminal law is concerned with punishing people for purposefully committing acts that are defined as crimes. People can be punished for doing an enormous number of things, from assaulting, wounding or murdering a person to stealing or fraud. The question is whether the criminal law should impose positive and mandatory obligations upon people and whether it is ever right that people should be punished for not doing something that the law rules that they should. In my opinion, it would not necessarily be wrong for the criminal law to impose punishments on people for failing to do certain things. This would be especially so when the doing of the act would cause no hardship to the person required to do it, but could, for example, help save the life of another. However, if this were to be done then the things that people were to be required to do would have to be very specific, there would have to be very carefully drafted defences to these offences and the possible punishments could not be unduly harsh.

Before proceeding, it is first necessary to overcome the semantic difficulties with the quote, 'criminal law should never seek to punish someone for not doing something'. On one level, there are many occasions where criminal law does punish people for not doing certain things. For example, if you take something from a shop and do not pay, then you can be punished for stealing. However, this is not the way criminal law sees this offence. The offence is the intentionally carried out act of taking something that belongs to another person with the dishonest intention to permanently deprive them of it. In other words, the crime is the stealing, not the failure to pay. There are also some situations, in English law at least, where people can be punished for not doing things. Sometimes the law considers that a person is under a duty to do something as a result of their position or something they have done. The first example of this is where a person enters into a contract; they can be under a contractual duty such that they will be liable for not doing something. The second example is where a person is under a tortious duty to do something and they fail to do it; for example, a person driving a car assumes duties to other road users to drive carefully and to obey road signs, and if they fail to do so they will be liable for the consequences. Thirdly, duties can be created by statute; for example, failure to provide a breath test is an offence. Finally, a person can be liable for purposefully not doing anything to stop something that they innocently started; for example, if a person accidentally drives on to someone's foot, but then purposefully refuses to drive off it, then they are liable for the continuing act.

This essay is concerned with the imposition of positive obligations upon people to do things, which they otherwise would have no obligation to do in order to avoid incurring a criminal penalty, such as the duty to give a breath test imposed by statute, which is discussed above. The question must be – to what extent should the criminal law be allowed to impose such obligations? For example, if a person sees a child drowning in six inches of water then should that person be under an obligation to try to save the child with the possible sanction of criminal punishment for failing to do so? Should the criminal law be allowed to go that far?

There are compelling arguments against imposing mandatory obligations, which have criminal sanctions, upon people. First, and perhaps most importantly, is the argument of freedom. If I am going about my business in a perfectly lawful way and I am unfortunate enough to come across the distressing sight of a child drowning in six inches of water then why should I be forced to try to save the child? I could panic and freeze in such a terrible situation – would it then be fair to punish me with a fine or even prison because I was unable to take control of my wits and save the child? What if I am looking after three other children at the time I find the drowning child and I have a legitimate fear that one or more of the children in my charge could injure themselves if I left them unattended in my attempts to save the drowning child? Even in this case, it is arguable that the law should not impose a criminal sanction simply because it would put too great a burden on my freedom. In this particular example, it could almost certainly be said that I have a moral obligation to try to help the child. In fact, in the vast majority of circumstances where the criminal law might seek to impose a sanction on a person for not doing something, there would arguably be a moral obligation for the person to do the specific act. However, having a moral obligation is very different to having a legal obligation to save the child because law and morals do not necessarily coincide. Apart from the negative responses of our peers, there are no sanctions for failure to meet moral standards. It is certainly arguable that the criminal law should not try to impose moral standards upon people. This is partly because people's moral standards vary so greatly and it hardly seems right to punish people for having differing moral standards.

Another argument against creating positive obligations in the drowning child situation is that the person upon whom the obligation to help falls could make a mistake, do something wrong and perhaps hurt the person they are supposed to be saving. In a lot of cases this will fall into the tortious duty area of the law – where a person involves themselves in a situation in a position of responsibility, they assume a duty to act with due care and skill and they can be held liable if they fail to do that. I would certainly accept that if criminal law intended to impose criminal sanctions for failing to help in the drowning child type of situation then there would have to be what some jurisdictions call 'the good Samaritan principle'. This rule is effective in the majority of American states and it means that someone who stops to help another person and, in some way, fails to help, or perhaps does something wrong, is immune from being sued for their mistake. In my opinion, a rule of this sort could easily be made to protect people upon whom positive obligations are imposed by the criminal law. In response to the argument that such obligations impinge upon the right to freedom, it could be said that anyone's freedom must be balanced against the rights of other people, including the drowning child's right to life. Further, the extent of the infringement of the right to freedom can be reduced by creating proper defences to the failure to comply with these mandatory obligations. I am also of the opinion that criminal offences should not be created for failing to do something that is required as a result of a moral standard, which could vary across society – instances where offences of not doing something could be created would have to be very clear cut.

There are several arguments in favour of creating offences of 'not doing' something: first, is that it will ensure that good things are done (saving children) and perhaps also that some wrongs are avoided (enforcing breath tests). In order to make sure that no bad comes out of the creation of such offences they would have to be very carefully defined to ensure that the person upon whom the obligation is put, and any other people involved, are not put at risk either physically, financially or even mentally and, further, limits on peoples' freedom must be carefully balanced and justified.

In my opinion, if criminal offences of omission are to be created then the following general rules should be applied: (1) the obligation should be of no financial cost to the person upon whom it is to be imposed; (2) the person should only be required to do that which is reasonable and this should be based on all their personal circumstances, including health and mental capacity; (3) the infringement of the person's right to liberty must be outweighed by rights of others; (4) the act which they are required to do should be considered necessary for the good of society; and, finally, (5) any such obligations imposed must be properly publicised so that everyone knows that they are obliged to fulfil the obligation and it must be a defence not to know that you were obliged to do it. Further still, the good Samaritan defence should be used and the punishments for breach of these obligations must be carefully thought out so as not to be unduly harsh, given that the person failed to meet a positive obligation rather than purposely going out of their way to do something unlawful.

Of course, codifying a set of rules, which meet all of these criteria, would be extremely time consuming and complicated and this may well be why it has not been attempted in the past. For this reason it is arguably more sensible to continue to rely on people's moral standards to ensure that things which should be done, and which cause the doer no hardship, should be done. Further, in the light of the recent developments in human rights law, it could become more and more difficult to legislate in such a way that would not reduce peoples' right to freedom.

Question 3: Have successive governments' policies of privatisation been successful with respect to their aims?

This is a topic that most people will have some knowledge of, but which is likely to be of most interest to those who have studied politics or modern history. The question itself is fairly self-contained with less room for interpretation than is the case with some titles, meaning that it is best suited to those that prefer factually based writing to that which calls for abstract thinking. It should be noted that the question refers to 'successive governments' policies' and therefore requires an understanding of events well before recent memory.

With any question that demands an evaluation of success to be made against a set of aims, it is crucial to make sure that the aims are clearly defined at the beginning of the essay. These are best included in a separate paragraph, rather than the introduction, but the introduction should make reference to the need to look at what the decision-makers were trying to achieve. There is then the choice of either going through the policies of successive governments chronologically, in turn, or running through all the arguments supporting the idea that a specific policy was a success, followed by all those suggesting the contrary. The former approach is on the whole to be preferred as it avoids mixing up a collection of disparate policies, although it is important not to lapse into narrative as can easily happen with chronological accounts.

The best answers will be the ones that challenge the wording of the question and, in particular, that look at what aims it is that we are referring to. A distinction can be made between the stated aims of successive governments, such as widening shareholding and improving services, and other aims, which include raising government finance. This can be linked with a discussion of the ideologies of the various governments that have followed privatisation policies as well as with a comparison of how privatisation has been used around the globe.

Sample Essay Plan

1   Introduction
   - ➤ identify need to evaluate evidence in relation to aims
   - ➤ definition of privatisation
   - ➤ political context of debate
   - ➤ approach to be taken in essay

2   Aims of privatisation
   - ➤ ideological aims (widening share ownership, reducing government interference in the market)
   - ➤ practical aims (improving services)
   - ➤ financial aims (realising capital for the government)
   - ➤ difference between stated and unstated aims

3   Arguments in favour of privatisation being successful
   - ➤ money raised
   - ➤ quality of services
   - ➤ cost of services
   - ➤ competition
   - ➤ widened share ownership
   - ➤ reduced dependence on government

4   Arguments against privatisations being successful
   - ➤ quality of services (for example, reliability of rail services)
   - ➤ lack of control (difficult task facing regulators)
   - ➤ continued government subsidies

- ➢ lost assets (arguably sold at an undervalue)
- ➢ difficulty of dividing up services (for example, different rail franchises)
- ➢ lost opportunity for profitability (private sector, not government, reaping rewards)
- ➢ benefits accruing to minority (growing divide between rich and poor)

5   Conclusion

- ➢ do the successes outweigh the problems?
- ➢ which aims are we measuring success against?
- ➢ were there any alternatives?

Question 4: Do human beings learn from their mistakes?

Open-ended and abstract questions like this are the perfect opportunity to demonstrate a real ability to think laterally and to cogently develop a range of arguments, and in that sense are ideal for a test of this type, given the limited opportunity that you will have to impress. At the same time, there is always the potential not to fully appreciate the scope of the question and therefore not to write a sufficiently well-developed answer, particularly given the time constraints involved. When deciding on your choice of question, you should therefore weigh up the pros and cons of tackling a more challenging essay, based on your own abilities and knowledge of the area.

The starting point should be to define what is understood by 'learning' and 'mistakes' as it is possible to construe these words in a wide or a narrow sense. The key to producing a good quality answer is to develop complex and well thought out arguments in the context of a simple structure. The question lends itself to being answered in two parts – how human beings do learn and how they do not – and it is an unnecessary risk to depart too far from this structure. Each of these parts will need to be considered both from a theoretical point of view and from the point of view of what can be learned from what has happened in practice.

To take the answer to a higher level, it is necessary to consider a number of subsidiary questions that arise from the main one. For example, some consideration could be given to the question of whether all human beings react in the same way, or, if not, whether it is possible to categorise them into certain groups. In addition, it would be interesting to look at what, if anything, human beings do learn from if it is not their mistakes. Finally, a more sophisticated issue is whether people should learn from their mistakes.

Sample Essay Plan

1   Introduction

- ➢ set question in context
- ➢ explanation of approach

2   Arguments for proposition

  ➢ principle of education
  ➢ cognitive function of brains
  ➢ evolution
  ➢ scientific advances
  ➢ principle of trial and error
  ➢ rewarding experience

3   Arguments against proposition

  ➢ where there is no disincentive not to make mistake again
  ➢ optimism that same consequences will not follow
  ➢ lack of understanding of nature of the mistake
  ➢ no alternative but to make future mistake
  ➢ human fallibility
  ➢ wars (in general, and successive conflicts over the same issue)

4   Conclusion

  ➢ do humans learn?
  ➢ should they?
  ➢ can they?

Question 5: What do you think should be done to solve the problem of overcrowding on Britain's roads?

This is a topic close to many people's hearts and one that we have nearly all had first hand experience of. As an essay question, it offers a good chance to develop some of your own opinions and allows for a greater degree of creativity than other questions. It is, however, a potentially difficult question to fully get to grips with, particularly given that no entirely successful solution has ever been found. Before choosing this question, you should ensure that you have enough evidence to back up your arguments, including if possible some statistical data on the various possible forms of transport.

It is often said that it ought to be possible to understand what point an essay is making without reference to the title and you should avoid the temptation of going straight into the arguments without first explaining what the problem is with Britain's roads. Try to go further than simply talking about them being very busy, by including information on how the situation has changed in recent years and how it compares with other countries. In setting out the measures that you believe could improve the situation, you should relate these measures to specific elements of the current problem and explain how you envisage each being resolved.

To take the essay to a higher level you need to show an appreciation of the difference between the theoretical arguments for and against different forms of transport and the practical issues, which can distort these theories, such as an in-built opposition to reducing use of the car despite the availability of alternatives. You should also consider the political factors at play, such as the revenue received from taxation on fuel and the government's obligations in respect of the Kyoto Protocol and similar agreements. Throughout the essay, you will need to identify ways in which transport issues differ from region to region and, more importantly, between rural and urban areas.

Sample Essay Plan

1   Introduction

> - explanation of what the problem is and its component parts
> - identify need to establish cause of component parts of problem
> - identify the parties involved and their respective roles (government, public, motoring groups, public transport operators, etc)
> - consider what has been done so far by all the parties involved
> - explain approach being adopted (organising by problem, solution, etc)

2   Public transport

> - different types
> - advantages
> - need to improve infrastructure
> - role of government
> - need to educate public
> - likely effectiveness

3   Charges and levies

> - explain what is meant (increased road tax, toll roads, levies on fuel, etc)
> - aim of such measures
> - who would organise and administer
> - public opposition
> - other advantages (raising money for government)
> - likely effectiveness

4   Limits on road usage

> - explain what is meant (rules to prevent vehicle use at certain times, places, etc)
> - aim of such measures
> - disadvantages
> - public opposition
> - likely effectiveness

5 Conclusion

➢ weigh up alternatives (and extent to which they are mutually exclusive)
➢ consider past experience and experience of other countries
➢ consider difference between theory and practice

SAMPLE TEST 4

Checklist of Answers to Multiple Choice Questions

Market Economies	The Crucifixion
1 (e)	10 (a)
2 (b)	11 (b)
3 (a)	12 (e)

Lutheranism	Racism
4 (d)	13 (e)
5 (c)	14 (b)
6 (e)	15 (d)

Insults in Schools	Leadership
7 (a)	16 (d)
8 (c)	17 (d)
9 (d)	18 (c)

Adoption	Existence of God
19 (b)	25 (a)
20 (b)	26 (d)
21 (a)	27 (a)

Frontlines	Mathematics and Biology
22 (d)	28 (e)
23 (b)	29 (b)
24 (b)	30 (e)

SECTION A: EXPLANATION OF ANSWERS TO MULTIPLE CHOICE QUESTIONS

1   Market Economies

Question 1

The very nature of the market economy, as explained in the first paragraph, is that it responds to consumer demand: 'If consumers want more of the good than is being supplied ... If consumers do not want a particular good ...' This mechanism would be irrelevant if consumers' preferences did not change. *The correct answer is therefore (e).*

On the other hand, the other assumptions given are all vital to the market economy. The operation of the system is described as follows: '... the price system acts ... like a marvellous computer, registering people's preferences for different goods, transmitting those preferences to firms, moving resources to produce the goods, and deciding who shall obtain the final products.' Inherent in this transmission of preferences is the fact that consumers and producers have perfect information about the state of the market as they are otherwise unable to express their preferences with maximum efficiency. *Answer (a) is therefore incorrect.* The theory works on the basis that consumers and producers will both act to maximise their profits; if they do not then the market would become distorted. *Answer (b) is therefore incorrect.* Freedom is central to the market economy in order that producers and consumers can express their preferences without interference. If there are barriers to mobility, it will not be possible, for example, for labour to move to the area where it will achieve the greatest return. *Answer (c) is therefore incorrect.* Similarly, if there is government interference, people will no longer be making a free choice and the market will be distorted. *Answer (d) is therefore incorrect.*

Question 2

The way merit goods are referred to, and the examples used (education, housing, museums and libraries), suggest that merit goods are beneficial and that it is desirable that they be provided. *The correct answer is therefore (b).*

It is not true to say that consumers have no incentive to spend on merit goods, as many will understand the benefit gained from such goods. If anything, the biggest incentive not to spend on them would be the fact that they would otherwise be provided by the government, thereby creating a circular argument. *Answer (a) is therefore incorrect.* Merit goods are more than capable of being provided by the private sector; private housing is the norm in the UK and private schools are commonplace. *Answer (c) is therefore incorrect.* It is not necessarily more efficient for merit goods to be provided by the government, as demonstrated by the fact that policies of privatisation have been pursued by successive governments, and internal markets introduced into publicly funded services. *Answer (d) is therefore incorrect.* The government may be able to obtain many goods for a good price by virtue of economies of scale, but equally, inefficiency and lack of competition may restrict their ability to do so. Certainly, there is no suggestion in the passage that this is the case. *Answer (e) is therefore incorrect.*

Question 3

It is stated in the passage that although the uneven distribution of wealth may bring about discrepancies in living standards, the market economy can increase such inequality. Inequality is something that most people would regard as undesirable, and there is a good reason for interfering with the market on this basis. *The correct answer is therefore (a).*

It would be an illogical argument to claim that the lack of a perfect market was a justification for distorting it further. *Answer (b) is therefore incorrect.* It is not that insufficient merit goods would be capable of being produced, as the theory of the market is that the supply of such goods would match the demand. *Answer (c) is therefore incorrect.* The problem is that not everyone would be able to afford to purchase merit goods privately in a pure market economy. The fact that consumers are influenced by advertising is not necessarily a bad thing and it is not suggested to be a reason for interfering with the market mechanism. *Answer (d) is therefore incorrect.* It is not true to say that no public goods can be provided by the market mechanism. The market would produce such goods if people were prepared to pay for them, and some wealthier people would always be prepared to do so. *Answer (e) is therefore incorrect.*

2   Lutheranism

Question 4

Something that is revolutionary is described as being 'a momentous event that within a short space of time overthrows an established order'. Of the alternatives, the one which is least likely to fall under this definition is the outbreak of an AIDS epidemic as even if this could be said to overthrow an established order, it would not do so within a short space of time. *The correct answer is therefore (d).*

The overthrow of a government would, by definition, lead to the overthrow of an established order and would normally take place within a short time. *Answer (a) is therefore incorrect.* A military coup would have the same effect, as would the assassination of a monarch. *Answers (b) and (c) are therefore incorrect.* A major terrorist attack, depending on its consequences, could overthrow an established order, and would by definition happen very quickly. *Answer (e) is therefore incorrect.*

Question 5

The article starts by putting forward the traditional view of Lutheranism as being revolutionary. The majority of it is, however, devoted to advancing arguments to counter this view, and concludes in a similar fashion. It follows from this that the writer is suggesting that Lutheranism is not as revolutionary as is often thought. *The correct answer is therefore (c).*

This necessitates it being incorrect to suggest that Lutheranism was revolutionary or more revolutionary than is often thought, but does not go as far as suggesting that Lutheranism was reactionary as there is still evidence given of how it could be considered revolutionary. *Answers (a), (b), and (d) are therefore incorrect, as must be answer (e).*

Question 6

The established position was that indulgences were part of religious life and were a way of getting into heaven. Luther advanced the opposite view, thereby directly and immediately attacking a fundamental pillar of the Church. This could be seen as falling into the definition of revolutionary, considered above. *The correct answer is therefore (e).*

The passage suggests that as the original 95 Theses was written in Latin, it could only have been intended for academic discussion and, as a result, would not have been intended to lead to any kind of overthrow of an established order. *Answer (a) is therefore incorrect.* The north German princes are said to have had a vested interest in keeping society stable and would not have wanted to support anything that could lead to revolution. *Answer (b) is therefore incorrect.* Luther's attitude towards peasants – that equality was not possible – was very much in keeping with widely held views at the time and could not be said to be revolutionary. *Answer (c) is therefore incorrect.* Similarly, his views on slavery did little to challenge the status quo. *Answer (d) is therefore incorrect.*

3   Insults in Schools

Question 7

The following quotation from Liz Rawsthorne identifies the intent behind the insult as being different between homophobic and racist insults in schools: 'If it's racist it's overtly aggressive. A lot of time when the word gay is used it's not used intentionally as a derogatory statement ...' None of the alternatives are identified as being such a difference. *The correct answer is therefore (a).*

The article contemplates the strong negative effect on the victim of gay insults and there is no reason to think that there would be any substantial difference in the effect of racist insults. *Answer (b) is therefore incorrect.* In the absence of more detailed evidence about the extent of the use of gay insults, it is impossible to comment on the difference in scale of usage. *Answer (c) is therefore incorrect.* Similarly, in the absence of information on the accuracy of racist insults or their tone it is impossible to comment on these potential differences. *Answers (d) and (e) are therefore incorrect.*

Question 8

In the context described, to use the word 'gay' in its literal sense would be to refer to something as being homosexual. Given that this is a characteristic that cannot be exhibited by inanimate objects, it must follow that children do not use the word in its literal sense. *The correct answer is therefore (c).*

The fact that the word is used in relation to inanimate objects does not in itself mean that the use is prevalent; this would depend on its usage in other situations as well. *Answer (a) is therefore incorrect.* Words are frequently used in different senses to their actual meaning and it does not necessarily follow that children do not understand its meaning. *Answer (b) is therefore incorrect.* To determine whether the word was used more frequently now than in the past would require a comparison of overall current usage and overall previous usage; details of its usage in one area does not provide this. *Answer (d) is therefore incorrect.* Whether or not the word is intended as an insult depends on a number of factors, and the fact that it is used in relation to inanimate objects does not on its own prove that it is not intended as an insult. *Answer (e) is therefore incorrect.*

Question 9

The only comparison of the treatment of homophobic and racist insults comes where it is said that teachers 'find homophobia far trickier to address than racism'. This does not imply that homophobic insults are not treated as seriously, and indeed the tone of the rest of the article suggests that this is probably not the case. *The correct answer is therefore (d).*

It is stated that '[t]he percentage of [young lesbians and gays] who had experience verbal abuse rose from around 8% in 1984 to 36% in 2001'. Combined with other comments about the increased problems in this area, this suggests that the use of homophobic insults has increased in the last 20 years. *Answer (a) is therefore incorrect.* Evidence is provided from a study that found that 72% of lesbian and gay adults had been regular truants. *Answer (b) is therefore incorrect.* Combined with the evidence of the homophobic abuse suffered by many of these groups and the specific example of Jamie, it is clear that such insults can impede academic progress. *Answer (c) is therefore incorrect.* It is stated that teachers blame the legacy of section 28 for some of the difficulties schools have in dealing with these problems. *Answer (e) is therefore incorrect.*

4   The Crucifixion

Question 10

The writer says that '[a]fter examining the biblical evidence I have come to believe that Pontius Pilate was responsible for saving Jesus'. This can be inferred not to be the traditional view, and necessarily dismisses the traditional view. *The correct answer is therefore (a).*

From this, it must be true to say that the traditional view has been superseded. *Answer (b) is therefore incorrect, as must be answer (c).* It is stated to be possible to draw support from the Bible for the view put forward. *Answer (d) is therefore incorrect.* The fact that the writer has reconsidered the view in this way suggests that she believes there to be a purpose in doing so. *Answer (e) is therefore incorrect.*

Question 11

Whether or not there were any independent witnesses to the crucifixion is somewhat irrelevant to the theory, given that the basis of the theory is that the events which took place were made to look like a real crucifixion, but in fact were not all that they seemed. *The correct answer is therefore (b).*

It is fundamental to a theory explaining Jesus's survival after execution that it is possible to survive crucifixion, and that Jesus was still alive when he was taken down from the cross. *Answers (a) and (c) are therefore incorrect.* The series of events necessary to explain his survival necessitate a number of the soldiers involved to have collaborated as it would not have been possible for anyone on their own to orchestrate this result. *Answer (d) is therefore incorrect.* In order for him to have survived it is necessary that he was removed from the cross before such time as he would have died. *Answer (e) is therefore incorrect.*

Question 12

In the first paragraph of the article, the writer says: 'I have set aside the traditional view to speculate on what could have happened.' This suggests, first, that she is not dismissing the traditional view out of hand and, secondly, that she considers there to be some merit in considering the alternatives to this. *The correct answer is therefore (e).*

It cannot be said that she thinks that the traditional view is definitely correct as otherwise there would be no merit in considering an alternative to it. *Answer (a) is therefore incorrect.* She does not say that the original view has been superseded, rather that she is putting it to the side to consider the alternative. *Answer (b) is therefore incorrect.* By definition, this means that she does not conclusively believe that Pilate saved Jesus. *Answer (c) is therefore incorrect.* Although she considers both views, she does not weigh them up in comparison with each other and it is impossible to say that she regards them as being of equal merit. *Answer (d) is therefore incorrect.*

5   Racism

Question 13

In the absence of an explicit definition of 'the Other', it is necessary to look at things the other way round and establish what is not included in the definition. It is said that the reverse side of the coin to 'the Other' is European 'whiteness'. This means that 'the Other' must refer to anyone who does not fall within this definition. None of the alternatives given correspond to such a group. *The correct answer is therefore (e).*

Blacks and Jews are likely to fall within the definition of 'the Other', but are only examples of two of a number of different groups that fall under this label. *Answer (a) is therefore incorrect.* The majority of Europeans are likely to be excluded from the definition by view of being part of the opposing definition. *Answer (b) is therefore incorrect.* It is not so much people of a different race to oneself, as that will vary according to who is making the judgment. *Answer (c) is therefore incorrect.* Westerners, if anything, are likely to fall into the category of European whiteness rather than the opposite. *Answer (d) is therefore incorrect.*

Question 14

The analysis of 'white' identity building on Jesus's depiction in Western images is based on the idea that he was immortalised as a blue-eyed Aryan, because of the perception of that being the norm, when in fact he was not. The point would be invalid if Jesus actually looked like that, as there would not have been the same degree of racial interpretation. *The correct answer is therefore (b).*

It is not of great consequence whether or not Jesus was or was not the son of God; what is important is that he is perceived as being of great religious significance. *Answer (a) is therefore incorrect*. Similarly, it does not matter whether or not those that depicted him in the way described were Christians or not, as what is being considered is the way racial stereotypes are used, irrespective of any issues of religion. *Answer (c) is therefore incorrect*. It does not matter whether or not the image used was originally created a long time ago; the significant thing is that it is still used. *Answer (d) is therefore incorrect*. It is irrelevant whether any alternative images exist, given that this image is described as being the predominant one. *Answer (e) is therefore incorrect*.

Question 15

It is said that '[a] key feature of racial categorizations of the Other is that they invariably represent a projection and a negative inversion of the central moral, aesthetic and cultural values of the dominant group ...'. This implies that stereotypes are based on the opposite of how those creating the stereotype perceive themselves to be. *The correct answer is therefore (d)*.

It is not said that it is impossible to define a race except by reference to another race; what is said is that racist ideologies often work on this basis. *Answer (a) is therefore incorrect*. Racialisation is said to be prevalent amongst Europeans, but no evidence is provided to compare this with other races. *Answer (b) is therefore incorrect*. Nowhere is it said that it is impossible for immigrants to become naturalised in reality; if anything, it is suggested that some racists claim this to be the case. *Answer (c) is therefore incorrect*. In order to claim that racism in Europe is increasing, it would be necessary to have statistical data for different periods, which could be compared. In the absence of such evidence, it is impossible to make such a claim. *Answer (e) is therefore incorrect*.

6   Leadership

Question 16

Following the introductory paragraph, which in essence just sets the scene for the debate, the question is posed of what leadership is, and it is this question that the writers devote a considerable amount of energy to answering in the next paragraphs. In particular, a number of different theories and ways of looking at the issue are outlined, both in the text and as a list. The subsequent text then goes on to relate such theories to the practical experience of leadership. *The correct answer is therefore (d)*.

The suggestion that no theory adequately explains successful leadership is almost inconsistent with the extract itself, as the writers are trying to determine which of the many theories of leadership put forward is accurate. Were they to conclude that it was impossible to formulate such a theory, then there would be a case for saying that this was the main idea in the passage, but in the absence of such a conclusion, this is not even a point being made, let alone the main one. *Answer (a) is therefore incorrect*. The issue of leadership during a conflict is dealt with quite prominently, forming an important part of the opening of the passage. What is said, though, is that many of the images associated with leadership have their roots in conflict, not that all the best leaders have led during a conflict. To make such an inference would in itself be difficult, and in any case is used more to provide background to the theories of leadership subsequently considered than as the main idea in itself. *Answer (b) is therefore incorrect*. The latter part of the passage goes on to consider those characteristics that make a good leader, and from the discussion on this point, there is some potential to infer that it is difficult to predict whether someone will be a good leader. There is, however, insufficient evidence to justify going as far as saying that it is impossible to make such a prediction, and in any case this is subsidiary to the main discussion about the different theories which can be followed. *Answer (c) is therefore incorrect*. Tied in with this is the issue of whether there is any merit in attempting to categorise those qualities which make a good leader. This is a potentially valid conclusion to reach, but it is not one that is explicitly made by the writers, and in the absence of clearer evidence that this reflects their opinion it is difficult to regard it as even a significant idea in the extract, let alone the main idea. *Answer (e) is therefore incorrect*.

Question 17

Nowhere in the extract is it suggested that a good leader does not share any of the qualities of a good manager. The only reference to this issue is where it is said that 'not all managers, for example, are leaders; and not all leaders are managers'. What this means is that being good at one does not necessarily mean that you will be good at the other. From this it is only clear that the two do not share every one of the same characteristics. It is not clear whether they share a few, lots, or a majority of the same qualities. Although it does not affect the answer, a likely conclusion, from the context of the article, is that they probably share a substantial number of characteristics. *The correct answer is therefore (d)*.

It is said that 'each generation has added something to the overall debate on leadership', suggesting that understanding of the theories underlying leadership has increased over time. *Answer (a) is therefore incorrect*. The first paragraph provides evidence to support the idea that conflict gives the opportunity to demonstrate leadership skills, citing specific examples of famous leaders and extrapolating a general principle. *Answer (b) is therefore incorrect*. The quotation at the end of the first paragraph, that 'the leader of armies is the arbiter of the people's fate, the man on whom it depends whether the nation shall be in peace or in peril', also provides evidence that leadership had traditionally been valued. *Answer (c) is therefore incorrect*. In the last paragraph, the evidence put forward from Peter Wright suggests that not all leaders share all of the same qualities, a view which the writers concur with in the last sentence of the extract. *Answer (e) is therefore incorrect*.

Question 18

In addition to the discussion of leadership, mention is also made in the article of followers, and it can be inferred that both are necessary for the success of society. Having all leaders or all followers would, by definition, render both roles pointless, and invalidate the distinction between them. *The correct answer is therefore (c).*

Given the need for followers, discussed above, simply having one excellent leader is not necessarily a formula for success if there is no one willing to be led. *Answer (a) is therefore incorrect.* Having a large number of very good leaders raises the same problem. *Answer (b) is therefore incorrect.* The converse position is where there are followers, but no leaders, and this would not be any more satisfactory. *Answer (d) is therefore incorrect.* It may be useful to have a good understanding of what constitutes good leadership, but it may be sufficient to simply exhibit the qualities without knowing why. *Answer (e) is therefore incorrect.*

7   Adoption

Question 19

Throughout the article, the writer suggests a number of concerns about homosexual couples adopting, whilst suggesting that the position is very different with unmarried heterosexual couples: '... a recent NCSR British Social Attitudes survey found 84% of the public would oppose the adoption of children by male homosexual couples ... But the position on co-habiting heterosexual couples is very different.' In the concluding sentence he then describes the Bill as one 'that in all respects but one is likely to generate significant public support'. Overall, it can be inferred that his opinion is that the government should allow adoption by unmarried heterosexual couples, but not by same-sex couples. *The correct answer is therefore (b).*

There is no suggestion that the writer feels that adoption should be prohibited for both types of couple, and for the reasons discussed above the remaining alternatives are incorrect. *Answers (a), (c), (d) and (e) are therefore incorrect.*

Question 20

It is stated that 66% of people believe that sex between a girl and a boy who are both under 16 is always wrong. This is the highest percentage of public opposition stated for any of the alternatives. *The correct answer is therefore (b).*

It is stated that 61% of people think that a married person having sex with someone other than their spouse is wrong. *Answer (a) is therefore incorrect.*

Although it is stated that 84% of people oppose adoption by male homosexual couples, the only combined figure given for same-sex couples is 55%. *Answer (c) is therefore incorrect.* It is stated that 64% of people agree that unmarried couples should be allowed to adopt, leaving a maximum of 36% disagreeing. *Answer (d) is therefore incorrect.* Only 9% of people are said to regard pre-marital sex as always wrong, and with 62% thinking that it is not wrong at all, a maximum of 38% of people can disagree with it to some extent. *Answer (e) is therefore incorrect.*

Question 21

In considering public opinions on adoption, it is said that 'most of the British public once found unmarried heterosexual couples and homosexuality alike morally unacceptable; but many now draw a distinction between the two and even those who have no wish to interfere with other people's sexual behaviour in private may have less "modern" views on suitability of couples to bring up children'. This suggests that attitudes have not shifted much in relation to adoption by same-sex couples, where as this and other evidence in the passage suggests that opinions have shifted in relation to the other alternatives. *The correct answer is therefore (a).*

It is said that 'British attitudes to co-habitation outside marriage are generally much more liberal than perhaps they once were, and there is wide support for extending many of the civil rights that come with marriage to those who are unmarried'. This and the subsequent paragraph suggest that attitudes towards the rights of unmarried parents and cohabiting couples have changed considerably. *Answers (b), (c), (d) and (e) are therefore incorrect.*

8   Frontlines

Question 22

It is stated that: 'The US has a different arm-twisting technique [to Saddam Hussein's regime] – to dangle offers of skills training, free college education and health care in the faces of poor Americans in order to get them to sign up … The sad result is a disproportionate number of "people of colour" on the US frontlines in the Gulf.' From the strong link implied between the two, it can be said that the writer felt that many ethnic minorities were enticed by the seemingly generous offers of the US government. *The correct answer is therefore (d).*

Nowhere is there any suggestion that ethnic minorities were less aware of the potential consequences of war or that they felt that they had less to lose. *Answers (a) and (b) are therefore incorrect.* It is not suggested, either, that they were coerced into fighting against their will; rather that their will was influenced by the offers made by the government. *Answer (c) is therefore incorrect.* There is no suggestion that loyalty played a major factor, and, in particular, there is no evidence that people of ethnic minorities felt a stronger sense of loyalty than other Americans. *Answer (e) is therefore incorrect.*

Question 23

Although it is implied that a substantial majority of those prevented from voting in Florida were likely to have voted Democrat, the actual reason why they were prevented from voting was because of their criminal records. Changing their political allegiance would not, consequently, have enabled them to vote, except in the absence of a change to the overall policy. Given that there is no conclusive evidence that the policy was implemented for purely political reasons – there is potential for the political allegiance of those affected to be a coincidence or at worst a helpful by-product – there is nothing to suggest that the policy would definitely be changed for this reason. *The correct answer is therefore (b).*

Given that at best the fact that so many of those disqualified were likely to vote Democrat could be seen as an unlikely coincidence and, at worse, it could be seen as verging on corruption; the appointment of a firm with strong Republican ties to implement the policy could be said to be open to criticism. *Answer (a) is therefore incorrect.* Any policy that allows for the imposition of a value judgment, rather than being a purely objective test, is bound to involve a degree of subjectivity. *Answer (c) is therefore incorrect.* The consequence of the policy is stated to be that a substantial number of black men were disqualified from voting. *Answer (d) is therefore incorrect.* The implication arising from this and the fact that 90 percent of black Florida residents have in the past voted Democrat, is that a majority of those disqualified were likely to vote Democrat. *Answer (e) is therefore incorrect.*

Question 24

It is specifically stated in the introductory paragraph of the article that, as the world's pre-eminent power, America is faced with an opportunity. The rest of the passage then highlights how this opportunity has arisen and the possible threats to it. From this, and the writer's tone, it can be concluded that the main idea in the passage is that America is faced with an opportunity which it must not waste. *The correct answer is therefore (b).*

It cannot be concluded from the evidence in the passage that American society as a whole discriminates against ethnic minorities. Only two examples are given of such discrimination and no evidence is put forward about the treatment of ethnic minorities in other areas. *Answer (a) is therefore incorrect.* The fact that there are some loose similarities in the way that people are recruited into the army does not for a moment suggest that America's military policies are the same as those pursued by other countries. In particular, clear contrasts can be found with Iraq, the example given. *Answer (c) is therefore incorrect.* Only one example is given of potential corruption in the American political system, and there is insufficient evidence to prove this. From this, it cannot be concluded that the American political system is corrupt. *Answer (d) is therefore incorrect.* It is suggested that US citizens are told that it is crucial to support George Bush's actions in Iraq. It is not clear whether this is a point which the writer agrees with, and, in any case, this is only a point made briefly at the end of the extract, and could not be said to be the main idea of the passage. *Answer (e) is therefore incorrect.*

9   Existence of God

Question 25

No evidence is put forward to support the assertion that everything that exists has a cause of action, and it is not deduced from anywhere. It must therefore be classed as a proposition. Similarly, there is no evidence or deduction leading to the assertion that the cause of the universe's existence is God. *The correct answer is therefore (a).*

That the universe exists is a well-established fact; (2) is therefore not merely a proposition. That the universe has a cause of its existence has been deduced from (1) and (2); (3) is therefore not merely a proposition. That God exists has been deduced from (1), (2), (3) and (4); (5) is therefore not merely a proposition. *Answers (b), (c), (d) and (e) are therefore incorrect.*

Question 26

The kalam cosmological argument draws a distinction between the universe and God by stating that the universe has a beginning in time. Inherent in a theory based on the concept of time is that such a concept is valid. That the universe has a beginning in time is not demonstrated by conclusive fact or deduction, yet it is central to the theory and must, therefore, be assumed. God is stated not to have a beginning in time, again without relying on any conclusive fact or deduction and is, as a result, also an assumption that must be made in order to follow the argument. *The correct answer is therefore (d).*

All three of these assumptions are central to the kalam cosmological argument and without any one of them the argument would be invalid. *Answers (a), (b), (c) and (e) are therefore incorrect.*

Question 27

It is stated that, under the simple cosmological argument, there is no answer to the question 'does God have a cause of his existence?'. This is an inherent flaw as either of the possible answers to the question exposes a gap in the logic of the argument. *The correct answer is therefore (a).*

It is neither stated in the passage that God does exist nor that God does not exist. *Answers (b) and (c) are therefore incorrect.* The cosmological argument is an argument that can be used to support the existence of God, but no conclusive proof is advanced. The kalam cosmological argument and the argument from contingency are more advanced forms of the simple cosmological argument and are not subject to the inherent flaw discussed above. No information is, however, included in the passage to compare the support for each and in the absence of such evidence it is impossible to claim that one argument is more popular than another. *Answer (d) is therefore incorrect.* There is nothing implicit or explicit in the passage to suggest that the kalam cosmological argument and the argument from contingency are inconsistent with each other. *Answer (e) is therefore incorrect.*

10   Mathematics and Biology

Question 28

In the first sentence of the extract, it is said that '[a]lthough mathematics has long been intertwined with the biological sciences, an explosive synergy between biology and mathematics seems poised to enrich and extend both fields greatly in the coming decades'. Throughout the passage, this point is picked up upon and examples are given of how the two disciplines can be mutually beneficial to each other. *The correct answer is therefore (e).*

Although much of the passage centres on the potential for mathematics to be as or more important to biology as the microscope and for biology to be as or more important to mathematics as physics, it is too early to say that one will prove more significant than the other and this kind of comparison is used to illustrate the relationship between the disciplines, not to be the main idea of the passage in itself. *Answers (a), (b), (c) and (d) are therefore incorrect.*

Question 29

In considering the similarity between mathematics and the microscope, the following is said: 'Mathematics broadly interpreted is a more general microscope. It can reveal otherwise invisible worlds in all kinds of data, not only optical.' From this, and the other comparisons made between the two in the passage, it can be gathered that both allow previously unknown data to be collected. *The correct answer is therefore (b).*

This is subtly different from allowing the viewing of previously unseen material, which strictly speaking mathematics does not do, given that it is a discipline rather than a piece of apparatus. *Answer (a) is therefore incorrect.* Both are identified as being major scientific advances, but largely only in the sphere of biology, and it is something of an exaggeration to regard them as the major scientific advances of their age. *Answer (c) is therefore incorrect.* Whilst the microscope may have been a relatively simple discovery in comparison to what it allows to be discovered, the field of mathematics cannot be regarded as simple. *Answer (d) is therefore incorrect.* There is nothing to suggest that the full benefit of both was not initially realised, and this is not an assumption that necessarily holds true. *Answer (e) is therefore incorrect.*

Question 30

It is said that 'biology will stimulate the creation of entirely new realms of mathematics', and this is followed by a comparison of the diversity of living and non-living nature. From this, it is tempting to make an inference as to which of these mathematics is better suited to, based perhaps on the greater potential afforded by the larger number of living species. Nowhere, however, is it considered which mathematics is actually best suited to, and simply because there is a quantitative advantage to one does not mean that there will not be a qualitative advantage to the other. *The correct answer is therefore (e).*

In order to prove any of the other alternatives to be correct, considerably more evidence of the effectiveness of mathematics as a tool in studying different types of nature would be required. *Answers (a), (b), (c) and (d) are therefore incorrect.*

SECTION B: EXPLANATION OF ANSWERS AND SAMPLES

Question 1: Is the House of Lords in need of further reform?

This is a topical question and one that most people will have some understanding of through the widespread media coverage of the issue. It is likely to prove a good choice for those who have a good understanding of domestic politics as it gives the opportunity to show off some specific knowledge as well as allowing for a discussion of wider political issues.

The question lends itself to a relatively straightforward structure. The first task is to set the question in context in the introduction by explaining that some reform has already taken place, but that this was relatively limited and there are calls for further changes to be made. It is then advisable to include a more detailed explanation of what these reforms involved at the beginning of the main section of the essay in order to have something to relate the subsequent argument to. This can either be dealt with issue by issue, explaining the implications of each, or the arguments on each side of the debate can be grouped together. In discussing the case for reform it is important to make clear exactly what has been proposed by the government and what alternatives exist.

To produce a more sophisticated answer it is necessary to look more deeply at the wording of the question and consider the issue of whether any reform was necessary in the first place, and if it was, whether the action taken was the most effective way to proceed. A distinction can be drawn between the theoretical arguments for having a particular form of second chamber and the political factors influencing the government, both when making the original reforms and when making any further changes. As much again could also be written on the House of Lords' role in the legal system and the proposed new Supreme Court; this may be too much to include in a single essay and you should make clear at the outset whether you intend to address this point.

Sample Essay

The House of Lords is one of the oldest political institutions in the world and its history can be traced back to the 14th century when two distinct houses of parliament began to develop: the Commons, consisting of shire and borough representatives, and the Upper House, consisting of religious leaders (Lords Spiritual) and magnates (Lords Temporal). Although various reforms took place over the next few centuries, as a result of events such as the Civil War, the actual constitution of the House remained almost unchanged until the 19th century with the Lords Temporal consisting exclusively of male hereditary peers. Even after this, the pace of change was slow, with women unable to sit in the House until the passing of the Life Peerages Act in 1958, which created the first class of non-hereditary peers apart from the Law Lords. It is against this backdrop of almost unparalleled tradition that many attempts to reform the second chamber failed, with Labour governments as early as 1968 unsuccessfully seeking to dramatically erode the traditional power of non-elected peers. By the time the current Labour government came into power in 1997, however, the country had undergone considerable social and political change and public support for reform had reached new levels, allowing Tony Blair to pass the House of Lords Act 1999, which removed the right of the vast majority of hereditary peers to sit and vote in the Lords. This nonetheless met with fierce opposition, especially from certain ranks of the Conservative Party, and was ultimately only passed once an amendment had been tabled by Lord Weatherill, which allowed 92 hereditary peers to remain for the time being. Since 1999, much further debate has taken place on the subject, and the government has subsequently made further proposals for sweeping reform. I shall therefore be considering the question of whether the Lords is in need of further reform, looking at the arguments put forward by both sides and also investigating what political and other factors are likely to have the most significant impact on the ultimate outcome of the process. In doing so, I shall focus only on the parliamentary aspects of the debate, but ultimately the subject must be considered in the broader context of constitutional reforms, which include the formation of a Supreme Court and the abolition of the role of the Lord Chancellor.

Before considering whether further reform is required, it is important to be clear what changes were made by the 1999 Act and what the government's intention was behind the policy. The latter is the more complicated of the two issues to address and goes a long way to explaining the current debate on the issue. Although the government was clear in its desire to remove hereditary peers, agreement could not be reached as to who the peers should be replaced with, thereby necessitating a two stage process to allow further consultation to take place. The 1999 Act was the first stage of this process and was ultimately a watered-down version of the original Bill, amended to leave behind 75 hereditary peers elected by their own groups, 15 elected by the whole House and the holders of two ancient offices – the Earl Marshal and the Lord Great Chamberlain. At the same time as the Bill was introduced, at the beginning of 1999, a government White Paper on modernising the House of Lords was published and a Royal Commission chaired by Lord Wakeham was set up to consider the role and function of the second chamber.

The main recommendations of the Royal Commission's report, 'A House for the Future', were that there should be a largely nominated chamber with three models of election for between 65 to 195 members, 12–15 year terms of service and a statutory Appointments Commission. In its manifesto for the 2001 election, Labour promised to complete the reforms and later that year published a White Paper detailing its plans. It was proposed that there should be a second chamber of 600 members, comprising of 120 members elected by the public, 120 appointed by an independent commission and the rest appointed by political parties in proportion to votes received by a party at the most recent general election. The remaining 92 hereditary peers would be removed and the second chamber would have no veto over government legislation, merely the right to delay its introduction. These proposals failed to meet with widespread support, however, with Lord Strathclyde, the Conservative leader in the House of Lords, on one side describing them as '... shoddy proposals cooked up in the Cabinet Office over a decanter of port, fit only to get a divided cabinet past the end of today ... ' and the Electoral Reform on the other side saying that '... the government started the process of Lords reform in the name of democracy, but it now appears they are reluctant to give up their powers of patronage'.

Such a lack of support has forced the government to shelve its plans for the time being, but that has done little to damp down the calls for change from many quarters. The principle argument advanced by those opposed to the House of Lords in its present form is that it is undemocratic and unrepresentative. This is a difficult argument to counter given that 92 members of the chamber are there simply by virtue of being born into particular families, whilst the other members, clergy aside, have simply been appointed by past governments. It also gives rise to a number of other criticisms, such as a lack of accountability, which is an inevitable result of the fact that none of the present members of the house can be voted out. This problem was highlighted by the controversy over Jeffrey Archer being able to continue to take his seat in the Lords even after being found guilty of a number of criminal offences, including those involving dishonesty. From a party political point of view, the situation as it stands is unsatisfactory given the influence that the government of the day has on the appointment of peers. Naturally this leads to a tendency to appoint a larger number of supporters of the party in power, often in an attempt to balance up representation in the house as a result of similar actions by previous governments. Tied in with this lack of independence in the current procedure for appointing peers is the problem that there is the potential for there to be allegations of corruption, something that reduces the legitimacy of the chamber.

Those who support the House of Lords in its current form do not, on the whole, seek to argue against any of these points, but instead focus on the advantages of maintaining the status quo. Indeed, it is the conceptually weakest argument, namely that the house works perfectly adequately as it is, that is often seen as being practically the strongest one in practice. This is largely the case because no satisfactory alternative has yet been proposed, with many of the suggestions for reform giving rise to as many problems as they solve. In this sense, the majority of arguments against reform are more arguments against the specific reforms planned, rather than the idea of reform in general.

It is difficult to attack the idea of having more appointed peers whilst also arguing that the existing ones should be retained, so much of the focus of attention for those opposed to change is directed towards the idea of having elected peers. The principal problem with this is that it could lead to the situation where both Houses of Parliament had the same political make-up, something that would undermine the bicameral nature of the UK Parliament and reduce the potential of the Lords effectively being able to hold the Commons to account where the government had a substantial majority. Another disadvantage is that elected peers would, almost by definition, have to act in a more political way in order to secure their re-election, thereby losing some of the independence that is held out to be an advantage of the current House. Indeed, this independence is cited as one of the principal reasons in favour of retaining a hereditary element to the house, as many hereditary peers were what are known as crossbenchers, with no fixed political allegiance. On this basis, there was an argument for retaining a larger number of hereditary peers, especially given that many were regarded as being very knowledgeable about a number of issues as a result of experience in the House or elsewhere and often had more time to devote to politics by virtue of not needing to pursue interests elsewhere in order to provide sufficient income in order to earn a living.

House of Lords reform is an issue divided very much down political lines, reflecting to a great extent the self-interest that each party has in their respective position. A very large number of the hereditary peers had Tory allegiances, and this contributed to a substantial Conservative majority in the House of Lords. Although not something that would be admitted in public, this was undoubtedly one of the main reasons behind Labour's desire to reform the chamber, facilitating as it did their plans for implementing a programme of legislation which might otherwise have been delayed by the Lords. The Conservatives on the other hand had much to lose if such reforms proceeded and are still largely opposed to future reform, due to the fact that the parties are so entrenched in their positions, which makes it very hard to achieve the kind of compromise that is necessary to resolve this debate.

In conclusion, I believe that the question needs to be looked at in several different parts. On the issue of whether reform was necessary in the first place, I would answer that it definitely was, given the difficulty in justifying allowing hereditary peers, many of whom did not even actively participate in the House, to remain regardless of their ability. The compromise ultimately reached was a sensible one, as it retained those hereditary peers who it could be justified retaining on the basis of their personal qualities in addition to their lineage. To simply stop reform here, though, would be something of a failure for the government, given the rather unsatisfactory way in which peers are currently appointed. I would therefore suggest that two key changes need to be made. First, appointments should be made by an independent body and open to public scrutiny. Secondly, there should be some elected members in the House, but this should extend only to perhaps half the total number in order that the problems of having two identically constituted houses are avoided. Where the 92 hereditary peers are making a valuable contribution to the House, I do not believe that it is necessary to remove them purely because of their origins, provided they would be among the best candidates for life peerages, as some element of stability is important to the functioning of the political process. Probably the most interesting question, and one that can only be speculated on, is what action will ultimately be taken by the government. Given the enormous opposition to previous proposals, it seems that a compromise is the only possible way forward and ultimately any agreement is likely to represent something of a feat of diplomacy.

Question 2: Do you think that depictions of sex and violence in the media should be more heavily censored?

This is a reasonably accessible question covering a topic that everyone has some experience of. It calls more for persuasive argument than detailed factual knowledge and offers a good opportunity to present a personal viewpoint. The flipside of this is that it can be difficult to provide sufficient evidence to back up any assertions made, and it is important to keep in mind the need to provide a balanced argument.

The starting point is to put arguments for and against the proposition contained in the question, although it is also possible to consider the question of whether censorship should be removed altogether, and in forming a conclusion it is perfectly acceptable to go beyond the narrow scope of the question. In your answer it is necessary to show an appreciation of the fact that this is not a black and white issue and it is very much a case of trying to decide where to draw a fine line in an emotional minefield.

A more sophisticated answer will pick up this last point and extrapolate it further, considering the different offences that can result from different types of material and how this is influenced by the type of media in which the material is carried. The issue of whose responsibility it is to censor should be addressed and, in conjunction with this, the issue of people taking personal responsibility and responsibility for their children. The historical dimension of censorship is worth considering and there is merit in contrasting the position in Britain with that in other countries.

Sample Essay

Most people would agree that it is no exaggeration to say that the Internet has changed the world over the last decade, offering new ways of communication, valuable educational tools, the chance to shop online and many more exciting opportunities. Such advances in technology have also been accompanied by massive changes in society as a whole and much of what now forms part of mainstream entertainment would have been considered wholly unacceptable 50 years ago. The harsh statistic remains, however, that as much as 60% of Internet traffic is pornography and this has sparked considerable debate about the role of censorship, both in relation to new and more traditional media. This is a subject on which opinions are very much polarised and it is impossible to completely isolate emotion from any discussion of the issues, in the same way that it is impossible to form a solution that encompasses the opinion of so many different people. I therefore intend to set out the arguments for and against each point of view, whilst also considering the differing standards used by different people and the different approaches taken to censorship in other countries over time.

Those who oppose censorship place considerable importance on the right of the individual to make judgments for themselves concerning what they watch or read. Arguably, this is a fundamental human right and one that the government or any other body does not have the right to take away. This being the case, such an argument could almost be said to trump other considerations, given the importance that we place on such rights in our society. Tied in with this is the idea that censorship is politically dangerous as a concept as it could spread to other areas and ultimately be used to suppress freedom of speech and other such rights.

From an aesthetic point of view, there are many problems with censorship in that it can stifle creativity and deter people from creating new material. Given the importance that we place on new material in order to permit cultural evolution, this is often regarded as a negative point, particularly where it could be said to distort taste and suppress the truth. Tied in with this is the argument that censorship can make sex appear to be dirty by suggesting that it is something that needs to be hidden. This is an unnatural way of viewing the subject and can develop unnecessary social problems as a consequence. The same is true where the view of violence is distorted. Often violence depicted on television can act as a deterrent to committing actual acts of violence, something which is clearly positive. In addition, there is said to be a cathartic effect from watching both sex and violence on television as it can provide a release from tension to view these things second hand.

Finally, one compelling argument against censorship is a matter of practicality, in that it is extremely difficult both to determine precisely what should be censored and then effectively put the policy into practice. Although this argument does not carry the same conceptual weight as other arguments, it is in many ways one of the stronger reasons for supporting this view on the basis that no idea is effective unless it can actually be put into practice. This is particularly the case with regard to online material where it can prove extremely difficult to identify the creator and can also raise some difficult jurisdictional issues.

Those who take the opposite view argue that sex and violence should be censored because of their potential to corrupt, particularly in relation to children. This again is a convincing argument and one that is impossible to dismiss out of hand, if for no other reason, on the basis that it is impossible to say that such material will definitely not harm anyone, a risk which is arguably too great to take. Supporters of this view take it a stage further and say that the availability of such material can precipitate a descent down a slippery slope and lead to the viewer becoming increasingly corrupted by other even more harmful content.

With regard to sex, censorship is seen not only as an effective way of preventing people from watching material deemed to be offensive, but also to safeguard those who could potentially appear in it by reducing the demand for the material. On a more emotional level, sex is to be regarded as a precious gift and one which should remain private, and there is a strong case for saying that the depiction of gratuitous acts on television cheapens this unacceptably. Depending on the nature of the material, it can also be straightforwardly offensive, particularly when directed toward the wrong target audience. Similar arguments are levelled in respect of violence, with which one of the main problems highlighted is the fact that violent acts shown on television are then replicated in real life.

To try to form a definitive view on the acceptability of all violent and sexual content as a whole is to fail to understand the nature of the issue and this is one of the major problems that arise when trying to have a reasoned debate. With, for example, a violent fight in a film, there is a world of difference between a scene which glorifies the violence and ignores the risks, and one which shows the horrendous consequences that can result, even if both show similarly explicit material. At the very least, this gives rise to the argument that censorship should focus on the impression created by material rather than just on the content, and arguably what would be more effective is for pressure to be put on film makers and other content providers not to produce material which glamourises violence and cheapens sex, but to produce that which portrays it in a more realistic light, which could actually educate people.

Censorship is not an issue that can be looked at in a vacuum and invariably a country's policy on the issue will closely reflect the religious and moral beliefs of that society. Many African nations take a very puritanical approach to censorship, with Zimbabwe, for example, banning not only the importation of pornographic videos, but also virtually every other form of media down to newspapers containing what is deemed to be inappropriate content. This is in sharp contrast to the approach taken in countries like America and Japan where material with explicit sexual and violent content is regarded as acceptable in some circles. Even between the latter two, though, there is considerable variation. Although Japan has more violence on TV, it does not have nearly as much actual violence as America does. This is partly attributable to cultural differences, but is also a reflection of the fact that in Japan the consequences of violence are much more extensively shown to the point that violence depicted in the media has the effect of discouraging actual violence.

In conclusion, it is clear that there are compelling arguments on both sides of this debate. I would tend to sympathise most strongly with the view that an individual's right to take responsibility for his own actions should come above all else, although I feel that it is vital to add a qualification to this in regard to children. This argument only works if the individual is capable of making reasoned judgments and this is not something that can be taken to be the case with a child. On this basis, I believe that the only cause for censorship is to prevent minors from viewing material that is unsuitable and that they are not equipped to fully deal with. Whether this responsibility should rest with governments or with parents is a difficult question to answer and on balance I would suggest that responsibility must be shared along the lines of what each can reasonably achieve. The government can prevent unsuitable material from being made available in such a way that children could gain easy access to it and parents can, on the whole, prevent their children from gaining access to material not intended for them. In relation to all other material, the remaining caveat to my suggestion that individuals should have the right to choose is that they should have sufficient information available to them in order to make their choice and I believe that this is only the case if all content that is capable of causing offence is labelled appropriately so that a person can make a reasoned decision whether to access it or not. In all cases, I believe that the ideal situation is for producers of material containing sex and violence to ensure that the impression created by such material is positive, not negative, and censorship as far as there is any should seek to further this aim.

Question 3: Which is more important: equality of opportunity or equality of outcome?

The advantage of more abstract questions such as this one is that they give a much greater opportunity to demonstrate original thinking and are much more open ended in terms of what can be included. There is no specific factual knowledge that is required to produce a good answer, but it is of course necessary to have sufficient information available to add credibility to the arguments that you put forward.

The starting point of the essay must be to define what you mean by equality of opportunity and equality of outcome and this should be followed by an explanation of how each can be achieved. This provides a basis for discussing not only which of the concepts is more important, but the practical potential for achieving each. In considering the arguments both ways, reference should be made to the individuals and groups that have supported one or the other as this can be used both to back up what you are saying and as something to argue against, as appropriate.

A good essay will not simply analyse the question in isolation, but will demonstrate an understanding of how such considerations are relevant to the policies adopted by different political parties. The recent realignment of ideologies in British politics, for example Labour's move to the centre of the political spectrum, provides a useful background against which to consider how the importance of these concepts has changed and where it is likely to go in the future. It is also useful to identify the difference between supporting ideas such as this in theory and actually successfully putting them into practice, perhaps making some comparison with the experience of other countries.

Sample Essay Plan

1   Introduction

   ➤ definition of equality of opportunity and equality of outcome
   ➤ context of debate (why either or both is desirable; extent to which they exist at the moment)
   ➤ political and social context (who is influenced; who can influence)

2   Equality of opportunity

   ➤ how this can be achieved
   ➤ to what extent it has been achieved
   ➤ how desirable it is
   ➤ political and other support
   ➤ experience of other countries

3   Equality of outcome

> how this can be achieved
> to what extent it has been achieved
> how desirable it is
> political and other support
> experience of other countries

4   Conclusion

> theoretical conclusion (based on evidence considered)
> potential to achieve in practice (and extent to which this differs from theory)
> can both be achieved (and circumstances in which this could be the case)?

Question 4: Should National Service be reintroduced in the UK?

This is the kind of question that is often superficially appealing as it has a largely non-academic theme and is not seeking to test any particular knowledge. These advantages must, however, be balanced against the potential difficulty in constructing a compelling enough argument, given the lack of conclusive proof either way. Ultimately, this title is likely to be better suited to those who enjoy extrapolating arguments out of limited factual evidence, than those who prefer a clearly defined set of parameters to work within.

Although National Service may seem like a straightforward enough concept, you should define what you mean by it, as there is the potential for it to include various different activities, different time periods and different participants, and this will influence your subsequent argument. The arguments for and against the reintroduction of National Service blend almost seamlessly into the arguments for and against abolishing it in the first place, but you should distinguish between these in order to identify what has changed in the intervening period.

The best answers to the question will seek to build both on past experience in the UK and on the experience in other countries when forming a conclusion, whilst demonstrating an appreciation of how the UK is different from other countries and how times have changed since National Service was last compulsory. This can be taken a stage further by considering what it is that is trying to be achieved through National Service and how this can be achieved through other, and potentially better, means.

Sample Essay Plan

1   Introduction

> ➢ explanation of what is meant by National Service
> ➢ current position in the UK
> ➢ context of debate
> ➢ approach to be taken in essay

2   Arguments in favour of reintroduction

> ➢ instils discipline (and consequent reduction of crime)
> ➢ reduces unemployment
> ➢ develops patriotism and loyalty
> ➢ role in education (teaches valuable skills)
> ➢ facilitates military recruitment (following compulsory period)
> ➢ motivates (and thereby increases self-worth)
> ➢ improves social skills
> ➢ increases strength of armed forces
> ➢ experience of other countries which have National Service

3   Arguments against reintroduction

> ➢ reduces freedom of choice
> ➢ wastes time
> ➢ detracts from other opportunities
> ➢ can teach brutality
> ➢ reduces quality of armed forces
> ➢ changing times
> ➢ experience of other countries which do not have National Service

4   Conclusion

> ➢ do advantages outweigh disadvantages?
> ➢ can aims be furthered by alternative methods?

Question 5: 'The overriding aim of government policy should be to ensure the greatest happiness for the greatest number of people.' Do you agree?

This is a philosophically based question, which demands an analysis of the theory of utilitarianism. This is a relatively straightforward theory to understand and the question should appeal even to those who have not studied philosophy in depth. It is a matter of personal preference whether it is approached from a largely theoretical point of view or whether more emphasis is put on the realities of government policy. Either way, it is important to have enough background knowledge of the basic principles of utilitarianism to be able to use this concept as a basis for discussion.

With more abstract essays like this, there is sometimes a feeling that the best way to impress is to adopt an unusually complicated structure. This is not the case and the best-written essays tend to be those that are approached in a straightforward way such that depth can be injected through the sophistication of the argument, without losing clarity. With this question, it is advisable to spend some time looking at the general concept of utilitarianism before putting forward the arguments for and against it being used as the aim of government policy.

A deeper analysis of the question is required in order to develop a top-class essay. Issues to be considered include whether such a theory should be an aim of government policy even if not the main one and whether such a theory should be the aim of any policy at all. It is always good to bring a personal opinion into an essay, particularly where the wording of the question specifically asks for one. You should not therefore be afraid to suggest any modifications to the theory, which you feel would make it more acceptable if it were to be used as an aim of government policy. For example, it could be said that it is a perfectly valid aim of government policy to ensure the greatest happiness for the greatest number of people providing that there is some minimum threshold that prevents anyone from being exploited. In addition, there is scope to discuss what should be the overriding aim of government policy if utilitarianism is rejected.

Sample Essay Plan

1 Introduction

  ➢ define what is meant by the question

  ➢ relate to concept of utilitarianism

  ➢ set out approach you intend to take (theoretical; reality of government policy)

2 Utilitarianism

  ➢ what it means

  ➢ how theory originated

  ➢ aims

  ➢ supporters of the view (originally and in modern times)

3 Arguments in favour of proposition

  ➢ can be applied to all situations

  ➢ easily understood

  ➢ fair (in one sense)

4   Arguments against proposition

> difficult to quantify
> merit of happiness being ultimate aim (could be seen to promote hedonism)
> does not protect human rights (for example, does not oppose slavery)
> difficulty in establishing who should judge effects of a policy

5   Possible alternatives

> modify theory (for example, by imposing minimum threshold of happiness for every person so as to protect human rights)
> use only as one aim (not overriding aim)
> issue of what else should be overriding aim

6   Conclusion

> balance arguments for and against proposition
> consider how alternatives would change the situation

SAMPLE TEST 5

Checklist of Answers to Multiple Choice Questions

Racial Stereotypes	American Political Parties
1 (d)	10 (b)
2 (a)	11 (c)
3 (c)	12 (b)

Home/Work Divide	Civil Society
4 (d)	13 (e)
5 (d)	14 (c)
6 (b)	15 (c)

Advertising	Life in Other Worlds
7 (d)	16 (e)
8 (a)	17 (c)
9 (c)	18 (d)

Ageing	Greek Gods
19 (a)	25 (b)
20 (b)	26 (c)
21 (a)	27 (d)

Population	Foreign Aid
22 (a)	28 (d)
23 (c)	29 (d)
24 (a)	30 (d)

SECTION A: EXPLANATION OF ANSWERS TO MULTIPLE CHOICE QUESTIONS

1   Racial Stereotypes

Question 1

In describing racial stereotypes, it is said that 'these highly distorted images, instead of being recognized for what they are, are understood as real-world entities'. This suggests that the stereotypes become understood as reality. *The correct answer is therefore (d).*

It is stated in the passage that such stereotypes are often incorrect, but this would not be as much of a problem if they were recognised as such. It is the fact that they are accepted as being the truth that leads to further problems. *Answer (a) is therefore incorrect.* It is not suggested that such stereotypes are always used in a derogatory fashion. This may often be the case, but it is also suggested that they are used by people without thinking, simply to describe others. *Answer (b) is therefore incorrect.* Although it is suggested that they become well established and difficult to change, this would not be a problem had they not been accepted as being true in the first place. *Answer (c) is therefore incorrect.* Similarly, overuse is identified as a problem, but would not be as serious a problem were it not for the fact that the stereotypes are accepted as reality. *Answer (e) is therefore incorrect.*

Question 2

Stereotypes are described as being 'distorted images' of reality. They cannot be said not to originate from the truth; they are effectively a distorted version of that truth. *The correct answer is therefore (a).*

It is said that stereotypes arise through the use of 'simplifying categories or patterns'. It is suggested that by regarding all those of a particular race in the same way, it is simpler than having to deal with the individual characteristics of each. *Answer (b) is therefore incorrect.* It is said that stereotypes of this nature 'can be transmitted from one generation to the next, or between classes, and geographically across society, with an astonishing durability'. This implies that not only do they pass freely through society, but that they permeate class. *Answers (c) and (e) are therefore incorrect.* It is inherent in the nature of stereotypes, as described, that they 'serve a conservative function' and are difficult to change. *Answer (d) is therefore incorrect.*

Question 3

It is not suggested that people do not realise that there are variations of colour, rather that they see them all as representing the same thing and lump them all into the same category rather than going to the effort of classifying them separately. *The correct answer is therefore (c).*

As mentioned above, it is not suggested that people do not realise that those described as black are not all the same. Ignorance is nevertheless clearly a factor in the use of the term, but is second in importance to laziness. *Answer (a) is therefore incorrect.* Similarly, it cannot be said to be more efficient to use the same term to describe a number of different categories; if anything, this is inefficient. *Answer (b) is therefore incorrect.* It is sometimes suggested that the word 'black' is more politically correct than 'coloured' or any of the other synonyms for the word. *Answer (d) is therefore incorrect.* Whilst this may explain its use in some contexts, that does not explain the use of the term to refer to such a spread of different peoples. The fact that it is suggested that the term is often used through ignorance leads to the conclusion that many people who use it do not do so out of any contempt or malice. *Answer (e) is therefore incorrect.*

2   Home/Work Divide

Question 4

It is said that '[r]esidences that contained separate rooms for eating, sleeping, cooking, bathing and relaxation gradually replaced large communal rooms that had contained all domestic activity'. This process can be seen as being relatively distant from industrialisation both in time and cause. That the change took place gradually suggests that it was not something that had to follow from industrialisation, a view supported by the fact that there is nothing to directly link the two changes, but for the fact that similar changes had been taking place in factories. In other words, it would have been perfectly possible for industrialisation to have taken place without the division of communal rooms having taken place. *The correct answer is therefore (d).*

The same is not true of the other alternatives. The building of factories is intrinsically linked with the process of industrialisation, and neither can stand separately from the other. *Answer (a) is therefore incorrect.* The move away from the home as the main productive unit was necessary to the achievement of industrialisation as well as being a direct result of it. *Answer (b) is therefore incorrect*. Given that industrialisation involved the simultaneous employment of labour, there was no alternative to there being a more synchronised way of life amongst the labour force. *Answer (c) is therefore incorrect*. Central to industrialisation was the payment of labour in exchange for their time, and it was unavoidable that time and money should become linked in this way. *Answer (e) is therefore incorrect*.

Question 5

Nowhere is it suggested that workers have a free choice of where they live. Such a view would imply a level of freedom for workers inconsistent with their portrayed status in society and is no way a necessary assumption of the home/work divide. *The correct answer is therefore (d)*.

The references to home as a 'haven in the heartless world' and a 'private sanctuary' arise from a belief held by some that it is desirable for there to be a distinction between home and work. *Answer (a) is therefore incorrect*. The examples of all the impediments to privacy, such as the 18th century legislation and the employment of staff, suggest that some regard privacy as an unattainable aim. *Answer (b) is therefore incorrect*. The fact that it is said that '[t]he newly centralised working environment was portrayed as rational, efficient and alienating, but the home, having become spatially and temporally separated was seen as something distinct' promotes the view that the two are different in character. *Answer (c) is therefore incorrect*. The comparison between family-run businesses, females working the 'double-shift' and the views articulated elsewhere in the passage suggest that home means different things to different people. *Answer (e) is therefore incorrect*.

Question 6

Although it is stated that workers were forced to adopt a more synchronised way of life, and spend a certain number of hours each day working in factories, it is impossible to gather whether or not this gave them more or less free time than before. Before, they may have been able to decide when they did their work, but in order to have produced sufficient crops it may have been necessary to work even longer hours in the fields than they later did in the factories. *The correct answer is therefore (b)*.

The 'vagaries of the climate' are mentioned in connection with agricultural work, and this is something that it can be inferred was eliminated by the move into factories. *Answer (a) is therefore incorrect*. Whilst before industrialisation people are described as having worked for themselves from home, it is said that, after industrialisation, 'workers exchanged their labour for wages in a centralised work place'. *Answer (c) is therefore incorrect*. Middle class capitalists would have relied on employing workers and stood to gain by people not simply working at home in the traditional way. *Answer (d) is therefore incorrect*. Hochchild's study of females 'working the "double-shift" of home and work' suggests an alternative view of how home and work could be perceived to that put forward in the rest of the extract. *Answer (e) is therefore incorrect.*

3   Advertising

Question 7

Nowhere in the article is it stated that it is difficult to make advertisements that appeal to all age groups. Indeed, there are several references to older people liking similar sorts of advertisements to young people. For example, it is said that '[b]y and large, in fact, the sorts of ads that old people like are the sorts of ads that everyone likes …'. *The correct answer is therefore (d).*

It is stated that the focus on older consumers is not a new thing, with the grey pound being described as 'a cliché of the advertising industry since at least the 1970s'. *Answer (a) is therefore incorrect.* It is said that the over-50s hold 80% of the nation's wealth and that '[o]lder people are far more rational customers than the flighty young, and need serious persuasion from anyone wanting their money'. *Answers (b) and (c) are therefore incorrect.* The fact that June Whitfield's regular appearances in advertisements are suggested to provoke cries of despair is to say that advertisements aimed at older consumers tend to perpetuate a stereotype. *Answer (e) is therefore incorrect.*

Question 8

Not only is it not mentioned in the article that younger people have a greater disposable income, but the only reference to money is to suggest that older people are wealthier. It follows that it cannot be true to say that younger consumers are targeted because of their greater disposable income, even if it could be asserted that younger people have fewer commitments for their money. *The correct answer is therefore (a).*

It is suggested that the typical profile of an advertising agency favours the young: 'If you see someone over 40 in an agency, chances are they're either a client or the chairman.' *Answer (b) is therefore incorrect.* Reference is made to older people needing more persuasion to part with their money. *Answer (c) is therefore incorrect.* Reference is also made to the 'flighty young', suggesting that young people are more impressionable and easier to persuade to buy things. *Answer (d) is therefore incorrect.* Several references are made to perceptions about the kind of advertisements that would appeal to older people, even though many are disproved. *Answer (e) is therefore incorrect.*

Question 9

John O'Sullivan, chairman of MWO Advertising, is quoted as saying the following with regard to older people and advertisements: 'Thing is, if there's a hole in an ad, they will spot it.' This, combined with the suggestion that 'older people want hard facts', suggests that the key difference between an effective advertisement aimed at a younger audience and one aimed at an older audience is factual content. *The correct answer is therefore (c).*

It is said that older people 'like a laugh as much as anyone else', suggesting that humour is not the difference between effective advertisements aimed at the different groups. *Answer (a) is therefore incorrect.* Celebrities are described as having the potential to appeal to all ages. *Answer (b) is therefore incorrect.* Quality, whilst clearly essential to effective advertisements, is not highlighted as a key difference specifically between the two advertising markets. *Answer (d) is therefore incorrect.* Nor, likewise, is creativity, which there is nothing to suggest is not equally applicable to both. *Answer (e) is therefore incorrect.*

4   American Political Parties

Question 10

The use of direct primaries is said to have 'encouraged the development of candidate-orientated elections which have helped to undermine party loyalty in congress'. It follows from this that direct primaries can be regarded as one of the causes of the weak party system that is described to be a feature of American politics. *The correct answer is therefore (b).*

The remaining alternatives can be gathered to be effects of, rather than causes of, the weak party system. It is suggested that elections have become more 'candidate-centred', and focused on personalities, since the strength of political parties declined and that '[o]ften, party workers at state and local levels will distance themselves from a presidential candidate who is unpopular in their state'. *Answers (a), (c) and (d) are therefore incorrect.* It is also said that '[n]ational parties in America do not lay down a strong party line because their control of the legislature is insufficiently strong to enable them to enforce the line'. *Answer (e) is therefore incorrect.*

Question 11

The example is given of Ross Perot, one of the leading independents in US political history who got 19% of national support, but no success in the Electoral College. Similarly, it is said that 'Ralph Nader failed to make any dent in the overall result in that the Electoral College only needed to take into account the results achieved by the Democrat Gore and the Republican Bush'. These comments suggest that the Electoral College poses the main obstacle to an independent party or candidate gaining power. *The correct answer is therefore (c).*

A lack of funding is identified as being a problem faced by independents, but is secondary to the problem of the Electoral College for two reasons. First, one of the reasons why independents struggle to raise funds is because of the perception that they are not capable of getting anywhere in the election. Secondly, even though Ross Perot did raise enough funds to compete with the main parties and secure a substantial proportion of the vote, he still only made very limited progress. *Answer (a) is therefore incorrect.* Nowhere is it suggested that independents struggle because they are unable to develop sufficient policies. *Answer (b) is therefore incorrect.* Although inexperience and the traditional strength of the two main parties are undoubtedly major factors, the example of Ross Perot, who effectively overcame these problems but was still unsuccessful as a result of the Electoral College, suggests that neither can be viewed as the main problem. *Answers (d) and (e) are therefore incorrect.*

Question 12

As discussed above, the electoral system and in particular the use of an Electoral College promote the strength of the main two parties. The fact that America has a federal system of government is not, however, related to this, and is more of an argument against the strength of political parties. The fact that America operates a federal system is identified to mean that parties 'tend to be broadly-based coalitions of interests organised in a decentralised way rather than tightly disciplined hierarchical structures'. This reduces their power. *The correct answer is therefore (b).*

The method of recruiting candidates whereby '[c]lose ties and a long history of party connections are usually needed to become a candidate to lead the party' allows parties to retain a higher level of influence than they would otherwise. *Answer (a) is therefore incorrect.* The limited success of independent candidates leaves power in the hands of the main parties. *Answer (c) is therefore incorrect.* The fact that '[t]he two main parties are ... capable of adjusting their policies to cope with policies raised by minority parties' makes it difficult for other parties to make progress in elections. *Answer (d) is therefore incorrect.* The main parties are also able to count on a level of financial support that smaller parties and independents have no chance of matching, thereby preventing there from being a level playing field. *Answer (e) is therefore incorrect.*

5   Civil Society

Question 13

At the very beginning of the article, three different possible definitions of civil society are put forward, and subsequently a plethora of different meaning are considered. This prompts the writer to pose the question: '[w]hat is to be done with a concept that seems so unsure of itself that definitions are akin to nailing jelly to the wall?' His response is that 'the time has come ... to at least be clearer with each other about the different interpretations in play'. From this it can be inferred that before any meaningful discussion can be had about civil society, it is necessary to define what is meant by the term. *The correct answer is therefore (e).*

It is suggested that civil society is used as a vague term, but the fact that the writer highlights the need to come up with an accepted definition shows that this is not his main point and that it is used more as an example of a wider theme. *Answer (a) is therefore incorrect*. Although there is some suggestion that some of the hopes placed on the success of civil society may be unrealistic, the fact that the writer is tackling the subject in this way suggests that he believes in the potential success of the concept. *Answer (b) is therefore incorrect*. That civil society influences business and family life may be true, but this is only a small part of what is being said overall and cannot be considered to be the main idea. *Answer (c) is therefore incorrect*. The same is true of the proposition that civil society is not a feature of all countries. This point is simply being made to show the wider context of the term. *Answer (d) is therefore incorrect*.

Question 14

The majority of conceptions of civil society are implied to promote various ideals or benefits for that society, and few would suggest that improving the quality of society was not a widely accepted aim. *The correct answer is therefore (c)*.

Cato's view of civil society is stated to involve 'fundamentally reducing the role of politics in society by expanding free markets and individual liberty'. This is not an idea that features in many of the other definitions put forward and is likely only to appeal to those with certain political beliefs. *Answer (a) is therefore incorrect*. Reducing conflict is implicit in some, but not all, definitions, as is the idea of promoting democracy. These are, however, relatively specific ideas and are not consistent with an all-encompassing definition. *Answers (b) and (d) are therefore incorrect*. Increasing individual freedom will again be an aim championed by the followers of some ideologies, but will be opposed by others and is likely to be controversial at least to some extent. *Answer (e) is therefore incorrect*.

Question 15

Nowhere in the extract is the suggestion found or relied upon that a perfect model of society can ultimately be found. Given that the writer has acknowledged the difficulty even in defining the term civil society and, in reconciling the many views which exist on the subject, it seems illogical to claim that he believes that underlying all of this is a perfect ideal. *The correct answer is therefore (c)*.

It is said that '[r]ecognizing that civil society does indeed mean different things to different people is one of the keys to moving forward', suggesting that he is assuming there to be some merit in studying the different definitions. *Answer (a) is therefore incorrect*. That so many people's views on the meaning and purpose of civil society are articulated suggests an underlying assumption that there is a common desire to seek more effective models of society. *Answer (b) is therefore incorrect*. That it is acknowledged that consensus is impossible, given the range of views on offer, suggests an appreciation that different people will always have different agendas in relation to civil society. *Answer (d) is therefore incorrect.* It is said that '… realizing these ideals … requires action across many different institutions …', suggesting an appreciation that co-operation is required. *Answer (e) is therefore incorrect.*

6   Life in Other Worlds

Question 16

It is said that '[t]here are only two properties that can determine if an object is alive: metabolism and motion', and examples are then given of each. It is also said, however, that 'both metabolism … and motion … occur in nature in the absence of biology'. From this, the only conclusion that can be drawn is that neither metabolism nor motion conclusively demonstrates the existence of life. *The correct answer is therefore (e).*

Examples are given of metabolism occurring in the form of fire, and motion occurring in the form of wind, showing that neither is capable on their own of providing the existence of life. *Answers (a), (b) and (c) are therefore incorrect.* There is also nothing to suggest that both together would necessarily be conclusive given that fire and wind can be combined to give a moving fire, which would satisfy both characteristics. *Answer (d) is therefore incorrect.*

Question 17

In the last sentence of the extract, it is stated that '[t]he presence of liquid water is a powerful indication that the ecological prerequisites for life are satisfied'. In other words, the presence of liquid water suggests a potential for life to exist. This is not, however, the same as saying that it indicates that life does exist. *The correct answer is therefore (c).*

It is suggested in the first sentence of the extract that it would be useful to have a 'tricorder', but that the author has no idea how such a device might work. *Answer (a) is therefore incorrect.* It is stated in the third paragraph that it has been suggested that 'life might be like fire, not water, hard to define phenomenologically, but easy to define at the fundamental level'. *Answer (b) is therefore incorrect.* It also suggested in the third paragraph that 'life is a material system' and that 'life … is a process'. *Answers (d) and (e) are therefore incorrect.*

Question 18

The following assessment of the difficulty in defining life is given at the end of the second paragraph: '… it is not all that surprising that we do not have a fundamental understanding of what life is. We don't know which features of

Earth life are essential and which are just accidents of history.' This supports the idea that the fact that we do not know which features of life are essential is a major reason why it is difficult to formulate a definition. *The correct answer is therefore (d).*

It is stated at the beginning of the last paragraph that we are able to identify a number of the components required for life. *Answer (a) is therefore incorrect.* In the penultimate paragraph, two properties that apply to all living things are defined. *Answer (b) is therefore incorrect.* That life is a process does not of itself make it hard to define, as we are more than capable of defining many other processes. *Answer (c) is therefore incorrect.* The fact that all forms of life are said to be formed from 20 amino acids ought to make it easier, rather than harder, to formulate a definition. *Answer (e) is therefore incorrect.*

7　Ageing

Question 19

The technique being advocated by the writer is said to 'repair all the types of molecular and cellular damage that happen to us over time', something that is described as having the potential effect of helping people live to over 1,000 years old. The fact that this technique could improve life expectancy by so much, despite all the other ways of dying still existing, suggests that the most common cause of death must be accumulated molecular and cellular damage. Although it is said that most people succumb to progressive diseases of old age, it can be inferred that they would not succumb to these were it not for the cellular and molecular damage. *The correct answer is therefore (a).*

The fact that a combination of accidents and disease is said to only have a fifty-fifty chance of killing someone before they reach 1,000, in comparison with the current life expectancy in our society which is near the 80-year-old mark, suggests that together these are a much less significant cause of death than the cellular damage mentioned above. *Answers (b), (c), (d) and (e) are therefore incorrect.*

Question 20

The introduction to the passage says that '[a]geing is a physical phenomenon happening to our bodies, so at some point in the future, as medicine becomes more and more powerful, we will inevitably be able to address ageing just as effectively as we address many diseases today'. The rest of the article goes on to consider the consequences and implications of curing ageing and whether it is right to do so. From this, it is clear that the prevention of ageing is the main result of the new technology. *The correct answer is therefore (b).*

By contrast, it is not entirely true to say that the technology prevents death because it is said that '[w]e will still die, of course – from crossing the road carelessly, being bitten by snakes, catching a new flu variant etcetera'. What it does is to prevent or dramatically reduce ageing, which is one factor in causing death. *Answer (a) is therefore incorrect.* There is nothing to suggest that the new technique will prevent illness and, as mentioned above, it is suggested that illness and disease will remain one of the most likely ways of dying. At most, it could perhaps be inferred to reduce susceptibility to the kinds of illnesses that tend to affect older people, but it is far too much of a generalisation to say that it will prevent disease altogether. *Answer (c) is therefore incorrect, as must be answers (d) and (e).*

Question 21

For younger people, the risk of imminent death arises from accidents and disease. These are not something which is addressed by the new technique, and there is no reason to think that there will be a dramatically reduced risk of such imminent death for young people. *The correct answer is therefore (a).*

On the other hand, for older people, one of the most likely causes of imminent death arises from accumulated cell damage. This is something that the new technology aims to prevent, with the consequence that there would be a dramatically reduced chance of dying imminently for older people. *Answer (b) is therefore incorrect.* As a result of the new technology, it is suggested that people would be 'youthful, both physically and mentally' right up until they die. This can be inferred to involve better health in old age, and a reduced or eliminated potential for frailty in old age. *Answers (c) and (e) are therefore incorrect.* An increased life expectancy is repeatedly suggested to be a consequence of the new technology: 'The average age will be in the region of a few thousand years.' *Answer (d) is therefore incorrect.*

8   Population

Question 22

It is stated near the beginning of the extract that Malthus believed that 'while the population multiplies in a geometric progression, food supplies increase in an arithmetic progression'. Later on, it is said that 'the means of subsistence must at least have increased in proportion'. From this it can be gathered that Malthus's prediction about available food supplies was incorrect. *The correct answer is therefore (a).*

It is suggested that there had been a rapid increase in the population over the 50 years before Malthus was writing. Given that his work largely sought to explain a rapidly increasing population, it is difficult to claim that this was not a period on which his predictions were based, and clearly the population did increase during this period. *Answer (b) is therefore incorrect*. It is said that 'by and large, a consumer is also a producer'. This suggests that all, or a majority, of consumers are capable of being producers, not that all actually are. *Answer (c) is therefore incorrect*. There is no suggestion that the historical evidence on which Malthus based his theories was flawed. If anything, the major flaw in his theory – that food supplies would only increase in arithmetic progression – was not supported by the evidence of people not getting any worse off despite the population increasing in the previous 50 years. *Answer (d) is therefore incorrect*. There is nothing to suggest that Malthus's two postulates were wrong. The flaw arose from his calculation of the available food, not the proposition that food was necessary. *Answer (e) is therefore incorrect*.

Question 23

Two aspects of Malthus's failure to foresee change are outlined: 'On the one hand the geometric increase in Britain's population did not come about, because of emigration and above all because of the reduction in the size of the family with rising living standards. On the other hand, improved agricultural techniques and the vast increase in imports meant that Britain's food supplies were not limited to increasing in an arithmetic progression.' None of these factors challenge the validity of his postulates, but all are external factors, which need to be considered in formulating a theory. By failing to recognise such externalities, Malthus was oversimplifying the calculation. *The correct answer is therefore (c)*.

This is not to say that the two initial postulates were too generalised. By definition, such propositions have to be all encompassing in nature and their whole purpose would have been undermined by making them more specific. There was no problem with building the theory on these postulates; the problem arose from not considering externalities whilst doing so. *Answer (a) is therefore incorrect*. It is not true to say that the 'checks' envisaged were incorrect. They were all relevant and, if anything, more such factors should have been contemplated. *Answer (b) is therefore incorrect*. It is stated that Malthus 'was virtually relying on the law of diminishing returns', although it had not been precisely stated at that time. Such a law is, in any case, not directly relevant to the 'change' that is being considered. *Answer (d) is therefore incorrect*. Although it is suggested that Malthus should have made reference in his theory to the total available land, it is not necessarily the case that he underestimated what was available and, in any case, this is not related to the idea of 'change'. *Answer (e) is therefore incorrect*.

Question 24

It is said that '[Malthus] failed to see that, by and large, a consumer is also a producer, for "with every mouth God sends a pair of hands"'. This suggests that he failed to appreciate the link between the size of the population and the amount of food that can be produced. *The correct answer is therefore (a)*.

It is said that the absolute limit on food production comes from the amount of available land, and that Malthus should have considered this. This suggests that it was not an assumption that he was making. *Answer (b) is therefore incorrect.* Although Malthus appears to have ignored some of the evidence arising from previous population growth, the fact that he based his theory largely on past experience of growth suggests that he cannot have regarded it as irrelevant. *Answer (c) is therefore incorrect.* Malthus's failure to consider externalities, such as improved farming techniques, is discussed above, and it cannot follow that he was assuming that methods of farming were likely to change. *Answer (d) is therefore incorrect.* There is no evidence to suggest that Malthus considered the relative yield of different pieces of land. *Answer (e) is therefore incorrect.*

9   Greek Gods

Question 25

It is said that 'language has a snake's tongue; it is good both in lying and in saying the truth'. This suggests that it can be used for two different purposes. *The correct answer is therefore (b).*

This is not the same thing as saying that words mean different things to different people, even though this may well be the case, as what the writer is suggesting is that people use language to say different things. It is not simply a case of the same thing being interpreted in different ways. *Answer (a) is therefore incorrect.* There is no suggestion that language is inherently inaccurate or ambiguous; this is something that will depend on its usage. *Answers (c) and (d) are therefore incorrect.* It may follow from what is said that language should be used with care, but this is a general inference and not one specifically reached from the reference to a snake's tongue. *Answer (e) is therefore incorrect.*

Question 26

The reference to a paradoxical conclusion relates to the sentence immediate before it, which is that '[t]here's a method in panic'. Not only is this consistent with the sense of what is written, but it is clear that this statement is a paradox, given that what is in effect being said is that there is order in disorder. *The correct answer is therefore (c).*

Not only are none of the alternatives necessarily paradoxes, but none fit in consistently with the particular reference in question. *Answers (a), (b), (d) and (e) are therefore incorrect.*

Question 27

Pan is described as having an influence on a number of different areas. Nowhere is his influence in financial matters referred to, however, and it is certainly not correct to say that this is an example of his main influence on society. *The correct answer is therefore (d).*

The question is posed of what is Pan in the era of the New Economy, and the writer goes on to consider this question, partly through the use of the example of financial crises. This shows that Pan is still relevant, at least to some extent, in the modern world. *Answer (a) is therefore incorrect.* Keynes' view of why people follow each other's judgment is put forward and this goes some way to explaining the herd mentality. *Answer (b) is therefore incorrect.* The financial crises to which the writer refers epitomise panic and are a good example of the phenomenon. *Answer (c) is therefore incorrect.* It is specifically said that '[w]e have come to this paradoxical conclusion studying the genealogy of financial crises'. This shows that the example is being used in part to explain how the paradoxical conclusion was reached. *Answer (e) is therefore incorrect.*

10   Foreign Aid

Question 28

In considering how attitudes had changed since 1996, one point identified was the clear signal sent to government 'that their citizens believed assistance to developing countries should be given a much higher priority'. *The correct answer is therefore (d).*

It is not the poverty itself that is said to have increased since 1996, but rather the perceived importance of the issue. *Answer (a) is therefore incorrect.* Awareness of Third World debt is only mentioned once, and there is nothing to compare the current figures with. As a result, it is impossible to say whether it has increased or decreased. *Answer (b) is therefore incorrect.* No causal link is stated or implied between Third World debt and poverty, and there is certainly nothing to suggest that such debt is the principal cause of poverty. *Answer (c) is therefore incorrect.* The evidence in the article suggests a lack of knowledge about foreign aid. Whether this lack of knowledge is increasing or decreasing is not considered. *Answer (e) is therefore incorrect.*

Question 29

Throughout the article, comparison is made of a change in public opinion towards foreign aid, between MORI's more recent work, and their study back in 1996. Virtually all the argument and factual evidence centres around this theme, and the conclusion reached is that there is increasing support for a more extensive foreign aid policy. As a result, it can be said that this is the main idea in the article. *The correct answer is therefore (d).*

The fact that public understanding of the foreign aid situation is generally poor is dealt with in only two sentences and is subsidiary to the main idea in the article. *Answer (a) is therefore incorrect.* There is survey evidence to suggest that many of the public think that not enough money is spent on foreign aid, but the writer puts forward no argument to support this and, in the absence of this, it is impossible to say that this is the main idea. *Answer (b) is therefore incorrect.* The fact that younger people tend to be stronger supporters of foreign aid is given as an example of the main point, but is only featured fairly briefly towards the end of the article and is not capable of being described as the main idea in itself. *Answer (c) is therefore incorrect.* The first paragraph suggests that domestic issues are still very important to people, and there is nothing to suggest that these have been subordinated by foreign politics, even though the latter is said to have risen in importance. *Answer (e) is therefore incorrect.*

Question 30

It is stated that 53 percent of Britons believe that the amount of money spent by the government on foreign aid is not enough. It follows that a majority of people would like to see more given in foreign aid. It is not implicit in this that the aid should definitely come from the government, simply that more should be given in total. *The correct answer is therefore (d).*

It is said that 'concern [about developing countries] was highest amongst 11–13 year olds, girls, and ethnic minorities'. No comparison is made between the levels of concern exhibited by each group, and there is nothing to suggest that each group exhibits equal concern. *Answer (a) is therefore incorrect.* Although a majority do not think that the amount of money spent by the government on foreign aid is sufficient, it does not follow that it would be a popular policy to increase spending in this area, given that this would inevitably involve reducing spending elsewhere or increasing taxation. It is possible that some of those surveyed had an idealistic perception of the potential to increase aid and had not considered the reality that it could cost them money. *Answer (b) is therefore incorrect.* Those that did think that enough money was being spent already are unlikely to be strong supporters of a policy to further increase spending. It is said that the mean estimate given for the proportion of government expenditure on foreign aid was 9 percent. In other words, this is the average estimate obtained by adding together all the estimates and dividing by the number of respondents. This is different from saying that 9 percent was the most common response; this would be the modal average. *Answer (c) is therefore incorrect.* It is said that 7 percent of people think that too much money is already spent on foreign aid. These 7 percent would be likely to support a policy not just to leave expenditure on foreign aid unchanged, but to reduce it. They would be likely to be joined in opposing an increase in expenditure in this area by the 32 percent who said that they thought the right amount was currently spent on foreign aid. *Answer (e) is therefore incorrect.*

SECTION B: EXPLANATION OF ANSWERS AND SAMPLES

Question 1: 'Preventing the illegal downloading of music and videos from the Internet is neither achievable nor desirable.' Do you agree?

The downloading of music and video from the Internet is a very topical issue and this question offers a good opportunity to show that you are in touch with current technological and legal issues in this field. The essay title lends itself to the writing of a top-class answer as it contains a number of different strands and offers the potential to include both a factual analysis and a more subjective discussion of the merits of the position. A cautionary note should, however, be sounded to those whose knowledge of this field is limited to the more general information gleaned from references in the media as there are a number of specialised issues which need to be considered in order to write a full answer.

It should not be taken for granted that it will be clear what you mean by the illegal downloading of content and this should be explained in the introduction of the essay. The most logical approach to the main section of the question would be to split it into arguments for and against the proposition that preventing the downloads is not achievable, and for and against the proposition that it is not desirable. There is the potential to combine the two, but this is unlikely to add anything to the essay and raises the risk that the arguments and issues will become confused.

To take the essay to a higher level you need to show an appreciation of the fact that this is a difficult area to look at in purely black and white terms. This will include consideration of the extent to which the prevention of downloads can be achieved and the factors that will affect the success of this. It is also desirable to question some of the subtleties in the title, such as whether the reducing of downloads is achievable even if prevention is not and whether it is desirable for there to be legal downloads of content and whether this impacts on the ability to prevent illegal downloads. You should also try to consider how the music and video industries have changed in recent years and how they are likely to evolve in the future, based on the experiences of the UK and other countries.

Sample Essay

The growth of the Internet has changed beyond recognition how people acquire music and videos. Whilst, just a few years ago, most people would have visited high street shops for the majority of their purchases, many are now looking into cyberspace for their entertainment needs. Every day, thousands of visitors visit legal sites, such as Napster and iTunes. Many more again, however, visit illegal sites, and an enormous problem exists with piracy of music and videos over the Internet. Essentially, the debate about whether such piracy should be tolerated involves balancing the rights of the people who create or own those songs and films and the right of the public at large to have access to such 'information'. I will argue that, for a number of reasons, in the majority of cases the rights of the owners should prevail over the rights of the public to have access to these works. The achievability of a system preventing such illegal downloads is a far more difficult question, which depends to a large extent on suitable legislation, adequate alternatives to file sharing and, to a certain extent, compliance by the public.

The very reason that downloading most music and videos is illegal is because it breaches the intellectual property rights belonging to the owners of those songs and films. Intellectual property rights are legal rights over intangible property that belong (usually) to its creator and such rights are protected by both statute and common law in the UK and the USA. There are a number of arguable rationales for the protection of intellectual property rights over works created by songwriters and film makers, all of which go some way to explaining the desirability of such protection. I would argue that there are two particularly compelling reasons in favour of the protection of the creators of music and videos from illegal downloads and that these two reasons are quite closely related. The first is that society should provide people with an incentive to create such works and the second is that people deserve to benefit from works that they have created. It is generally considered that the creation of artistic works, such as songs and videos, is an inherently good thing because it contributes to society and to the works and ideas therein. The more ideas and works to which people have access, the more informed is debate, and society is richer as a whole. Creators spend a lot of time, and sometimes (in the case of films in particular) money, on creating music and videos. It is vital that they have some way of recouping the investment which they make in their works. Further, it is arguable, at least, that the more successful their work is, the more they should get in return.

If the law did not protect creators of music and videos from unlawful copying, then the creators would have absolutely no way of recouping their outlay and no way of benefiting from successful works that they created. Without such protection, therefore, there would be no incentive for anyone to make music or videos and this would, in turn, lead to fewer works being created. If this were to be the case, then, based on the above arguments, society would be poorer as a whole because there would be fewer works created and therefore fewer ideas disseminated. There is also a common sense argument that if a person creates something then they must be the owner of it. If I take wood from my garden and carve a toy train then the train would belong to me. Equally therefore, if I take ideas from my head and write a song then that song must belong to me. This argument is, of course, made more complicated by the fact that the song that I have written is intangible – I can let my friends play with my train, but then I can take it back and lock it away to protect it. As for my song, if I email it to my friend as a piece of digital media it is then very much more difficult for me to ensure that I get it back and to prevent anyone else from playing it. Further, it is possible to challenge this argument on the basis that the ideas in my head are not my own ideas, but, instead, ideas that I have been given by society. Take for example the character of Crocodile Dundee, a fair-haired, tanned Australian with a broad accent and a hat with corks hanging from it, who wrestles crocodiles. That character is a stereotype created by Australian society and which existed long before the film was made. Aside from a few refinements, the character of Crocodile Dundee can hardly be said to have been created by the person who made the film: it was made by society. On this basis, does the creator of the character really 'own' the character and does he really deserve to benefit from it?

There are, of course, arguments in favour of refusing to protect creators of films and music from people illegally downloading their works. The most compelling of these arguments, in my opinion, is that if ideas and information are inherently good and useful things in society then society should do everything it can to ensure free use and maximum dissemination of them. This idea is reflected in the concept of the 'marketplace of ideas'. The 'marketplace of ideas' is a concept based on the ideas of John Stuart Mill, a social theorist, and it is a metaphor for the free exchange of information. The more information that is passed back and forth between people, the more they know and the better informed they are; this must, in turn, mean that they are more likely to make the right decisions. As I have discussed above, it is also extremely difficult to protect music and videos once they are recorded in digital media. Along with such protection being extremely difficult, it could also be very expensive to create a successful regime of protection and to police it properly. These are factors that must be considered when deciding if it is desirable to protect creators from illegal downloading.

In my opinion, none of the arguments in favour of free movement of information or maximum dissemination of works are strong enough to override the arguments of desert and incentive which are in favour of protecting creators. I don't find the arguments that protection is difficult and possibly expensive to be compelling. Just because something is difficult to do does not mean it is not the right thing to do. Further, in my opinion, the incentive argument must win over all other arguments because it is generally accepted that ideas and works are a good thing for society – without the incentive afforded by the protection of creators' rights such works will not be created, or at least will not be created in such high numbers. Without such creation society will suffer because the information and works will not be there to be distributed – even if there are no laws to prevent distribution.

I now turn to whether a system of prevention of illegal downloading is possible. In my opinion this is a much more difficult issue and is not one that can be completely resolved in this essay. I will review the problems caused by 'peer-to-peer' ('p2p') file sharing and the attempts that have been made to overcome them. Finally, I will consider their chances of success. It is necessary to note that the creation of the Internet was a massive technological revolution, which grew very quickly, particularly during the mid- to late-1990s. It is now a massively successful tool for the dissemination of information in a great many ways, most of which were totally unforeseen at the outset of its use. For both of these reasons, the British government was in a very difficult position as far as legislating to regulate use of the Internet. As a result, the system of protection currently in place is rather slow growing and piecemeal and, thus, relatively ineffective considering the enormous capabilities of the Internet.

This leads us to the major problem at which this essay is directed. Websites were set up on the Internet which allowed people to swap music over the Internet without paying the owners. The most famous of these websites was Napster, set up by a former student named Shawn Fanning. He invented a system called 'peer-to-peer' file sharing, which made it possible for anyone to download music files from someone else's computer, for his own use and for free. This led to such high levels of music 'swapping' that the music industry claimed CD sales dropped 15% in 2000 after Napster was set up in 1999. Whilst users clamoured to use the site because it meant they could download all the music they wanted for free, the music industry did all that it could to destroy it for precisely the same reason. Napster was eventually sued out of business (although it is now up and running again as a legitimate download site). Attempts to solve the 'p2p' file sharing problem have, thus far, involved attempts to make 'p2p' file sharing illegal. This has been done in conjunction with setting up official download sites, such as iTunes and the new Napster, where music can be bought for roughly 79 pence per track. The music on these sites is there by permission of the holders of the copyright. This works extremely well and is a very good compromise between the public, who do not wish to spend £15 on a CD, and the music industry, which wants a return on its input into the products.

Unfortunately, there are still a number of illegal 'p2p' websites that allow file sharing. As a result of these websites, creators will continue to suffer losses in respect of their intellectual property rights. Practically, it has tended to be very difficult to prevent people sharing their files in this way, especially when they consider that they should be allowed to do it. Various technological measures, such as file spoofing and interception, are, however, now being developed which may offer an additional weapon to content providers who have seen their market carved apart. Until such measures are better developed, though, it seems that the only way to stop illegal downloading happening will be for the owners of the intellectual property rights to litigate against the website administrators in order to discourage the practice and, if all else fails, to put them out of business. It remains to be seen how effective the advertising campaigns, by companies such as Apple, trying to discourage people from 'stealing music' will be, but I am inclined to the opinion that there will be a sufficient number of people who are unaffected by the campaigns or who feel they should be allowed to share files that 'p2p' file sharing will continue to be a problem.

In conclusion, I am of the opinion that preventing illegal downloading of music and videos is not only desirable, but is very important, in order to create an incentive for the creation of further works and to reward creators for their work. Further, I think that banning 'p2p' file sharing would be a sound step towards the creation of proper regulation of downloads from the Internet and I believe that the music industry is to be commended for its compromise in allowing legitimate downloading of tracks. Unfortunately, I believe it will be very difficult to eradicate 'p2p' file sharing altogether because of the scale and diverse nature of the Internet and the enormous number of users who support the practice of illegal downloads. I do, however, believe that the new wave of technological measures, developed by the record and film industry, will soon begin to level the playing field and redress the current imbalance in favour of the illegal sharers.

Question 2: Should there be such a thing as a war crime?

This is one of the most intellectually demanding questions that you will come across, and for strong candidates it provides the ideal opportunity to write a deep and thought-provoking essay. It is the kind of question that has a number of dimensions and you should be wary of only contemplating it on the level of whether there is such a thing as a crime during a war, as there is more to the issue than this. You should also appreciate the need to provide some specific examples of past acts that have been classified as war crimes and how these have been dealt with.

By way of introduction it is, of course, necessary to define what you mean by a war crime, but given the different ways in which this can be interpreted this should not just be hurried over in a sentence or two and will certainly merit its own paragraph. You need to make clear that your answer will consider both the label 'war crime', as applied to certain acts, and also the underlying concept of a war crime and whether it is a theoretically sustainable idea. The subsequent arguments can then be divided up along similar lines.

To write a top-class answer, you will need to look at the wider context and consider the justification for war generally and whether there should be any rules of engagement during a conflict and, if so, what they should be. This is likely to mean qualifying your conclusion one way or the other to show an appreciation of what is trying to be achieved through the concept of a war crime, and whether this is possible and/or desirable.

Sample Essay

War has been an unavoidable part of human culture since ancient times. As unfortunate as this may be, I write this essay from what I consider to be the undeniable proposition that war will always exist. War involves a suspension of ordinary rules and law. With war comes fighting between armies, and fighting will always lead to loss of life. These evils are simply facts resulting from the inevitable existence of war, but that does not mean that they should not be controlled and monitored in some way to prevent excessive inhumanity. Further, there are some things that should never be tolerated, even in times of war, for example torture and murder of innocents or non-combatants. For these reasons, it is important that there is such a thing as a war crime, so that individuals guilty of committing or ordering humanitarian atrocities can be punished for causing to happen that which should never be tolerated, even in times of war.

It is difficult to think of any reasons at all why there should not be such a thing as a war crime. It might be arguable that in times of war each side should be allowed to do whatever it takes to win the war and thus achieve that which it considered so valuable as to be worth fighting for. This was certainly the widely-held view in ancient times when warring nations or groups would expose their enemies to the most horrendous atrocities. It is my view that, if anything, this provides the strongest case for the existence of defined war crimes – we have seen what people are capable of, and some such things are so horrific that they should never be contemplated. If people are willing to go to these terrible lengths to win wars, then they must be stopped in whatever way possible.

An argument against defining and legislating against war crimes is that the rules would be impossible to enforce and so would be meaningless. Such rules must necessarily be international laws, since the vast majority of fighting is between different countries, and fighting within a country is generally considered a domestic issue, rather than an international one. It is unfortunately the case that, although there are international laws, they are very difficult to enforce because countries are generally only governed by conventions and treaties to which they have voluntarily signed up, so countries who do not wish to comply with the rules laid down in them cannot be forced to do so. There is no international criminal law that automatically applies to all nations and, even if there was, it would be extremely difficult to enforce because there is no international court that has universal jurisdiction to deal with breaches of international law. In my opinion, however, the fact that rules might be difficult to enforce is not a good enough reason not to create the rules in the first place. Political pressure by other countries is a very powerful tool, and as long as there is universal disapproval of countries that breach international laws there will be an incentive for nations to comply with those laws.

It must be remembered that steps have been taken to ensure there is a properly organised international mechanism to deal with war criminals. The International Criminal Court (La Cour Pénale Internationale) at The Hague has been set up to deal with breaches of the laws of war. It is the first treaty-based international criminal court and it has been established in order to promote international laws and to ensure that perpetrators of international crimes of genocide, crimes against humanity, war crimes and crimes of aggression do not go unpunished. As of 16 May 2005, 99 countries have signed up to the International Criminal Court. The 99 states include 26 African states, 11 Asian states, 15 Eastern European states, 19 states from Latin America and the Caribbean, and 26 are Western Europe and other states. Article 8 of the Statute of Rome, under which the ICC was set up, defines war crimes as grave breaches of the Geneva Convention of 1949 and other violations of the laws and customs applicable in international armed conflict within the established framework of international law. These definitions specifically include, for example, torture, inhumane treatment, extensive destruction of property not justified by military necessity and carried out willfully and wantonly, willful deprivation of a prisoner of war's right to fair and regular trial, unlawful deportation, intentionally directing attacks against the civilian population and killing or wounding a combatant who has surrendered. The same provision also defines certain weapons, the use of which amounts to a war crime. They include poison or poisoned weapons, asphyxiating devices, bullets that expand or flatten easily in the human body, and weapons that cause superfluous injury or unnecessary suffering.

The statute is carefully drafted to cover all people who may be responsible for war crimes, including military leaders and heads of government. Further, it creates a number of defences for those who may have been forced to commit international crimes through duress or other threats to themselves or others. There is no jurisdiction to convict a person of an international crime if that person was under the age of 18 when the crime was committed. Where a statute is as well drafted as this one is, and where it is approved by 99 countries around the world, I am of the opinion that it is an excellent mechanism to prevent international atrocities and to ensure that the people responsible for them, when they do occur, are punished. The proper policing of international crimes is particularly important in the present international climate where it seems that more international crimes are being committed than ever before. Even if this increase is only perceived because of the new awareness of these wrongs, it is still vitally important that any instances of international crime are dealt with swiftly and strictly. Numerous leaders have been accused of international crimes: Slobodan Milosevic, Saddam Hussein and General Pinochet, to name but three. For the first time in history, people guilty of these despicable acts are being properly held responsible for their actions; in my view this can only be a good thing.

Unfortunately, there are teething problems with the ICC. Perhaps most obviously, the trials of international criminals take an extraordinarily long time. The case against Milosevic started in February 2002, the prosecution finally finished putting its case two years later in February 2004. Milosevic, who started presenting his own defence, has been unwell, partly as a result of the trial and although the Court insists that his defence must be completed by October 2005, the meeting of this deadline remains to be seen. I do not think it could be argued that this is a reason why alleged international criminals should not be tried and, if necessary, punished. The allegations made against Milosevic are many and varied and his crimes spanned many years and took place across all of the former Yugoslavia: the case against him is a complicated one and will take a long time to prove. Of course, Milosevic must have a fair trial and this means he must be allowed to mount the best defence he possibly can. Again, this will take a long time, but that is a necessary result of ensuring he has a fair trial.

In conclusion, the definition of, and punishment for, war crimes is not just a good thing, it is an absolute necessity for the long-term, and properly organised, protection of combatants and non-combatants alike in war time. In times of war it is all too easy for states to lose sight of humanity in favour of beating the enemy; it is vital that this is prevented. Further still, although it might seem somewhat trite to say that power corrupts and absolute power corrupts absolutely, behind every war crime is a person who makes the conscious decision to commit these crimes or to lead others to commit them.

Whilst there is the possibility that people in power might resort to war crimes for their own ends or for what they consider to be the good of their country, it is vital that possible prosecution looms over them, initially as a deterrent and, if this fails, then as a means to mete out punishment.

Question 3: What are the arguments for and against the present system of jury trial?

This is one of the few questions with a direct legal basis and provides a relatively straightforward option for those wanting to demonstrate the kind of general knowledge of the legal system that should be second nature to anyone applying for an undergraduate degree course in law. It also offers the chance to demonstrate a wider appreciation of UK politics and of how it impacts on the law.

Given the wording of the question, it is fairly clear how this essay should be structured. Having started by explaining what the present system of jury trial is, you then have the option of either presenting all the arguments for the present system followed by all those against it, or of taking the different issues one by one and explaining the positive and negative factors associated with each. In doing so, it is important to identify which of the issues is of greatest significance and, in particular, whether there are any overriding principles that should take precedence over less significant factors. Your conclusion should take account of the fact that there are a variety of different options that could be taken in relation to jury trial, ranging from the extreme, for example abolishing the whole system, to the relatively minor, such as who is eligible for jury service, and that not all reform is inconsistent with the assertion that the current system is working well.

Although this style of question does not particularly lend itself to being approached in a novel way, it is nevertheless desirable to bring some original thinking to your answer. Instead of simply advancing points in favour of each side of the argument, try to back up these points with details of where the argument has or is likely to receive support from and how it has or is likely to be received by different groups. This may require details of how the present system came into being and what reforms have already been made by previous governments. A comparison with the position in other jurisdictions will add to the balance of the answer and help to set the debate in context.

Sample Essay Plan

1   Introduction

   ➢ background of jury trial
   ➢ context of debate
   ➢ approach to question

2 Current system

- explanation
- recent reforms
- proposals for reform

3 Arguments in favour of present system

- fairness (majority or unanimous decision required)
- independent decision (tried by peers, not affected by legal knowledge; separates fact from law)
- limited potential for corruption (juries kept away from media)
- tradition (perceived success of British justice)

4 Arguments against present system

- cost
- efficiency
- lack of knowledge by jurors (for example, in complex fraud cases)
- disruptive effect of being called for jury service
- possible reforms

5 Support for each side of debate

- political parties
- judiciary
- public opinion
- experience of other counties

6 Conclusion

- theoretical view (consideration of priorities; importance of having confidence in legal system)
- practical issues (likelihood of change in political climate)

Question 4: Is fame a valid aspiration?

This is one of the least academic and most subjective questions and, as such, entails a more creative piece of writing than the majority of other essay titles you are likely to be offered. In deciding whether to answer this question you should consider whether this is where your strength lies or whether you would be better with a more structured and more factually based questions. In particular, it is important not to think of this kind of abstract title as being an easy option, as it is not a simple question to answer coherently and completely in a short space of time. It is, however, likely to be a more unique and memorable answer if you do attempt it successfully.

The most obvious approach would be to look at the arguments for fame being a valid aspiration followed by the opposite arguments, or vice versa, although other approaches are equally as valid. From the outset it is crucial to explain clearly what is meant by fame and to develop the idea by looking at different ways in which people can become famous. A likely conclusion is that some of them would be regarded as more valid than others and this is a point that should be investigated.

Given how open-ended the question is, there is the potential to develop your answer in a number of different ways and this is an ideal opportunity to use some ideas of your own. One of the key points to consider will be whose judgment is important in determining validity and, in doing so, it would be desirable to look at how aspirations have changed over recent decades. There is also the potential to consider what else could be seen to be a valid aspiration and the more general issue of what role aspirations play in people's development and whether they are of importance.

Sample Essay Plan

1   Introduction

   ➢ definition of what is meant by fame (and how this has changed)
   ➢ context of debate (TV reality shows; media interest in celebrities, etc)
   ➢ approach to be taken to question

2   Arguments for fame being a valid aspiration

   ➢ need for something to aim at
   ➢ ability to succeed in other areas
   ➢ positive characteristics of fame

3   Arguments against fame being a valid aspiration

   ➢ nature of the fame achieved
   ➢ duration of fame
   ➢ happiness or otherwise of celebrities
   ➢ impression set for children
   ➢ decline in academic standards
   ➢ lifestyle

4   Other potential aspirations

   ➢ financial success
   ➢ academic success
   ➢ sporting success
   ➢ family
   ➢ happiness
   ➢ philanthropy

5   Conclusion

> is fame a valid aspiration?

> what other valid aspirations are there?

> overlap of different aspirations

> personal opinion

Question 5: 'Appearance is more important than substance to the modern politician.' Do you agree?

This is a question that will appeal both to those with an in-depth knowledge of politics and also those who are familiar with current affairs more generally and have formed a view on the subject. It provides a good opportunity to discuss a more subjective issue, but is potentially a fairly difficult question to tackle given its indefinite nature. Before choosing the question, you should make sure that you have sufficient arguments to put forward to form a reasoned answer rather than just resorting to a general discussion of the principles, which may not read very convincingly.

In the introduction you should set the quotation in context by looking at who is likely to have said something like this and whether this proposition has received any support. As part of the introduction, you need to explain what you understand by the quotation as there are different interpretations which could be put on it and it should never be assumed that the reader will be able to read your mind. The main part of the essay is likely to be divided into two parts, the first looking at the arguments for the proposition and the second looking at arguments against, or vice versa. Alternatively, you may wish to put forward various pieces of evidence and then consider for each one whether they are in support of or against the proposition. Either way, it is open to argue that the two are not mutually exclusive and to consider the degree of overlap.

A high-quality answer will seek to analyse each different part of the question, looking at what is meant by a modern politician and considering what else may be of importance to them, and of importance in achieving what. This will inevitably include some analysis of past politics as it is impossible to talk about the modern politician without having something to compare him against. You may also wish to look at the deeper issue of what should be of importance to a politician and how much divergence there is between theory and practice.

Sample Essay Plan

1   Introduction

> definition of 'modern politician'

> explanation of what is meant by 'substance' and 'appearance'

> context of how proposition has arisen

> explanation of approach to be taken in essay

2   Arguments for appearance being more important

> ➢ diminished role of debate in House of Commons
> ➢ increased reliance on the media (so called 'sound-bite' politics)
> ➢ increased focus by politicians on their physical appearance
> ➢ reduced time spent by some MPs on constituency business

3   Arguments for substance being more important

> ➢ media scrutiny of politicians' actions
> ➢ characteristics of successful leaders
> ➢ importance of confidence in leaders (potentially justifying need to present policies in a certain way)
> ➢ the need to explain policies to the public (and whether this justifies the need to focus on presentation)

4   Differences from the past

> ➢ the changing nature of politics (advances in society; changing global politics; modern technology)
> ➢ differences in politicians (and the extent to which these changes have resulted from the changing nature of politics)

5   Conclusion

> ➢ what should we expect of a politician?
> ➢ what do we expect?
> ➢ how achievable is this in reality?

USEFUL CONTACTS

LNAT Consortium

www.lnat.ac.uk

Participating Universities

University of Birmingham

The School of Law
University of Birmingham
Edgbaston
Birmingham
B15 2TT
Tel: 0121 414 3637
Fax: 0121 414 3585
email: law@bham.ac.uk

University of Bristol

The School of Law
University of Bristol
Wills Memorial Building
Queens Road
Bristol
BS8 1RJ
Tel: 0117 954 5356
Fax: 0117 925 1870
email: law-ug-admissions@bris.ac.uk

University of Cambridge

Law Faculty
University of Cambridge
10 West Road
Cambridge
CB3 9DZ
Tel: 01223 330 033
Fax: 01223 330 055
email: enquiries@law.cam.ac.uk

University of Durham

Law Faculty
University of Durham
50 North Bailey
Durham
DH1 3ET
Tel: 0191 334 2833
Fax: 0191 334 2842
email: law-ug-admiss@durham.ac.uk

University of East Anglia

The General Office
School of Law
University of East Anglia
Norwich
NR4 7TJ
Tel: 01603 592 520
Fax: 01603 250 245
email: law@uea.ac.uk

University of Glasgow

Stair Building
5–8 The Square
University of Glasgow
G12 8QQ
Tel: 0141 330 6075
Fax: 0141 330 4900
email: faculty@law.gla.ac.uk

King's College London

School of Law
King's College London
Strand
London
WC2R 2LS
Tel: 020 7836 5454
Fax: 020 7848 3460
email: enq.genlaw@kcl.ac.uk

University College London

Faculty of Law
UCL
Bentham House
Endsleigh Gardens
London
WC1H 0EG
Tel: 020 7679 1492
Fax: 020 7679 1414
email: uctlgpo@ucl.ac.uk

Manchester Metropolitan University

The School of Law
Manchester Metropolitan University
All Saints West
Lower Ormond Street
Manchester
M15 6HB
Tel: 0161 247 3046
Fax: 0161 247 6309
email: law-hums@mmu.ac.uk

University of Nottingham

School of Law
University Park
Nottingham
NG7 2RD
Tel: 0115 951 5700
Fax: 0115 951 5696
email: law-enquiries@nottingham.ac.uk

University of Oxford

The Faculty of Law
St Cross Building
St Cross Road
Oxford OX1 3UL
Tel: 01865 271 490
Fax: 01865 271 493
email: lawfac@law.ox.ac.uk

Advice on University Applications

Oxbridge Applications
13–14 New Bond Street
London
W1S 3SX
Tel: 0870 080 1940
Fax: 0870 080 1941
entry@oxbridgeapplications.com
www.oxbridgeapplications.com